e-Service

e-Service

New Directions
in Theory and Practice

edited by
Roland T. Rust and P.K. Kannan

M.E. Sharpe
Armonk, New York
London, England

Library of Congress Cataloging-in-Publication Data

E-Service : new directions in theory and practice / Roland T. Rust and P.K. Kannan, editors.
  p. cm.
Includes bibliographical references and index.
ISBN 0-7656-0806-5 (hc : alk. paper) — ISBN 0-7656-0807-3 (pbk : alk paper)
  1. Electronic commerce. 2. Customer services. I. Title: E-Service : new directions in
theory and practice. II. Rust, Roland T. III. Kannan, P. K.

HF5548.32 .E1875 2002
658.8′4—dc21

2002022192

Printed in the United States of America

The paper used in this publication meets the minimum requirements of
American National Standard for Information Sciences
Permanence of Paper for Printed Library Materials,
ANSI Z 39.48-1984.

BM (c) 10 9 8 7 6 5 4 3 2 1
BM (p) 10 9 8 7 6 5 4 3 2 1

Contents

v

Part II Business Opportunities and Strategies

Part III Public-Sector Opportunities

List of Tables and Figures

Tables

Figures

Preface

The beginning of the twenty-first century has seen the confluence of two powerful, long-term trends in the business world: the shifting of the economy from goods to services and the rapid expansion of the information economy and electronic networks. This confluence has given rise to the era of "e-Service," which is defined as the provision of services over the Web. E-Service has tremendous potential to change the business landscape in the twenty-first century. As Microsoft Chairman Bill Gates has commented, "Everything in the world will be in Web services" (Burrows 2001). The demise of the "gold-rush phase" of Internet commerce and the shift from a techno-centric focus to a customer-centric focus of online businesses only reinforces the importance and potential of e-Service in transforming business.

This opportunity has generated significant interest in both practitioner and academic communities in understanding how the Web and the network environment can be harnessed in providing e-Service. Companies in consumer markets are investing in information technology (IT) infrastructure to build electronic–customer relationship management (e-CRM) systems and one-on-one marketing systems, to apply "data mining tools" to understand their customers better, and to provide focused service. In the business markets, Internet service providers (ISPs), application service providers (ASPs), and procurement service organizations are charting new models and methods in providing services to their customers. In the public sector, organizations and agencies are rapidly setting up "e-government" systems to provide services to citizens. In the academic community there is an increased interest among researchers in understanding how e-Service impacts consumers—their satisfaction, their loyalty, and their expectations about service quality—and how this knowledge can be used to design better frameworks and systems for service provision.

The simultaneous e-Service developments in different sectors of industry and academia have led to two important initiatives. The first initiative is this book, aimed at providing a collection of the different emerging perspectives on e-Service and a unified framework to understand e-Service, even as practitioners and researchers are grappling with this concept. Some private-sector organizations view e-Service narrowly as information services, while such IT organizations as Hewlett-Packard have been using e-Service as their marketing theme in order to move away from a product-centered focus to a service-centered focus. In some government agencies, e-Service is viewed as a means of holding government accountable to its citizens. In the academic community, e-Service is seen as an overarching customer-centric concept with a strong technology emphasis. Given the many perspectives, we have solicited contributions from leaders in these various communities and have created a book that synthesizes the complementary perspectives under an overarching framework.

The second initiative is the founding of the Center for e-Service in September 2000 at the Robert H. Smith School of Business, University of Maryland. The center's mission is to be "the world's leading e-Service strategy and research center." The center was designed to help companies develop leading-edge e-Service strategies and research capabilities in e-Service. It features more than two dozen faculty members from leading schools and departments with research expertise in the specific aspects of e-Service. The center is well connected to e-Service thinking, through its faculty research effort and through key industry alliances with such leading e-Service exponents as CommerceNet, Wireless Data Forum, e-Gov, International Academy of Services, and the American Marketing Association (AMA). It also provides a forum for the exposition and exchange of emerging e-Service ideas through its sponsorship of the AMA's Frontiers in Services Conference and the *Journal of Service Research*. In addition, Smith School of Business has instituted an innovative curriculum in e-Service to provide executives and MBA students with the best e-Service education currently available.

E-Service: New Directions in Theory and Practice focuses on three key areas: (Part I) the customer–technology interface, (Part II) business opportunities and strategies, and (Part III) public-sector opportunities. It features many of the researchers and practitioners associated with the Center for e-Service and other key researchers and exponents who are making leading-edge contributions to the field. The contributors include practitioners and consultants spanning both private and public sectors and academics from the fields of Marketing, Information Systems, and Computer Science. Topics range from understanding the impact of self-service technologies, to wireless rules for e-Service, to e-Service in government. This book provides a collection of fresh and emerging perspectives on e-Service that should be useful to managers and academics alike. Happy reading!

Roland Rust
P.K. Kannan

Reference

Burrows, Peter. 2001. "Sun's Defiant Face-Off." *Business Week,* November 19, p. 47.

e-Service

1

The Era of e-Service

Roland T. Rust and P.K. Kannan

Amid the rapid advent and subsequent failure of many Internet-based e-businesses, a significant transformation has been taking place in the business world, almost unnoticed in the surrounding din. This transformation has led to the emergence of the era of "e-Service," a concept that is at the confluence of two most important long-term trends—the shifting of the overall economy from goods to services and the rapid expansion of the information economy and electronic networks. New technologies—wireless, broadband, data-warehousing, data-mining, agent technologies—are providing businesses with new opportunities and capabilities to reach and serve customers. As customer expectations are shaped by these technologies and possibilities, businesses are increasingly using the information technology (IT) and electronic networks to improve the efficiency and efficacy of their business processes, to develop new markets, and to improve their competitive positions. This trend, in turn, is fueling the movement from goods- to service-based businesses and economy. In this introductory chapter, we focus on the trends leading to the era of e-Service and set the stage for rest of the book by providing an overview of the concept of e-Service, outlining its importance to businesses in today's economy, and considering the opportunities and challenges the era of e-Service is opening up.

In the next section, we first define the concept of e-Service and its scope, then relate it to different contexts within which the term has been used and to other common terminologies such as customer/citizen relationship management and relationship marketing. We continue, in Section 3, with a discussion of the technological, economic, and organizational trends that contribute to the emerging importance of the era of e-Service. In Section 4, we focus on issues of substantive importance to organizations in both the public and private sectors, as they embrace the concept of e-Service as a path to competitive advantage and meeting customer/citizen expectations. In Section 5, we present our concluding comments.

e-Service—The Concept

In the broadest sense, e-Service can be defined as the provision of service over electronic networks such as the Internet (Rust and Lemon 2001). This notion of e-Service includes not only the services provided by a typical service organization, but also those provided by goods manufacturers whose success vitally depends on the quality of their service. Thus, it is an overarching customer-centric concept. The scope of e-Service can be described in the context of Figure 1.1, which illustrates the upstream and downstream channels of an organization. The organization, which could be in the private or public sector, interacts with its customers/citizens in the downstream channel and with its suppliers in the upstream channel. The types of interaction can include all or some of the following: information-based interactive exchanges, negotiation interactions, promotion flows, title exchanges, and product/service flows (Kannan 2001). E-Service includes all of the above interactions and flows except for the physical product and its transfer in both the downstream and upstream channels (see Rust et al. 1996). Thus, in the downstream channel, it subsumes concepts such as customer/citizen relationship management (CRM and e-CRM), relationship marketing, one-on-one marketing, customer care, and so on. In the upstream channel, e-Service subsumes e-procurement, supply chain functionalities, just-in-time inventory, and the like. However, there is one important philosophical difference in the upstream channel focus. While the focus of supply chain and e-procurement has been to increase efficiency and reduce costs, e-Service focuses on improving service to customers and expanding the market. In addition to the domains of business-to-business, business-to-consumers, and government-to-public, the e-Service concept can be applied in an intra-organizational context. In Figure 1.1, within the organization each cell or department is a customer of another cell or department, and the e-Service concept subsumes such intra-organizational interactions.

Given the interest in e-Service and the simultaneous, albeit fractured, evolution of the concept in various sectors and industries, it is important to examine the many definitions and perspectives of "e-Service" that have emerged. Some companies in the IT sector view e-Service narrowly to imply information services and Web services provided by consulting companies (e.g., Viant,

Figure 1.1 **The Scope of e-Service**

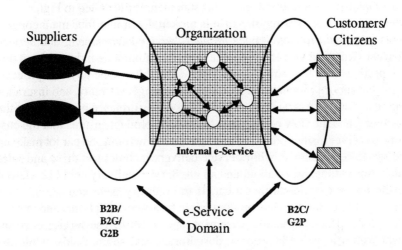

Note: B2B=Business-to-Business; B2G=Business-to-Government; G2B=Government-to-Business; B2C=Business-to-Consumer; G2P=Government-to-Public.

Scient, IBM). Many IT infrastructure companies in the telecommunications sector have also been viewed as providing "e-Service"—electronic services such as connectivity and related services. Other companies, such as Hewlett-Packard, have been using "e-Service" as their marketing theme in order to move its focus from products to services. In some government agencies, e-Service is viewed as a means of holding government accountable to its citizens. Many other companies view e-Service as a purely IT-driven concept.

Our notion of e-Service is much broader than IT services, Web services, or infrastructure services. While it includes all the IT-based services provided over electronic networks, it also encompasses the service product, service environment, and service delivery that comprise any business model, whether it belongs to a goods manufacturer or a pure service provider (Rust et al. 1996). The fundamental philosophy of e-Service is the focus on customers/citizens—meeting their needs and thereby growing the markets and revenue. Technology is an enabler in e-Service and not an end in itself. The next section illustrates the concept of e-Service with concrete examples.

Transformation to e-Service

It is conventional wisdom that, whether a firm is marketing products or services, the intangible components of its offering play a pivotal role in winning and maintaining a satisfied customer. A commonly used perspective that emphasizes the importance of this statement is illustrated in Figure 1.2a, where the market offering of a firm is broken down into four main components: *physical product, service product, service environment,* and *service delivery* (Rust and Oliver 1994). Viewing the automobile industry from this perspective, we can readily identify the automobile as the physical product, while the service product consists of title exchange, warranty, and insurance and financing. The service product is the core performance purchased by the customer, and the flow of events in the service product ensures that the customer receives his/her preferred product. The showroom and car lot make up the service environment while service delivery includes test drive and sales pitch, repair time, negotiation, and so on. Service delivery could be viewed as the *process* of purchasing a car. If the industry were education, say a university, then the physical product might be a degree/diploma, and the service product fields of study, placement, and so forth. The service environment would include classrooms, dormitories, and sports fields, while the service delivery component would be teaching performance, job interview schedules, and so on.

With the Internet becoming a viable alternative marketing channel and businesses exploiting the power of electronic networks, many service components have been transformed to e-Service. In the automobile industry, it is now possible to purchase a car on the Internet alone, and the car is then delivered to the customer's home. How are the service components of Figure 1.2a transformed on the Internet? The service product components of title, warranty, insurance, and financing can all be obtained over the Internet. The Web site of the car manufacturer providing detailed information on the car, using digital images and videos, replaces the traditional service environment of showroom and car lots with an e-Service environment (Figure 1.2b). Some of the service delivery components of sales pitch and negotiation are replaced by simpler processes of customer self-service processes, price comparison agents, name-your-own-price models, and so on. While some service delivery components such as test drive and repair process still remain in the traditional channel, many have transformed to e-Service (Figure 1.2b).

A similar transformation occurs in the second example, when e-learning replaces traditional classroom-based education. However, it is important to note that this transformation is not a simple one-to-one transformation. The nature of e-Service components is substantively different from traditional service—they give customers more control, they include many more self-service features, the service environment is qualitatively very different, and the e-Service delivery processes themselves are philosophically different. Such differences are challenging and difficult to manage, given that many businesses operate in both the traditional channel and the e-channel and thus have traditional service components alongside e-Service components. Rapid technological advances characterizing the information economy only make this problem more complex.

In addition to creating a complex mix of service components, technology advances and change contribute to the transformation to e-Service in three important, interrelated ways: changing the physical product to a service product, creating service intermediaries, and creating new markets.

Transformation of the Physical Product

The advent of electronic networks and channels as a means of distribution has had a significant impact on digital and information-based products. Physical *products* such as telephone answering machines can now be easily replaced by telephone answering *services* offered by telecom companies. This is a not a simple one-for-one substitution, as service connectivity offers greater opportunity to cross-sell and up-sell services and build stronger relationships with the customers (Rayport and Sviokla 1994). Marketing of individual printed books is being replaced by marketing of e-book subscription services. Record companies are contemplating selling music online using subscription-based services in addition to physical records and CDs. Individual software packaged and sold through physical distribution channels is being slowly replaced by software subscription services on the electronic networks. For example, Microsoft has been contemplating changing its business model of selling individual software products and product upgrades to a subscription-based software service with service delivery using the Web ("Microsoft Changes Terms" 2001). This transformation of physical products to pure e-Service components (Figure 1.2c) has significant implications for building customer relationships and for exploring new opportunities and markets, especially in the domain of network-based, digital, and information-based products.

Creation of Service Intermediaries

The transformation of physical products to service products has also led to the creation of service intermediaries—either new organizations such as the e-book companies or firms such as Marimba that deliver software services directly to desktops, or existing firms such as Hewlett-Packard taking on a new service marketing role. In addition, the rapid development of technologies, their complexity, and the rapid pace of obsolescence have made it very difficult for firms to install and maintain state-of-the-art technologies and

Figure 1.2 **Transformation to e-Service**

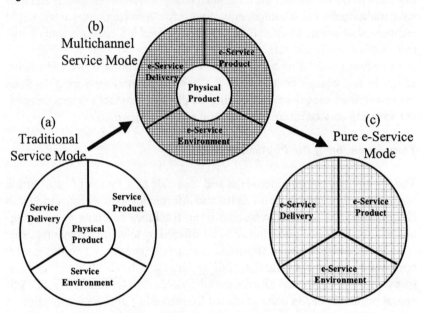

information services in-house. This outcome has forced many firms to outsource their technology-based services, including e-Service, to outsourcers and application service providers (ASPs) (see Shugan 1994). This has led to the creation of credible and capable service providers, especially in the high-technology areas, which, along with connectivity providers such as telecom firms and Internet Service Providers (ISPs), are leading the transformation to an e-Service-based economy. In fact, companies such as IBM are increasingly focusing on services as their prime revenue source rather than their traditional products ("Package Deals" 2001).

Creation of New Markets

Ubiquitous network connectivity has led to creation of new markets and organizations hitherto unimaginable. Markets enabling such auctions as e-Bay in the consumer-to-consumer (C2C) sector and FreeMarket in the business-to-business (B2B) sector, firms such as Autobytel and Priceline and consortiums such as Orbitz in the business-to-consumer (B2C) sector and Covisint in the B2B sector are good examples of e-Service created as a result of network connectivity. New markets provide e-Service to both upstream and downstream channel partners.

Impact of Technology

Technology development is also contributing to the importance of e-Service by creating other new opportunities. For example, developments such as mobile phones, personal data assistants (PDAs), and pagers facilitate real-time information delivery to customers when and where they want it. Speech recognition systems, natural language parsers, and user-friendly interfaces, combined with developments in database technology and data mining, allow businesses to provide personalized, self-help systems to customers to enable rapid response, real-time, and remote interaction possibilities. As businesses use the opportunity provided by technological advances to gain competitive advantage, new forms of e-Service open up, providing greater convenience and support services to customers. And as e-Service becomes the source for a sustainable competitive advantage for businesses, it will play a crucial role in determining the success of the overall economy—first, through rendering the processes, organization, and markets more efficient, and second, through reducing costs for customers.

Impact of Customer Expectations

An important element of the transformation to e-Service is the reinforcing impact of customer expectations. As organizations start using e-Service as leverage for competitive advantage, it also raises the bar for other organizations with increasing customer expectations regarding the possibilities and quality of e-Service. These expectations, in turn, fuel the need for greater efficiency and effectiveness in customer/citizen contact areas and service components, leading to a greater emphasis on e-Service within organizations in both private and public sectors. The positive impact of increasing customer expectations on the growth of e-Service is well supported by the many new e-Service/e-government initiatives being launched by organizations in different industries and sectors ("Web Site Offers" 2001). The next section discusses the opportunities and challenges that await these organizations as they embark on the era of e-Service.

Opportunities and Challenges

E-Service presents significant opportunities and equally significant challenges in taking advantage of these opportunities for organizations operating in the B2C and B2B markets as well as in the government-to-citizen (G2C) and government-to-business (G2B) sectors. We will first examine some issues that are more relevant in the B2C and G2C spaces and then shift our focus to issues common to all spaces.

Personalization and Customization

In the context of e-Service, customization implies targeting of customers as part of a group or segment, while personalization implies one-to-one direct marketing on an individual customer basis. Both initiatives rely heavily on collecting data/information about customers. Technological developments have enabled the creation of value for customers and the building of customer equity (Rust et al. 2000). The developments in data mining tools are also enabling businesses to identify their top customers and create value for this group through personalization and customization (Reichheld and Schefter 2000). Collaborative filtering, clickstream analysis, customer surveys, and data warehousing capabilities are opening up immense opportunities to provide personalized e-Service to retain targeted customers and increase lifetime value of customers.

However, personalization and customization initiatives are quite challenging to implement successfully. The reason is that e-channel lacks the human touch to build relationships, as is evidenced in other offline service settings. While many businesses view these initiatives as good substitutes for human relationships (Barlow 2000a), it is important to understand that the success of these initiatives depends on good, reliable information from customers themselves, which can happen only if customers trust the online businesses in the first place. Thus, there is an element of catch-22 in this process.

If personalization and customization initiatives are based on unreliable information, they could be perceived as gimmicks or tricks. Furthermore, if they are based on information collected without the knowledge of customers, they could lead to distrust (Billington 1996). Recent studies (e.g., Frels and Kannan 2001) have also shown that personalization/customization initiatives could lead to higher overall perceived risks in conducting online transactions with online customers, especially in high-involvement services (e.g., financial services). Thus, the challenge for businesses in the era of e-Service will be how to derive the benefits of personalization and customization technologies without the serious fallout that could accompany them.

Privacy and Security Risk Management

Privacy and security risks are emerging as serious concerns in the era of e-Service, and if they are not properly managed, they could pose a threat to the viability of e-Service. Privacy risk is defined as a consumer's concern that information that he/she has willingly provided about himself/herself to a marketer, through either conducting a transaction, answering surveys, or surfing the company's Web site, could be misused by the marketer. "Security risk" refers to a consumer's concern that an unknown third party will obtain the consumer's personal or financial information without his knowledge while he is transacting business online or the third party will disrupt his transactions online (Frels and Kannan 2001). In the online environment, privacy and security risks cause the most concern of all risks for not only consumers but also marketers (Hair and Keep 1997). Thus, they influence not only the acceptance of e-Service by customers, but also the design of e-Service by organizations. Security concerns play an important role in whether a customer will adopt the e-channel for transactions (Parasuraman 2000). Additionally, many consumers still feel discomfort with technology in general and some degree of insecurity regarding specific online transactions (Parasuraman 2000). The publicity regarding credit-card information theft, "denial-of-service" hacker attacks, and misuse of private information by high-profile marketers has increased consumers' awareness and concern regarding these risks.

While similar concerns exist with regard to transactions in nonelectronic service settings, there is a heightened sensitivity regarding these risks online. For example, in traditional channels, consumer attitude toward privacy invasion ranges from "tolerance to resigned disgust," but in the online environment consumers' need for control and protection of privacy is quite intense (Hoffman et al. 1999). In fact, recent studies (e.g., Zeithaml et al. 2000) reveal that security and privacy concerns have a critical impact on consumers' perceived control in online situations, which in turn determines consumers' perceived e-Service quality. Therefore, the challenge for online organizations is to appropriately manage and relieve these concerns amid the heightened publicity and sensitivity brought about by high-profile mishaps in these areas. Organizations are using self-regulation and instituting formal positions such as chief privacy officer within their organizations to oversee their privacy policies and practices. This approach may help build their reputation for privacy protection. A recent study shows that while customization and a large user base (strength in numbers) may mitigate privacy and security concerns of new and less experienced users of the online channel, only organization reputation seems to be universally effective in reducing consumers' overall perception of risk across all segments of online users (Frels and Kannan 2001).

The heightened concern regarding privacy risks in the online environment is also spawning a new type of service industry—privacy protection services—and an emerging market for privacy. Intermediaries such as Zero-Knowledge and Privada provide anonymity for consumers as they surf online and use e-mail (Petersen 2001), while "infomediary" organizations, such as Lumeria and Persona, allow consumers to store their personal information in their own so-called "profiles" and to "opt-in" with marketers of their choice (Lester 2001). Other organizations, such as TrustE, authenticate organizations' privacy practices and provide "seals of approval" that organizations can display at their Web site. The efficacy of such seals and privacy statements displayed at Web sites in relieving privacy concerns is still an open issue. But, given the technological progress, and resultant decreasing costs, in collecting, processing, and disseminating consumer information, Roland Rust et al. (Forthcoming) show that the market for privacy will continue to decline over time till little privacy remains.

e-Government and Digital Divide

E-Service initiatives within the government that are focused on citizens hold significant promise. Examples of such initiatives (see Bollettino [chap. 12, this volume] and Steyaert [chap. 13, this volume]) indicate that they make it simpler for citizens to receive high-quality service from federal, state, and local governments, while reducing the cost of delivering those services. The expected results of an e-government initiative within the federal government include private and secure electronic transactions with and within government using Public Key Infrastructure (PKI), provision of high-quality service to citizens regardless of mode of access (phone, in person, or the Web), reduction of expense and difficulty of doing business with the government, provision of ready access to government services through the Web, and making the government more transparent and accountable (U.S. Office of Management and Budget 2001).

While e-Service has immense potential for government processes, it also creates significant challenges for the government because of the digital divide. A U.S. government report issued in 1995 indicated that a significant proportion of rural and urban America does not have access to the Web and thus cannot take advantage of e-government (Grimes 2001). Minorities, the disabled, and rural residents in the United States and many countries around the world still lag behind in their use of computers and speedier access to the Web. While a for-profit business can pick and choose the channel it finds most profitable to operate (Web or phone or brick-and-mortar) and choose not to offer services in channels where the potential for losses is high, democratic governments do not have the option of picking and choosing channels due to citizen equity considerations. In many instances, governments will be forced to offer the same citizen services in all channels and will be facing multichannel service integration challenges. While the goal of e-government initiative is to provide a "one-face" government no matter through which channel citizens access government services, governments will have to face issues such as: (1) how to provide uniform services across all channels, (2) how to seamlessly integrate services across channels to increase efficiency and minimize costs of service provision, and (3) how to educate and encourage citizens in the use of technology-based, self-service options and move them up from less efficient to more efficient service channels.

Self-Service Technologies

The last two decades have seen an explosive growth in the use of self-service technologies (SSTs) triggered mainly by the increasing costs of manual service provision combined with technological advances and with the possibilities of Web-based and wireless-based services. Many of the service offerings such as "24x7 service," order status transparency, and remote problem diagnosis, are based on self-service technologies (see Meuter et al. 2000 for a review of SSTs). The use of technology has significant implications for the types of self-service that could be offered and the level of support in terms of resources needed for such technologies (Dabholkar 2000). These factors, in turn, impact the success and failure of self-service technologies and the degree of satisfaction that consumers derive from their use. Amy Ostrom et al. (chap. 3, this volume) address issues such as reasons for success or failure of SSTs, the propensity of consumers to readily adopt some types of SSTs versus others, and the sources of customer satisfaction and dissatisfaction with SSTs. Consumers' technology-readiness (Parasuraman 2000) might well play a critical role in determining their adoption and satisfaction with SSTs.

Within the context of a multichannel service strategy, the above questions assume greater significance. With the emergence of multi-touch-point service systems, the satisfaction or dissatisfaction with SST can spill over to other touch-point encounters. For example, bank automatic teller machine (ATM) failures could result in dissatisfaction with other channels of service. Thus, service encounters with SST may impact customers' perceptions of overall service from an organization. This effect calls for clear strategies for designing and managing expectations of self-service technologies. Additionally, the ownership and branding of self-service technologies is an important issue that organizations cannot overlook. Jeffrey Rayport and John Sviokla (1994) cite the example of commercial banks using the ATM technology in the early 1970s and 1980s to reduce customers' reliance on costly human teller service, which resulted in the large ATM networks owning the customer relationships, thereby diluting the brand equity of the banks with the customers. This result highlights the importance of e-Service strategy in designing SSTs.

With the emergence of the Internet, many PC-based self-service technologies incorporate personalization and customization features. An interesting issue is whether such personalization and customization could positively impact customers' satisfaction with SSTs. Research is also needed on how the level of self-service impacts (positively or negatively) customers' interpersonal relationship with service providers, and what is the optimum level of self-service in the context of multiple touch-point service. This is an important issue because one of the main objectives of e-Service is to increase customers' loyalty and lifetime value, and an appropriately designed service mix can contribute significantly toward building customer loyalty.

Customer Loyalty

It is a well-known argument in the popular press that it is difficult to engender loyalty online because the online environment makes it very easy for consumers to compare competitive offerings, price shop, and switch between Web sites (e.g., Barlow 2000b). We counter that an appropriate e-Service strategy and implementation can take advantage of the very characteristics of the online channel to build e-loyalty. This is an issue that many e-tailers are grappling with, as one of the key elements of relationship building— human interaction—is absent on the Web. Lacking personal relationships between sales associates and customers, many Internet retailers are seeking technical solutions to the problem of building loyalty. Some of these technology-based initiatives include designing user-friendly Web sites, incorporating personalization and customization software, building secure transaction platforms, incorporating privacy features, providing search functions, creating communities, and instituting online loyalty programs. The key issue is whether these technology solutions really build loyalty, and if so, what is their relative importance. To foster customer loyalty to a Web site, e-tailers need to understand how these elements contribute to customers' assessment of the site's quality of e-Service and how it affects customer loyalty outcome measures (Zeithaml et al. 2000).

A recent study (Kannan et al., Forthcoming) argues that the technological initiatives could be viewed as part of the overall "investments" toward building customer relationships. Other investments could include information provision, good price, and reliable fulfillment. These investments are necessary for creating a relationship "equity"—viewed in terms of the trust the customers have with regard to the Web site, the value they perceive in its offerings, and the commitment they feel toward the online organization. This equity manifests itself in e-loyalty outcomes, both attitudinal (repeat-purchase intention, willingness to share information, and positive word of mouth) and behavioral (repeat-purchase behavior, frequency of visits, cumulative sales, and e-tailer share of customer spending). Many e-tailers put too much emphasis on the behavioral measures of "stickiness" and "repeat visits" through gimmicky loyalty programs and promotions without much emphasis on building relationship equity and true loyalty, and they were swept away during the online shakeout phase (Jupiter Media Metrix 2001).

An issue of research is to examine how effective the different investments are in building relationship equity and what should be an optimum mix of investments that would build true loyalty—attitudinal as well as behavioral. Extant research suggests that loyalty programs may not always be effective in building e-loyalty (Dowling and Uncles 1997).

Experience Engineering

The importance of e-Service in creating loyalty has also given rise to a new way of thinking about specifically designing for good customer experiences in a service setting. Proponents of "total customer experience" hypothesize that "business strategies centered on design and delivery of total customer experiences can persistently create superior customer value and establish sustainable customer preference" (in other words, customer loyalty) as compared to traditional product and service-centric strategies (Haeckel and Carbone 2001). This total experience implies the take-away customer experience evoked by the interaction of product, service, and the "atmospheric" stimuli. In an e-Service setting, "atmospheric" stimuli could include the many dimensions of Web-site features, which have been shown to play an important role in determining e-Service quality (Zeithaml et al. 2000). The engineering of Web-site experience is an emerging issue, and two chapters in this book devote considerable attention to it. Irina Ceaparu et al. (chap. 5) focus on designing Web sites for creating "trust," and Weiyin Hong et al. (chap. 6) examine how Web-site design impacts consumer behavior online. It is important to understand how specific Web-site experiences can be designed by controlling design factors—access, navigation, site aesthetics, response, reliability, "trust" insurance, and information—and how the specific experiences relate to customers' perceived value. This knowledge is especially valuable in the e-tail setting, given online retail's state of flux recently.

e-Markets and Procurement Services

Moving on to the B2B and G2B spaces, there have been significant developments, such as evolution of electronic markets, exchanges, and third-party procurement services, and pricing mechanisms such as online auctions based on Internet connectivity. The electronic markets, exchanges, and online procurement services have created new forms of e-Service that did not exist before. These services provide the opportunity to increase the liquidity of the market, reduce trading costs, make procurement and selling more efficient, and enable organizations in the B2B as well as G2B space to focus on increasing the quality of services. The market is still evolving as the first wave of such independent marketplaces as e-Steel, PaperExchange, PlasticNet, and Chemdex latched onto the model of third-party market makers and floundered; and the powerful buyers started forming their own consortiums. Analysts argue that a more stable model of e-distributors, lying somewhere in the middle of the two extremes of stand-alone markets and consortiums, will emerge (Berryman and Heck 2001). The e-distributors will provide services such as title transfer, aggregation/disaggregation of goods for the convenience of buyers, and advise buyers on which products and services to choose. They may also perform a critical service for the sellers by finding markets for their goods and thus adding value in the transactional value chain. For example, companies like FreeMarkets.com are already providing similar procurement services to buyers by enabling auction-based procurement to take advantage of lower prices, and identifying and prequalifying sellers to participate in the auctions. The product categories for which they provide such services are not traditional commodities but complex products for which auctions have not been used previously.

As the above opportunities arise, many questions arise in analyzing e-Service in the upstream channel. As more businesses start using e-markets, the impact on overall procurement and procurement using traditional models would be an interesting area to study. Would e-markets increase liquidity by increasing the number of players? Would an auction-based pricing mechanism be detrimental to buyer-seller relationship? The irony of a B2B marketplace is that, while in the B2C market the focus seems to be on a one-on-one relationship with customers with the use of Web technologies, in the B2B market the Web is being used to replace the traditional one-on-one relationship with suppliers, with procurement through exchanges and auctions. Obviously, this has been counterproductive and has led to failures of many e-markets. An e-Service perspective would suggest alternative forms of markets where the focus would be to create value for both buyers and sellers and not just one of them.

Connectivity Services, ASPs, and Online Media

One of the most significant creations of new services is network connectivity and the associated opportunities for providing information, content, media, and IT services through the Web. Traditional products are now being transformed into services and offered through the Web—print books and music, multimedia CD/DVDs are being transformed to subscription services for content, be it text, music or video. In addition to the numerous Internet service providers that offer connectivity to both business and consumer markets, there are application service providers that provide reliable service-outsourcing opportunities to many organizations. Online advertising, publishing, and information services have become a significant proportion of the new economy (Barua et al. 2001). These network-based new opportunities have also raised important questions regarding service provision. What does quality of service mean in the network connectivity arena? In the event of congestion in networks, what kinds of reliability assurances can be given regarding connectivity services? What pricing schemes are the best to offer connectivity services? How should service-level agreements be drawn up, and what impact do they have on customer expectations? Who should bear the responsibility for service failures through denial-of-service (DOS) attack? How should organizations segment consumers for service offerings? In the area of content provision on the Web, in addition to the above questions, there are issues of digital rights management, pricing of content, and service guarantees. Many of these questions are significant issues for managers as well as researchers. This is one aspect of e-Service that needs critical attention in the coming years even as the network-based economy grows rapidly in both upstream and downstream channels and in both business and consumer markets.

e-Service Measurement

Measurements in the context of service provision consist of a set of internal measures that focus on the service delivery, engineering, and operational dimensions, and a set of external measures based on sales and profit and customer assessment of services (Bolton and Drew 1994). The measurement of customer assessment of services, in turn, consists of customer satisfaction/dissatisfaction measurement (Holbrook and Corfman 1985; Oliver 1981) and perceived service quality (Parasuraman et al. 1985, 1988; Zeithaml 1988). In the context of e-Service, many internal measures are being designed and used—ranging from effective access and response times to delivery times, reliability, time spent in the system, and so on. Internal measures of consumers' online behavior are also being employed—stickiness of the Web site, clickstream analysis, response to promotions, switching away to competitor sites, and so forth. Many online organizations are also using customer satisfaction surveys on the Web to supplement internal measures to better design Web sites and fulfillment systems. In practice, many of such surveys have been developed on the fly with no real focus on their reliability and validity

(Miller and Dickson 2001). In the realm of measurement of perceived overall quality, Valarie Zeithaml et al. (2000) have developed a measure of e-Service quality (e-SQ) that is similar to the SERVQUAL measure that focuses on traditional service channels (Parasuraman et al. 1988).

There has been extant research, in the context of traditional service channels, that focuses on how useful the customer satisfaction measures are in predicting the external measures of sales, market shares, and profit (see, for example, Bolton and Drew 1994). A similar question can be raised in the context of e-Service. First, there is the issue of identifying the relevant dimensions on which customer satisfaction can be measured and how customer satisfaction relates to overall perceived quality of service. Second, the nature of the relationship between the internal measures and customer satisfaction measures needs to be established. Is this relationship any different from what we find in the traditional channel settings? Should it be? The answer to these questions is key to establishing a reliable and valid feedback loop from customers. The objective of the research should be to aid managers in improving the overall quality of e-Service by identifying the important elements of internal measures that impact customer satisfaction and overall perceived quality. While notable effort is under way in measuring e-Service quality, there is still a critical need for research and development of new measures in this area, especially in the context of B2B space. In chapter 13 of this volume, Joan Steyaert presents some of the issues in measuring e-Service in a government environment.

Multichannel Service Strategies

The Internet is increasingly being used as one among many channels and touch-points used to service customers. The days of pure-play Internet organizations are almost over, and organizations are desperately seeking to integrate the multiple channels through which they operate and to provide consistent and comparable service in all channels. While this capability provides opportunities for organization to be more accessible to customers and to strengthen their relationships with them, it also creates unique problems. Some of them are technological in nature, such as the need to create integrated databases containing customer data that can be accessed easily and quickly no matter through which channel the customer accesses the service, and to create uniform service experiences across channels. For example, a customer could access her broker through multiple channels—wireless, online, phone, or in person—and should be able to transact seamlessly across channels. The second issue is setting realistic expectations regarding the capability and limitations of service delivery through the different channels. For example, if a customer wishes to access a bank teller in person, the wait could be minutes, whereas online the information could be obtained instantaneously. The third issue is to ensure that the customer environments are properly managed to provide consistent experiences across channels.

Some considerations to be taken into account in designing multichannel service options include: how much spillover can the organizations expect from customer experiences in one channel to the other? Do positive and negative experiences have the same spillover effect? What should be the optimal design of the multichannel options to minimize negative spillover? How can customer expectations be managed across channels to maximize total customer experience and customer loyalty? How and through which channel should customer feedback be obtained to maximize reliability of the feedback? These questions become more significant as technological advances, such as wireless and telematics, create more options for customers to stay in touch with their service providers. This is also a rich area for academic research.

Conclusions

The rapid technological changes and the emerging new forms of service have made it imperative that both academic and practitioner attention is focused on all facets of e-Service—strategy, research, and implementation—and the individual components that we discussed in the previous section. Many novel ideas and technologies have characterized the last few years of e-commerce, but it is very clear that a technology focus alone cannot put a business on the path to success. The key to success still remains a continued focus on the customers and winning them over with a superior value proposition of product and service. Researchers have made great progress in the last two decades understanding and measuring the concepts of service quality, customer satisfaction, and customer value in the context of service in traditional channels. The challenge is to understand how those concepts can be applied and used in the context of the Internet-based service. Online businesses have long experimented with the different components of e-Service using trial and error, but with the focus on research, they can now cut out the downside risk and embark on reliable e-Service strategies and implementations.

References

Barlow, Richard G. 2000a. "Today's Loyalty Leaders Won't Last." *Marketing News* 35(6):13.

———. 2000b. "Online Loyalty Programs Losing Traction." *Brandweek*, September 18, 30–32.

Barua, Anitesh; P. Konana; A.B. Whinston; and F. Yin. 2001. "Driving E-Business Excellence." MIT *Sloan Management Review* 43(1) (fall): 36–45.

Berryman and Heck. 2001. *McKinsey Quarterly*: www.mckinseyquarterly.com/article.

Billington, Jim. 1996. "Five Keys to Keeping Your Best Customers." *Harvard Management Update* (July): 3–6.

Bolton, Ruth N., and James Drew. 1994. "Linking Customer Satisfaction to Service Operations and Outcomes." In *Service Quality: New Directions in Theory and Practice*, ed. Roland T. Rust and Richard L. Oliver. Thousand Oaks, CA: Sage, 173–200.

Dabholkar, Pratibha A. 2000. "Technology in Service Delivery: Implications for Self-Service and Service Support." In *Handbook of Services Marketing and Management*, ed. Teresa A. Swartz and Dawn Iacobucci. Thousand Oaks, CA: Sage.

Dowling, Grahame R., and Mark Uncles. 1997. "Do Customer Loyalty Programs Really Work?" *Sloan Management Review* 38(4) (summer): 71–82.

Frels, Judy, and P.K. Kannan. 2001. "Consumers' Risk Perceptions in Conducting Online Transactions: An Experimental Investigation." Working paper, Smith School of Business, University of Maryland, College Park, MD 20742 (available at www.rhsmith.umd.edu).

Grimes, Ann. 2001. "Closing the Gap." *Wall Street Journal*, Special Report on I-Commerce, October 29: http://interactive.wsj.com/articles/SB10041174211 69724720.htm.

Haeckel, Stephan H., and Lewis P. Carbone. 2001. "Designing and Delivering Total Customer Experiences: A Holistic Approach." Presented at the Frontiers in Services Conference, Bethesda, MD, October 25–28 (abstract available at www.rhsmith.umd.edu/ces/).

Hair, Joseph F., Jr., and William W. Keep. 1997. "Electronic Marketing: Future Possibilities." In *Electronic Marketing and the Consumer*, ed. Robert A. Peterson. Thousand Oaks, CA: Sage.

Hoffman, Donna L.; Thomas P. Novak; and Marco Peralta. 1999. "Building Consumer Trust Online." *Communications of the ACM* 42(4): 80–85.

Holbrook, M.B., and Kim P. Corfman. 1985. "Quality and Value in the Consumption Experience: Phaedrus Rides Again." In *Perceived Quality*, ed. J. Jacoby and J. Olson. Lexington, MA: Lexington Books, 31–57.

Jupiter Media Metrix. 2001. "The Jupiter Media Metrix February 2001 Ratings." *jup.com —Press Releases*, February 13.

———. 2000. "Jupiter: Loyalty Programs Alone Fail to Create Loyal Customers." *jup.com—Press Releases*, April 8.

Kannan, P.K. 2001. "Introduction to the Special Issue: Marketing in the E-Channel." *International Journal of Electronic Commerce* 5(3) (spring): 3–6.

Kannan, P.K., Janet Wagner, and Cristina Velarde. Forthcoming. "Initiatives for Building e-Loyalty: A Framework and Research Issues." In *e-Business Management: State-of-the-Art Research, Management Strategy, and Best Business Practices*, ed. Michael Shaw. New York: Kluwer.

Lester, Toby. 2001. "The Reinvention of Privacy." *Atlantic Monthly* (March): 27–39.

Meuter, Matthew L.; Amy L. Ostrom; Robert I. Roundtree; and Mary Jo Bitner. 2000. "Self-service Technologies: A Critical Incident Investigation of Technology-Based Service Encounters." *Journal of Marketing* 64(3): 50–64.

"Microsoft Changes Terms of Pacts Under Which Firms Buy Software." 2001. *Wall Street Journal*, May 11, p. B4.

Miller, Thomas W., and Peter R. Dickson. 2001. "Online Market Research." *International Journal of Electronic Commerce* 5(3) (spring): 139–168.

Oliver, Richard L. 1981. "Measurement and Evaluation of Satisfaction Processes in Retail Settings." *Journal of Retailing* 57: 25–48.

"Package Deals: These Days Big Blue Is About Big Services Not Just Big Boxes." 2001. *Wall Street Journal*, June 11, p. B2.

Parasuraman, A. 2000. "Technology Readiness Index (TRI), A Multiple-Item Scale to Measure Readiness to Embrace New Technologies." *Journal of Services Research* 2(4): 307–320.

Parasuraman, A.; V.A. Zeithaml; and L.L. Berry. 1988. "SERVQUAL: A Multiple Item Scale for Measuring Consumer Perceptions of Service Quality." *Journal of Retailing* 64: 12–37.

———. 1985. "A Conceptual Model of Service Quality and Its Implications for Future Research." *Journal of Marketing* 49: 41–50.

Petersen, Andrea. 2001. "E-Commerce (A Special Report): Industry by Industry— Privacy—Private Matters: It Seems that Trust Equals Revenue, Even Online." *Wall Street Journal*, February 12, R-24.

Rayport, Jeffrey F., and John J. Sviokla. 1994. "Managing in the Marketspace." *Harvard Business Review* (November–December): 141–150.

Reichheld, Frederick F., and Phil Schefter. 2000. "E-Loyalty: Your Secret Weapon on the Web." *Harvard Business Review* (July–August): 105–113.

Rust, Roland, and Katherine N. Lemon. 2001. "E-Service and the Consumer." *International Journal of Electronic Commerce* 5(3) (spring): 85–102.

Rust, Roland, and Richard L. Oliver, eds. 1994. *Service Quality: New Directions in Theory and Practice*. Thousand Oaks, CA: Sage.

Rust, Roland T., P.K. Kannan, and Na Peng. Forthcoming. "The Customer Economics of Internet Privacy." *Journal of Academy of Marketing Science*.

Rust, Roland; Anthony J. Zahorik; and Timothy L. Keiningham. 1996. *Service Marketing*. New York: HarperCollins.

Rust, Roland T.; Valerie Zeithaml; and Katherine Lemon. 2000. *Driving Customer Equity: How Customer Lifetime Value Is Reshaping Corporate Strategy*. New York: Free Press.

Shugan, Steven M. 1994. "Explanations for the Growth of Services." In *Service Quality: New Directions in Theory and Practice*, ed. Roland T. Rust and Richard L. Oliver. Thousand Oaks, CA: Sage, 223–240.

"Web Site Offers Taxpayers Direct Access for Filing." 2001. *Wall Street Journal*, September 5, p. B1.

U.S. Office of Management and Budget. 2001. *President's Management Agenda: Fiscal Year 2002*. Washington, DC: Executive Office of the President, Office of Management and Budget, 23–25.

Zeithaml, V.A. 1988. "Consumer Perceptions of Price, Quality and Value: A Means-End Model and Synthesis of Evidence." *Journal of Marketing* 52: 2–22.

Zeithaml, Valarie A.; A. Parasuraman; and Arvind Malhotra. 2000. "A Conceptual Framework for Understanding E-Service Quality." MSI Working paper.

Part I

The Customer–Technology Interface

2

Techno-Ready Marketing of e-Services

Customer Beliefs About Technology and the Implications for Marketing e-Services

Charles L. Colby

Why e-Services Succeed

Why do e-Services succeed? Since the dot.com shake out in 2000–2001, we have heard more about failures than about the stunning successes of e-Service companies. Some e-Services are so successful that they are household names, such as America Online, eBay and E*Trade. Many of the success stories are occurring behind the scenes within established companies, part of a massive movement toward an e-Service mode of doing business. For example:

- Credit card companies like Capital One Financial Services allow their customers to apply for credit and manage their accounts online.
- The travel industry is being turned upside down with the plethora of online sites for booking travel. In addition to freestanding sites such as Expedia.com, major airlines such as United and hotel chains such as Marriott International offer their own systems for booking online reservations.
- Some telecommunications providers allow customers to sign up for services online and access information on their accounts.
- Banks are successfully converting their customers to online banking, and some, like E*Trade Bank (a subsidiary of E*Trade), are able to operate

without any branches at all. Banks with commercial services, like Bank of America and Wells Fargo, are now offering expanded services to businesses, ranging from online shopping to payroll management.

- Verizon Communications has created a powerhouse brand with its SuperPages, a name that refers not only to its paper Yellow Pages directories but also to its comprehensive online directory of businesses and shopping services.
- LendingTree provides an online marketplace for consumers seeking a range of loan services, including mortgages, home equity loans, and auto financing. The firm also provides a technology platform, Lend-X, which allows financial institutions to provide their own privately branded online lending.

In answering the question "Why do e-Services succeed?" we would have to cite a range of factors, including luck, determination, and the ability to build a stable technology system. But one very important reason that certain companies surge ahead of their competition is that they *listen to the customer*. The successful companies understand basic consumer needs and consumer psychology, and apply this understanding in every phase of their growth.

Returning to the case of the failures, many of the e-Service companies that perished when they reached the limits of their capitalization treated customers as an abstraction, a section of a business plan that assumed that consumers and intermediaries could not resist the tidal wave of technological change. The only role of market research was to produce fuzzy numbers for making a case to investors.

The idea of listening to customers and addressing their needs in the marketing mix is not novel; it is the core of any disciplined, professional marketing organization. However, the challenge is greater for an e-Service because this type of business is innovative and cutting-edge. Markets for innovations behave differently than the mature markets for stable technologies, requiring a different approach to marketing.

Before delving into the differences, it should be noted that *e-Services are likely to be innovative for years to come because the technologies on which they are based are evolving.* In the near future, we will see advances in areas such as data security, streaming video, broadband, and portability. As an example, consider online banking, which is now a cumbersome process fixed to the home computer. Future technology will free consumers from a fixed location, providing expanded financial transaction capabilities that can be activated wherever the consumer goes. Consumers can potentially discard their checkbooks and debit cards and handle all their business through portable devices. The concept behind online banking has undergone transformation in the past as well. E*Trade Bank, while known for its Internet model, has a history dating back to the 1930s; it was formerly known as Telebank, and overcame the barriers of time and space long before the Internet existed.

The fact that e-Services are innovative and will continue to be so in the foreseeable future has ramifications for how they should be marketed. The author and his colleague, A. Parasuraman, have studied the adoption process for innovative products and services for several years. We have found that consumer behavior for cutting-edge technology is distinctly different than for a mature, traditional product or service. For example, contrast a trip to a bookstore to purchasing a book on the Internet. While the e-Service purchase offers convenience, new complexities arise, such as: learning to master an online store with limited personal help; fears about the safety of financial information sent out into cyberspace; the potential for confusion over fees and charges; and insecurity over whether the seller will carry out promises.

The following section presents our learning regarding the behavior process that consumers and businesses go through for an e-Service. It presents the concept of "technology readiness," identifies the five types of technology buyers, and discusses how markets for new innovations change over time. The chapter frequently quotes the National Technology Readiness Survey (NTRS), a tracking study conducted by the author and A. Parasuraman, and sponsored by the University of Maryland Center for e-Service.[1] This study is updated annually with a random sample of U.S. adults.[2]

How Customers Buy Technology

Technology Readiness

At the heart of the adoption process for cutting-edge technology is the construct of "technology readiness" (or TR). Technology readiness refers to the propensity of an individual to adopt and embrace new technology for personal use or at work. The technology in question would be defined as anything that is (1) cutting-edge and (2) removes a significant part of the human element from a product or service it replaces. Virtually all e-Services are cutting-edge, as are most of the systems that enable consumers to use e-Services, such as computers, Internet access, software, and portable devices. E-Services also remove the human element, reducing contact with salespeople, bank tellers, brokers, service reps, and so on. Technology readiness may be a factor even for service technologies that enhance the ease of use by automating tasks: this is because *self-service technologies* often significantly change the process consumers are familiar with or eliminate some degree of the human element in a transaction.

As with other traits, individuals vary in their level of technology readiness, and the variation approximates a classic bell curve, or normal distribution. We have quantified this with a Technology Readiness Index, which has a mean of 100—over time the index has remained much the same in the United States, demonstrating an inherent stability. One feature that distinguishes more highly techno-ready consumers from others is that they tend to adopt commercially available technologies sooner. To illustrate, the penetration of Internet access at home in 2000 was 75 percent among the most techno-ready one-third of the population, 46 percent among the middle one-third, and 30 percent among the lowest one-third. A similar pattern is found among many other technology-based products and services.

Technology readiness influences not only the adoption of technology but also the degree to which one embraces a new technology, making full use of its capabilities. As an example, over half the population have access to the Internet at home. However, the least techno-ready consumers may barely rely on the Internet for e-mail and basic research. Highly techno-ready users are more inclined to explore advanced capabilities, such as changing their home page, customizing Web portals, creating their own Web site, and making telephone calls over the Internet. Any e-Service provider will find that a segment of the customer base lobbies for advanced capabilities, particularly those that provide greater control.

Technology readiness applies in both a consumer and business context. For example, more techno-ready workers are more inclined to procure goods and services over the Internet. They are also more likely to show an interest in helping clients and coworkers with technology problems. Technology readiness also applies to nonprofit situations. For example, the share of the one-third highest technology-ready adults who have visited a Web site for a nonprofit organization was 46 percent in 2000, compared to only 9 percent for the lowest one-third.

Technology readiness is not a measure of competence. Highly techno-ready consumers may feel more comfortable with e-Services, but they are not necessarily smarter or better trained. For example, a person low in technology readiness may be introduced to certain technologies because of his or her occupation. Another person high in technology readiness may desire advanced technology but lack the financial means to acquire it. In addition, one should not imply a judgment of whether it is "good" or "bad" to be highly techno-ready. In some contexts, a person may not want to be too techno-ready; workers in an office with a limited capital budget may fare better if they do not require a lot of updating of equipment and software.

As a final point, marketers need to recognize that *anyone* can be techno-ready, lest they overlook entire segments of the market. More technology-ready consumers are younger, more affluent, and more likely to be male. Yet, older consumers, the middle class, and the poor can be important markets if given the encouragement and capabilities to use an e-Service. Recent research shows that females equal males in purchasing on the Internet, a shift from the earlier years when most purchasers were male.

The Facets of Technology Readiness

Research has shown that people have a paradoxical relationship with technology, holding both positive and negative feelings at the same time. To illustrate, 70 percent of U.S. adults find new technologies to be mentally stimulating, but at the same time, 56 percent feel that technology always seems to fail at the worst possible time. A love affair with technology exists among the public, but one that is colored by a healthy dose of skepticism about the potential downsides of technology in regard to safety and privacy. The public desires the convenience afforded by e-Services but also has a nostalgia for the "personal touch."

Our research on technology beliefs reveals that TR is multifaceted, consisting of four relatively independent dimensions of belief about technology (see Figure 2.1). Two of these are "contributors" to technology adoption and two are "inhibitors." Each dimension is represented by beliefs that are uniquely intertwined with the benefits and limitations of e-Services. The contributors, which propel consumers toward adopting and using e-Services, consist of *optimism* and *innovativeness.*

Optimism is the degree of faith an individual has in the benefits of cutting-edge technology. Optimistic consumers believe that technology gives them greater control and flexibility in their lives. They feel that technology will make them more efficient at home and work, provide them with greater convenience in their schedules, and offer more freedom of mobility. They also enjoy new innovations, finding them to be stimulating and fun. To illustrate, two individuals may each spend a full hour learning to use a new e-Service (say, uploading pictures to a photo-processing service on the Internet). The more optimistic consumer may barely notice the time investment, and would laud the benefits of being able to perform the task twenty-four hours a day without leaving home. The less optimistic consumer would complain of the time wasted learning a new way to do something when the old way worked fine, and would need to be reminded of the benefits of the new way. (See Table 2.1 for examples of optimistic beliefs.)

Another contributor to technology readiness is innovativeness, the degree to which an individual likes to explore and experiment with new technology. Innovative consumers like to learn about new technologies, and will keep

Figure 2.1 **Multiple Facets of Technology Readiness**

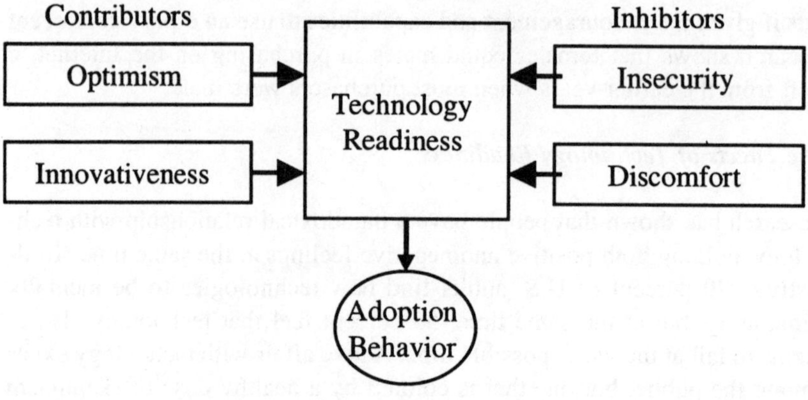

Contributors   Inhibitors

| Optimism | | Insecurity |

Technology
Readiness

| Innovativeness | | Discomfort |

Adoption
Behavior

up-to-date through personal reading and research. These individuals also like to share their knowledge, and are a source of information for others. To a truly innovative individual, the process of experimentation can be a reward in itself: in fact, innovativeness and optimism are to some extent independent, that is, one does not necessarily have to be optimistic in order to be innovative. Finally, innovative consumers tend to be self-learners. In the case of an e-Service, a more innovative customer would be more inclined to tinker with its capabilities and figure out its features without help. (See Table 2.2 for examples of innovativeness beliefs.)

While optimism and innovativeness propel consumers to adopt technology, *insecurity* and *discomfort* inhibit them. Insecurity is perhaps the biggest drag on the advancement of e-Services today. When a commercial process is unfamiliar and there is an absence of a personal representative, physical location, or corporate history, consumers get nervous. When the e-Service is entrusted with personal and financial information, the perceived risk is magnified even further. At one level, there appears to be an archetypal fear of any new technology, although the level of concern varies by the individual. Some consumers may greatly exaggerate the risks; for example, some will gather information on the Internet about a service but refuse to enter their credit card to initiate a transaction. Instead, they will provide the information over the telephone to a complete stranger. Others may underestimate the risk, conducting business online with a company they have never heard of and which does not offer an address or phone number.

Another element of insecurity is the need for assurance that a process is working properly. Depending on the insecurity level of the individual, there is a need for feedback cues throughout the transaction process and at the

Table 2.1

Examples of Optimistic Beliefs

79 percent of consumers believe that technology gives them more freedom of mobility.

71 percent feel that products and services that use the newest technologies are much more convenient to use.

67 percent think that technology gives people more control over their daily lives.

76 percent believe that technology makes them more efficient in their occupation.

Source: Colby and Parasuraman 2000.

end. One frustration of some e-Services trying to minimize costs in their business model is the demand by some consumers for a written receipt. In addition, the need for a personal contact is greater among the more insecure customers. An insecure customer finds the human element reassuring; people can be held accountable and will be motivated to help the customer. A customer who lacks security concerns may actually find the human element to be a distraction, a chance for an error that a computer would not make. Some new technologies allow personalization or customization to make the service interaction more intimate, but this capability is no substitute for the reassurance offered by a human presence.

In the current business environment, there is a great degree of insecurity about conducting business over the Internet. This issue is unavoidable because of the inherent nature of e-commerce, but it poses a significant obstacle to the expansion of e-Services. To illustrate, in the 1999 National Technology Readiness Survey, 77 percent of consumers expressed concern about giving out a credit card number over a computer; a year later, the figure had barely changed and stood at 73 percent. (See Table 2.3 for examples of insecurity beliefs.)

The other inhibitor to technology adoption is discomfort, the degree of anxiety consumers feel when they are unable to control technology. Consumers with a high discomfort level perceive themselves to have difficulty learning and mastering technology. They will feel a sense of embarrassment when it fails. These consumers tend to distrust tech support, considering the group to be uncommunicative or arrogant. Yet, these same consumers need and demand tech support for e-Services if they are to use them successfully.

An e-Service is, for all practical purposes, a "self-service," relying on users to navigate through options and help themselves. The discomfort factor manifests itself when the technology is not customer-focused and therefore is difficult to learn, navigate, and use. The greater the degree of discomfort, the

Table 2.2

Examples of Innovative Beliefs

85 percent agree that learning about technology can be as rewarding as the technology itself.

32 percent feel they are among the first in their circle of friends to acquire new technology when it appears.

63 percent enjoy the challenge of figuring out high-tech gadgets.

Source: Colby and Parasuraman 2000.

greater the need for a more interpersonal model of support. While users who are comfortable with technology can figure things out on their own with manuals and experimentation, users with high discomfort seek a person to sit down with them or talk to them over the phone. (See Table 2.4 for examples of discomfort.)

The four factors described here—optimism, innovativeness, insecurity, and discomfort—combine to determine an individual's overall technology readiness. The Technology Readiness Index developed from the research by A. Parasuraman and the author combines beliefs in each of these areas to create an overall measure of technology adoption propensity. It is important to recognize that the elements are relatively independent of each other. A customer can be optimistic but uncomfortable, innovative but insecure. The balance of contributors and inhibitors determines the overall technology readiness of the consumer, but the particular combination of factors determines the role the consumer plays in the marketplace for an e-Service.

A Technology Segmentation

A traditional way of classifying consumers of cutting-edge technology has been to array them by their stage of market entry—as innovators, early adopters, early majority, late majority, and laggards. This approach simplifies what appears to be a more complex process. In their 1999 book *Crossing the Chasm: Marketing and Selling High-Tech Products to Mainstream Customers*, authors Geoffrey Moore and Regis McKenna discuss how many technology marketers fail in moving their products beyond a small base of tech-savvy customers to the mainstream market. Innovative new products and services will not automatically follow an adoption curve but may require a concerted, comprehensive strategy to push demand to the mainstream market of more pragmatic consumers.

The markets for innovative products and services can be segmented based

Table 2.3

Examples of Insecurity Beliefs

74 percent of U.S. adults worry that information they send over the Internet will be seen by other people.

70 percent of U.S. adults do not feel confident doing business with a place that can only be reached online.

59 percent of U.S. adults do not consider it safe to do any kind of financial business online.

Source: Colby and Parasuraman 2000.

on the four technology-belief dimensions described in the previous section, showing that the marketplace is more complex than a simple continuum. Instead of arraying consumers by their stage of market entry, we have identified five basic types of customers, each possessing different levels of optimism, innovativeness, insecurity, and discomfort. The segments, which individually account for anywhere from 14 percent to 27 percent of the market, are Explorers, Pioneers, Skeptics, Paranoids, and Laggards (Figure 2.2). The share of individuals in each segment remains relatively stable over time.

The following provides a brief description of each segment:

• Explorers—These consumers are the first to adopt cutting-edge technology, including e-Services, and are the most techno-ready. Explorers are highly motivated toward adoption, with little inhibition: they are highly optimistic and innovative, while having little insecurity or discomfort with technology. Explorers are more likely to be male and younger, and to have more education, a higher income, and a higher incidence of employment in technology professions. They are more success-oriented, more oriented to cerebral activities as opposed to physical activities, and interested in exploring their world. They are consistently the first to adopt new e-Services; for example, in the 2000 National Technology Readiness Survey, they have a much higher usage rate of online banking, online investing, signing up for telecommunications services online, subscribing to online publications, buying merchandise over the Internet, and so on.

• Pioneers—The second most techno-ready segment, Pioneers share the optimism and innovativeness of Explorers but possess a degree of discomfort and insecurity about cutting-edge technology. They desire the latest innovations but must overcome inherent fears and need help mastering the unfamiliar. Pioneers are relatively young and are middle-class. They like to try new things, and are impulsive and success-oriented. This important segment accounts for over a fourth of the market, and awaits on the other side of

---

Table 2.4

Examples of Discomfort Beliefs

65 percent of U.S. adults sometimes think that technology systems are not designed for use by ordinary people.

44 percent of U.S. adults believe that when they get technical support from a provider of a high-tech product or service, they sometimes feel as if they are being taken advantage of by someone who knows more than they do.

Source: Colby and Parasuraman 2000.

---

the chasm to adopt new e-Services. Unlike Explorers, they need help adopting these new services.

• Skeptics—Almost as techno-ready as Pioneers, this segment needs to be convinced of the benefits of new technology. Skeptics do not involve their lives with technology. They lack optimism about its benefits and are not particularly innovative, but at the same time, they do not have major issues of insecurity or discomfort. Skeptics have average income and education (slightly higher than Pioneers on both), are about the same age as the general population, and are less likely than others to work in technology professions. Not surprisingly, they tend to be less impulsive than other consumers. Depending on the e-Service, they adopt a little behind or at the same time as Explorers. The major marketing challenge is to convince these customers of the underlying benefits of the e-Service.

• Paranoids—Below average in technology readiness, Paranoids are distinguished by their optimism about technology. Yet, they are held back by a lack of innovative tendencies and a high level of insecurity and discomfort. Paranoids are lower-income, lower-education, older, and mostly female. They feel pressure from the fast pace of life and are conscious about their self-image. This is a viable segment for the e-Service marketer, but one that will adopt later than others and only after reassurance and help with adopting.

• Laggards—As the name implies, this is the last group to adopt cutting-edge technology and the lowest in technology readiness. Laggards possess little motivation to adopt, being low in optimism and innovativeness, but they have ample resistance in the form of insecurity and discomfort. Laggards are the oldest segment, with a large portion of senior citizens. They are also the least educated and the lowest-income. They tend to be more brand loyal and do not like to try new things. This segment has the lowest incidence of usage of e-Services of any group, and is the lowest priority for a marketer.

Each of the segments above tends to adopt cutting-edge services at different speeds. An example is the point in time at which each segment achieved 10 percent penetration of Internet access at home. The Explorers reached

Figure 2.2 **Technology Belief Segments**

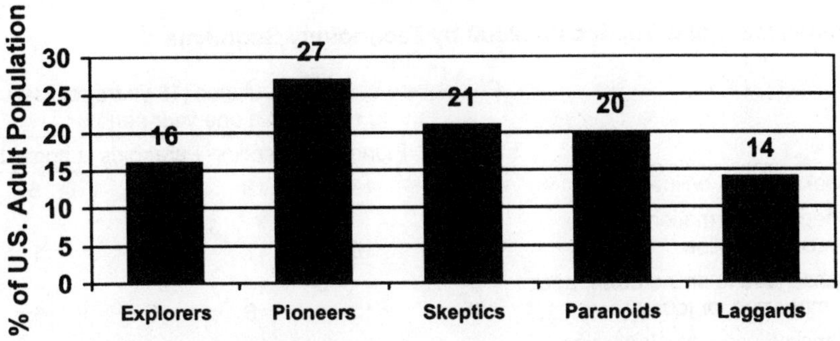

Source: Colby and Parasuraman 1999.

this milestone first around July 1995. Pioneers reached this mark thirteen months later; Skeptics reached it seven months after the Pioneers; Paranoids eight months after the Skeptics; and Laggards eight months after the Paranoids. The entire process spanned thirty-eight months, with the Explorers in the forefront and the Laggards in the vanguard. This pattern is similar to many categories of e-Services, as evidenced by the 2000 National Technology Readiness Survey (see Table 2.5). In some cases, Skeptics and Pioneers adopt at about the same rate, though Pioneers are usually a little ahead.

The differential timing of the segments suggests a final and important observation about the customer for an e-Service (or any innovative technology). The newest customer is always changing. In other words, each segment can be viewed more as a "wave" rather than as a static group. A marketer should not try to target one single segment, but should assume that each segment will eventually enter the market in its respective time frame.

To illustrate, for a mature service that is not technology intensive, the newest customers will always be those who have entered the life cycle where they first encounter a need. For example, the new customers for mortgage bankers will be first-time home buyers. However, many mortgage providers are shifting to an online process that collects and approves applications over the Internet. Because this is a relatively new form of e-Service, the first customers will be Explorers (including experienced home buyers trading up or refinancing), borrowers who are unusually optimistic, confident, and self-reliant. As time progresses, the newer customers will be Pioneers and Skeptics, and finally Paranoids and Laggards. With this change in the customer base, lenders can expect customers who need more help and reassurance and more selling on the benefits of getting a mortgage online.

The first part of this chapter has presented an empirically based theory, on how and why consumers adopt technology. The major points covered so far are:

Table 2.5

Penetration of e-Services in 2000 by Technology Segments

	Percentage of adult population (18 years or older) using service in a one-year period				
	Explorers	Pioneers	Skeptics	Paranoids	Laggards
Booked travel online	48	19	18	7	5
Checked information on bank account online	41	18	17	5	1
Subscribed to online newspaper, magazine, or journal	35	13	9	5	1
Checked account information with utility online	16	7	3	1	0
Applied for credit card online	12	8	3	1	1

Source: Colby and Parasuraman 2000.

- Customers for an e-Service can be scored by their level of TR, or propensity to adopt new technologies.
- Technology readiness is multifaceted, being higher based on the degree of consumer optimism and innovativeness, and lower based on the degree of insecurity and discomfort.
- Taken together, the facets of TR define five different types of technology consumers—Explorers, Pioneers, Skeptics, Paranoids, and Laggards.
- The technology-customer segments vary greatly in how much and how soon they adopt e-Services.

From the above, it follows that an e-Service marketer can achieve faster market penetration by focusing on the specific contributors and inhibitors to technology adoption, taking into account the unique needs and concerns of each technology segment.

The next part of the discussion introduces some strategies that address specific contributors or inhibitors to technology adoption to ensure successful marketing of an e-Service.

Techno-Ready Marketing

Definition of Techno-Ready Marketing

"Techno-Ready Marketing" is a term we use to describe the successful application of principles for marketing an innovative technology. A "techno-ready marketer" recognizes the unique consumer behavior for cutting-edge products and services and applies this knowledge in the marketing mix and in servicing customers. The following discussion identifies some of the distinctive strategies that an e-Service marketer should consider, along with some examples of success stories. These are organized by strategies for acquiring customers and strategies for satisfying and retaining them.

Strategies for Acquiring Customers

Technology Evangelism

Explorers can make or break an e-Service, depending on their reactions when it is first introduced to the market. First of all, they are the most likely to adopt a new e-Service. If a company cannot penetrate this segment, it will most likely fail to gain the critical mass in the market needed to move to other less techno-ready segments.

In addition, Explorers are important influencers of other segments, since they relish gathering information and offering their opinions. Because the process of gathering information is time-consuming and burdensome, Explorers have a ready audience for their views. While the highly techno-ready Explorers like to do their own research, other potential users of e-Services will prefer personal sources of information, such as a recommendation from a knowledgeable friend or coworker.

Technology evangelism is one strategy for leveraging the energy of Explorers, ensuring their early adoption and eliciting their support for the new service. One early user of this approach was Apple Computer, which dispatched a force of paid, professional evangelists to preach its platform to the media and to influencers in the market. An e-Service company could similarly hire its own paid professionals to reach out to influential groups, including journalists, user groups, and technology enthusiasts. One important target for evangelists would be the groups that influence the end-users. In the case of online mortgages, an example referred to earlier, a logical target market might be tech-savvy real estate agents because they render advice to home buyers on where to obtain financing. A provider of e-Services for small businesses might reach out to chambers of commerce, initially seeking a forum with the most techno-ready members who will advise their peers.

While not every e-Service company has its own force of evangelists, many of them practice similar strategies that have the same impact. The Internet provides new opportunities that are relatively cost-effective. A common method is to create educational Web sites and online communities focused on the problem addressed by the e-Service. These communities often include a feature where a visitor can e-mail a link to a friend. Another method is a viral marketing campaign, a strategy of encouraging Internet users to share information, creating the potential for exponential growth in the number of recipients of information. The ultimate goal is to disseminate a message about a service, perhaps getting prospective users to visit a sell-site where they can sign up. The process can be facilitated by offering something compelling with the message—useful consumer information, amusing graphics, or a giveaway—and creating an easy-to-use medium for disseminating the message.

Designing Services to Be Future-Ready

Because e-Services tend to be cutting-edge, customers will have differing needs based on their level of techno-readiness. More techno-ready consumers not only adopt e-Services earlier, but also make greater use of their features and functionality. For example, while a low-techno-ready customer may limit use of an e-commerce site to moderate-size purchases (e.g., books and music), a more techno-ready customer may use the site for tickets to events and large purchases such as cars and appliances. The more techno-ready consumer may also use special features of the site, such as customization, signing up for newsletters, downloading products like e-books, and allowing the site to send products automatically.

The more features that are built into an e-Service, the more expensive and difficult it will be to develop and implement. The dilemma faced by the marketer is that customer needs change over time as less techno-ready users become more comfortable with the service and begin to expect it to do more. The challenge for the marketer is to make the service "future ready," identifying features that will be required in the near future, while not making it overly complex.

An example is the customized (or personalized) portal, which allows users to tailor the content and appearance of a Web site to meet their own interests. One of the best-known examples is "My Yahoo," the personalized version of Yahoo!, a leading portal offering news, information, entertainment, and online shopping. The concept is an important feature in many online services, from Web publications to e-commerce sites.

How can companies determine which features they need to develop now to ensure acceptance in the future? The key is to study the expectations and behaviors of highly techno-ready customers. In its market research, a company should rely on a structured approach that compares on a feature-by-feature basis these more innovative customers with those who are less techno-ready. Features for which there are few differences by level of techno-readiness are more likely to have reached their long-term potential; if they are not popular now among the more techno-ready users, they are not that likely to grow in popularity in the future. Features for which there is a high degree of divergence of interest by level of techno-readiness have future-ready potential. The more techno-ready consumers recognize the value of these features, while the rest of the market may desire them in the not too distant future. Obviously, there is no oracle that allows a marketer to predict the future with certainty, but a careful focus on the opinions and usage patterns of the techno-ready segment will help to achieve a good balance between the risks of obsolescence and overengineering.

Proving Benefits

An important segment of the market for an e-Service consists of Skeptics who lack the inherent optimism and innovative tendencies of Explorers and Pioneers. Skeptics need to be convinced of the underlying benefits of innovative technology, but, once sold, will adopt quickly because they have few inhibitions. An e-Service must clearly articulate how it can have a positive impact on the lives of consumers. In the case of an e-Service targeted to businesses, it must present a compelling business case with financials.

Take, for example, an online directory such as Verizon's SuperPages.com. A consumer may ask, why bother to turn on a computer when a hard copy of the same directory is right at their fingertips. Only a person who is optimistic about technology or has actually used an online version can imagine the real benefits. For example, with the online version, a user can search within a radius of a specified area, or look for a business by name instead of category. Information is also more up-to-date and includes listings outside the immediate area covered by the paper version. These features result in more shopping options, which in turn lead to better value and quality. The benefits are important enough to draw users to SuperPages, but only if they are educated about them.

Some companies are particularly effective at communicating the benefits of their e-Service. One of the most profitable firms on the Web today is Quixtar, an online shopping portal that allows Independent Business Owners (IBOs) to develop their own e-commerce businesses. Independent business owners succeed by selling products through the Quixtar site and its partner stores, and by recruiting, training, and supporting other IBOs. New visitors to Quixtar are immediately presented with a flashy interactive presentation that begins with the words "Your future is loading" and positions the site as a path to achieving dreams. The site content carefully presents the benefits for starting a Quixtar business—"low start-up costs, a totally flexible time commitment, support of other IBOs." In sum, the company does an effective job of clearly stating its business proposition to a potentially unsure audience.

Strategies for Satisfying and Retaining Customers

The challenges of marketing e-Services encompass not only acquiring customers, but also satisfying and retaining them. Our research has shown that technology readiness is associated with satisfaction with technology—while more techno-ready customers have a relatively easy time mastering e-Services, less techno-ready users have special problems related to their higher level of discomfort and insecurity. In order for an e-Service not to stall in its early stages, a marketer must design it to be customer-focused, provide responsive customer care, and offer reassuring communication.

Customer-Focused Design

As noted earlier, an e-Service is by nature a form of "self-service" that requires customers to help themselves. Instead of stating their requests to an employee behind a counter or at the other end of a telephone line, customers must typically enter information and commands on their own with the expectation that the service will deliver as required. For this reason, e-Services must be designed to be customer-focused. The user must be able to learn how to use the service in minimal time with minimal help, and find continued use to be relatively effortless.

A case in point is an online publication such as a newspaper or magazine. In the early days of the World Wide Web, publications were converted into an online format to take advantage of the new medium, but tended to resemble their paper prototypes, providing static designs that were difficult to navigate. Over time, leading publishers such as Cox Interactive Media and Washington Post Newsweek Interactive offered variations that were extremely user-friendly. Elements that Web users now take for granted include neatly organized and clearly labeled content and efficient search tools. Such designs did not occur by accident. These sophisticated media concerns invested heavily in testing their designs in front of readers and continually refining them.

When is an e-Service designed to be truly customer-focused? The following are some criteria to consider when evaluating e-Services:

- First of all, the service should be *intuitive*, so that the protocols for its operation match what users expect. For example, the labels on links should lead to the functions or content that are consistent with their meaning to users.

- The service should also be *efficient*, taking minimum time to master. For example, a lending service that requires a lot of entry of personal data should have an easy-to-use template. One such service tested by the author would erase all the data entered by the user if the back key on a browser were clicked, a clearly inefficient process.
- An e-Service should also be *responsive*, avoiding delays due to downloads, slow servers, or design problems.
- Because there is no employee to tell the customer to wait, an e-Service needs to be *assuring*, providing feedback throughout the process that the service is working as it should. For example, many services will provide a printable receipt or send a confirmation e-mail.
- Finally, the e-Service should be *compatible* with other technology and *reliable*. While more techno-ready users will be able to solve problems by failures in these areas, mainstream users will become frustrated and seek out a more user-friendly alternative.

The best way to ensure that an e-Service is customer-focused is to test it throughout various stages of development. One common approach is usability testing in a laboratory environment. In a typical test, users are asked to complete various tasks on their own, while researchers watch for potential problems. Ultimately, changes are made, such as in fonts, labeling, layouts, instructions, and so on, and tasks are repeated to validate whether the user experience is improved. Marketers of e-Services will gather feedback in other forms as well. These include more qualitative, open-ended methods such as navigational focus groups to identify strategic issues affecting usability. They also include more structured methods of feedback, including ongoing tracking surveys of user satisfaction.

Responsive Customer Care

The level and quality of customer support for an e-Service can be as important as its design in ensuring acceptance by all customers, particularly those who are uncomfortable with technology. Customer care can be provided in many forms in an e-Service, including "help" areas on a site, written documentation, e-mail, online chat, telephone support, and even in-person customer support.

An unfortunate irony is that many companies embark on e-Service models in order to keep costs low and therefore steer away from more personal service, when the technological nature of the offering makes this element important. A real example is the author's experience consulting for a large company that would offer Internet access to businesses, but stipulated that all customer service must be accessed online. The provider never considered what customers would do if they needed to report that their Internet access was not working. While this is an extreme case, e-Services vary in the level of customer care they offer, and the more successful ones seem to offer personalized service, usually in the form of a 1-800 telephone number.

In the 2000 NTRS, 58 percent of consumers indicated that telephone customer support was an "extremely" or "very" important feature for an e-commerce site, while 53 percent considered online customer service to be important. The same study showed that a telephone service rep is the most desirable form of obtaining help of any kind, ahead of online chats, automated help features, e-mails, and so on.

There are a couple of reasons that personal customer care is essential for many e-Services. First, only the most techno-ready customers are true self-learners. Other customers want at least the comfort of knowing that they can turn to an informed source for help if they need it. Second, while people often turn to technology solutions, they are also inherently high touch, desiring the reassurance of a human voice. The 2000 NTRS reveals that 90 percent of adults consider the "human touch" to be important when doing business with a company, and agreement is high even among the highly techno-ready Explorers.

AccentCare is one of the leading home care companies in the United States that provide a wide range of options to enable seniors to live at home independently. Since the company's main customers are seniors, it is critical to provide them with real-time, responsive customer service. The company's Web site is a one-stop resource for planning, implementing, and monitoring the care of a person with age-related disabilities. The company initiated a LivePerson's initiative, creating a nonintimidating online tool that enables even users who are not computer-savvy to interact directly online. One of the benefits of this one-on-one dialog conducted through LivePerson is that it provides a level of anonymity sometimes needed by people discussing health issues and personal concerns.

Another company that has made strides in this area is Allfirst Financial, a Baltimore-based diversified financial services company offering online banking and brokerage services on the Web. Allfirst introduced customer care using a technology called Voice over Internet Protocol (VoIP), which allows customers to surf the web and ask questions in a voice mode at the same time. Customers with one phone line can resolve their problems with a service representative while remaining online, ensuring faster resolution.

Reassuring Communication

Another issue inherent to e-Services is that customers experience a high level of insecurity, creating the need to reassure them through messages and protective policies. By nature, buyers are more secure when they enter a physical location or deal with a human being. To the extent that an e-Service is a new brand (or an existing company that trades under a new and unfamiliar brand name), the problem is exacerbated. Insecurity can take many forms, including fear that a service will not work, that there is fraud, or that information will be stolen or misused.

Insecurity is a huge issue that holds back the potential of e-Services, making it a priority for marketers to address. In the 2000 NTRS, the top reason for not purchasing online was the belief that it was not safe and secure. The single most important feature of an e-commerce site was its privacy policy (considered "extremely" or "very" important by 79 percent of adults).

Some of the more successful e-Services realized early on that buyers need reassurance, and addressed this issue in various ways, including policing mechanisms to avoid fraud, as well as guarantees and clearly stated privacy policies. For example, the online auction firm eBay offers a comprehensive safety resource called SafeHarbor, which includes a clear statement of security policies, departments for monitoring abuse, and protection services such as insurance and escrows.

VeriSign is a leader in services that make online commerce secure. The company's services range from certificates of authenticity that reassure customers about an e-commerce site to sophisticated encryption systems that protect the integrity of online transactions. Aside from the real impact that VeriSign's services have on the safety of commerce, its official seal also serves as a reassuring sign to customers nervous about doing business online. Another organization offering assurance for users of e-Services is the Council of Better Business Bureaus. In the cyber age, a link to the BBB site can send a message to customers that an e-Service is a legitimate concern.

This chapter has presented two ideas—a theory of consumer behavior for innovations that is applicable to e-Services, and a managerial framework for acting on this theory. It is impossible in this short space to provide a comprehensive marketing text—the book by the author and A. Parasuraman, *Techno-Ready Marketing: How and Why Your Customers Adopt Technology* (2001), provides a deeper treatment of the subject. Nor is it the goal here to identify everything a marketer of e-Services must know to be successful, since a lot of valuable information will also come from traditional marketing texts. The emphasis here has been on the issues that are unique to e-Services. In sum, marketers and scholars need to recognize that e-Services in today's environment are cutting-edge, challenging customers with new ways of conducting business while removing more of the human element from the transaction. This requires a new understanding of consumer beliefs and how to apply them in the context of techno-ready marketing.

Notes

1. The National Technology Readiness Survey is conducted by Rockbridge Associates, a market research firm based in Great Falls, VA; It is sponsored by the University of Maryland Center for e-Service.
2. The survey is conducted by telephone. The sample is based on random-digit dialing among a different group of individuals each year.

References

Colby, Charles L., and A. Parasuraman. 1999. *1999 National Technology Readiness Survey: Research Report*. Great Falls, VA: Rockbridge Associates.
———. 2000. *2000 National Technology Readiness Survey: Research Report*. Great Falls, VA: Rockbridge Associates.
Moore, Geoffrey A., and Regis McKenna. 1999. *Crossing the Chasm: Marketing and Selling High-Tech Products to Mainstream Customers*. New York: HarperBusiness.
Parasuraman, A. 2000. "Technology Readiness Index (TRI): A Multiple Item Scale to Measure Readiness to Embrace New Technologies." *Journal of Service Research* 2(4): 307–320.
Parasuraman A., and Charles L. Colby. 2001. *Techno-Ready Marketing: How and Why Your Customers Adopt Technology*. New York: Free Press.

3

Self-Service Technologies

Amy L. Ostrom, Mary Jo Bitner, and Matthew L. Meuter

Introduction

The Internet has vastly changed the ways in which consumers interact with companies, and the ways companies deliver services to customers. Think about the last time you needed to transfer money from one bank account to another. Did you go to a bank branch and actually speak with a teller? Or did you go online to your bank's Web site? How about the last time you needed to get an airline ticket? Did you speak with a travel agent or an airline representative? Or did you visit an online travel agency or an airline-specific Web site to get flight schedule and pricing information, possibly making the purchase of the ticket online as well? When you were last confronted with a health question, did you call your physician, or did you first check a health-oriented Web site to try to find an answer?

With even a cursory glance at how we personally interact with companies on a day-to-day basis, it is readily clear that the Internet is playing an increasingly important role in how services are being delivered to customers. Researchers have begun to address many issues related to e-Service, including how customers respond to e-Service and the implications for consumer behavior (Rust and Lemon 2001), how best to capture and measure customers' experience in online environments (Novak et al. 2000), the impact that interactive decision aids have on online decision-making (Haubl and Trifts 2000), and the key steps that must be taken to develop a successful e-Service strategy (Voss 2000).

Although the Internet has garnered most of the spotlight when it comes to technology used by consumers to get service from an organization, in actuality it is just one of several technologies that enable customers to get service for themselves. For example, besides the Internet, it is common for consumers to get service from kiosks such as automatic teller machines (ATMs) or pay-at-the-pump or through automated phone systems. In this chapter, we look broadly at consumers' evaluation and adoption of self-service technologies (SSTs) so we can gain insight into how to enhance the success of self-service technologies in general and e-Service in particular.

Self-Service Technologies

As described above, services once delivered by employees through an interpersonal interaction are now commonly obtained by customers through the use of self-service technologies. Self-service technologies are defined as any technology interface that enables a customer to produce and consume services without direct assistance from firm employees (Meuter et al. 2000). Figure 3.1 shows an array of some of the SSTs that exist today. While this is not an exhaustive list, it does illustrate the range of technologies that are available to customers. The primary SST interfaces include automated phone systems, interactive freestanding kiosks, video or compact disk (CD) technologies, and Internet-based systems. For example, a customer might use an automated phone-based "menu" system to order a prescription refill. Or she might buy gas at a pay-at-the-pump kiosk or get store coupons from an information kiosk at a mall. And, both business and end consumers might review company product and service information via a CD or track the delivery time of a package on a Web site that provides automated package-tracking capabilities.

Furthermore, the figure highlights the fact that these technologies are enabling customers to accomplish a variety of different goals (Meuter et al. 2000). First (goal 1), they can be used by customers to attain basic customer service, often twenty-four hours a day. For example, customers can use SSTs to get information concerning their accounts or to get answers to frequently asked questions. In the past, much of customer service could be provided only through an interpersonal interaction either in a face-to-face encounter or over the telephone. Self-service technologies also can be used by customers to engage in direct transactions with companies where they purchase a company's products or services via technology (goal 2). Again, in the past these types of transactions could be completed only by visiting a store, by placing an order over the telephone by speaking to a customer service representative (CSR), or through the mail. Finally (goal 3), SSTs enable customers to get "self-help." This service entails technologies that allow customers to learn or train themselves about issues that are important to them. Many companies provide SSTs that can help customers achieve each of these goals.

Figure 3.1 **Categories and Examples of SSTs in Use**

Purpose \ Interface	Telephone/Interactive voice response	Online/Internet	Interactive kiosks	Video/CD*
Customer service	- Telephone banking - Flight information - Order status	- Package tracking - Account information	- ATMs - Hotel checkout	
Transactions	- Telephone banking - Prescription refills	- Retail purchasing - Financial transactions	- Pay at the pump - Hotel checkout - Car rental	
Self-help	- Information telephone lines	- Internet information search - Distance learning	- Blood pressure machines - Tourist information	- Tax preparation software - Television/CD-based training

Source: Meuter et al. 2000, 50–64. Reprinted with permission from the *Journal of Marketing,* published by the American Marketing Association.

*Video/CD is typically linked to other technologies to provide customer service and transactions.

For example, through its Web site, Federal Express helps customers to achieve all three. It is easy to order supplies or request a package pickup from the corporate Web site (goal 2). In addition, an increasing number of customers track shipped packages through the Web site instead of talking to a CSR (goal 1). Finally, Federal Express provides many self-help resources on its Web site such as its eBusiness tools (goal 3). These include tips and pointers such as domain name registration information that can be used by small and medium-sized businesses to create and manage an e-commerce site.

As Figure 3.1 and this brief introduction suggest, there exist endless opportunities for companies to interact with customers using each of these technologies and to help customers accomplish many goals. In some industries such as banking, companies are strategically focused on using different technologies to create multiple touch points with their customers (e.g., through ATMs, online banking, automated phone systems). However, as mentioned earlier, much of the focus on technology and interest in SSTs has centered on the Internet and online applications delivered by personal computer or other Web-enabled devices. This is not surprising given that half the adults in the United States have Internet access (Lenhart et al. 2000). Of those with Internet access, on a typical day 16 percent search for the answer to a question, 13 percent get financial information, 13 percent do research before a purchase, and 4 percent buy a product (Pew Internet and American Life Project 2000). This is an enormous number of people interacting with companies online. The numerous wireless devices available will only serve to increase the likelihood of people's using the Internet to achieve their customer service, transaction, and self-help goals.

While there are endless opportunities for SST applications, they are expensive to develop, implement, and maintain. Not all will succeed. The deluge of recent failures of Internet-based services makes this abundantly clear. In large part, the potential for success depends on customer acceptance and usage. Thus, it is of paramount importance for firms to understand how customers evaluate SSTs, the factors that will encourage them to adopt and use these new service technologies, and what will drive their satisfaction and loyalty to SSTs and the firms that offer them. A number of years ago, we began a research program to understand SSTs and to answer the following types of questions:

- Why do some SSTs succeed while others do not?
- What are the sources of customer satisfaction and dissatisfaction with SSTs?
- Why do customers readily adopt some SSTs and not others?

Other researchers, many represented in this book, are addressing similar types of questions as we all seek to understand the challenges and opportunities of e-Service. Here we summarize the results of our research program to date, organized around two themes: Consumer dis/satisfaction with SST encounters, and consumer adoption of SSTs. We end this chapter with specific managerial implications for implementing SSTs, with a special emphasis on e-Service and directions for future research.

Customer Satisfaction and Dissatisfaction with SSTs

In this section, we examine the factors driving customer satisfaction and dissatisfaction with SST encounters. We first discuss prior research that has investigated consumer evaluations of SSTs and then focus specifically on research we conducted to study the underlying sources of customer dis/satisfaction with a variety of different SSTs.

Previous Research

Although SSTs are increasingly integral to how companies interact with their customers, SSTs have not been extensively explored in the academic literature. While considerable work has been done examining interpersonal service encounters between customers and employees (e.g., Bitner et al. 1990; Price and Arnould 1999; Solomon et al. 1985; Surprenant and Solomon 1987), only recently have researchers begun to investigate customers' evaluations of technology-based encounters. For example, Pratibha Dabholkar (1996) investigated whether using an SST increased or decreased customers' perceptions of control and whether perceived control in turn impacted customer quality perceptions (also see Dabholkar 2000).

Given the explosion of online services, much of the recent focus on SST evaluations has been on how customers evaluate online service encounters. Valarie Zeithaml et al. (2001) developed a conceptual model of e-Service quality highlighting dimensions (e.g., reliability, responsiveness, ease of navigation) likely to impact customer quality perceptions of Internet shopping sites. David Szymanski and Richard Hise (2000) investigated the determinants of satisfaction with e-retailing. Their results indicate that convenience, site design, and financial security influence online shoppers' assessment of satisfaction, with convenience the strongest predictor of e-satisfaction. Ko de Ruyter et al. (2001) studied the impact of organizational reputation, relative advantage, and perceived risk on perceived quality of and intention to use a travel-oriented e-Service. The results suggest that all three factors play a role in influencing customers' attitudes and behaviors toward e-Services (Ruyter et al. 2001). Mitzi Montoya-Weiss et al. (2001) examined consumer attitudes toward using an online retail channel in a multichannel retail context (i.e., bricks and clicks). Based on a study of a financial institution's customers, they found that attitude toward use of an online retail channel was impacted by perceptions of risk and of online and branch service quality. Online service quality and risk perceptions were influenced by customer perceptions of Web-site design elements such as information content and navigation structure.

Although insightful, the difficulty with much of the prior research on technology-based encounters is that it tends to examine a single technology (e.g., Dabholkar 1992, 1996). Existing research has not investigated the proliferation of new technologies available to customers today and how they affect customer satisfaction.

Critical SST Encounters Research

Given the importance of understanding customer satisfaction and dissatisfaction with SSTs, we set out to further examine the influential factors. In this study, described in detail in Meuter et al. (2000), we used the critical incident technique. This technique involved asking respondents to describe a time when they had either a satisfying or a dissatisfying encounter using an SST. The stories that the respondents provided, via a Web-based survey, were subjected to a classification process in order to determine the underlying themes leading to the respondents' dis/satisfaction. In this study, more than 800 respondents participated, with 56 percent describing a satisfying encounter and 44 percent describing a dissatisfying one. It is important to keep in mind that not only were the respondents a diverse group of individuals (e.g., their age ranged from younger than 18 to older than 64, income ranged from below $15,000 to over $75,000), but the experiences the respondents described were not focused on just one type of SST or the SSTs available from one particular company. Instead, respondents reported a wide range of SSTs being provided by a host of different companies. The most commonly described SSTs in the sample were ATMs, pay-at-the-pump gas, various automated phone services, and various Internet shopping services. This is not surprising, given that these are the types of SSTs people use most frequently in their daily lives. But many others were mentioned as well, including automated hotel checkout, automated car rental pickup and return, online package tracking, and online brokerage services.

Themes Underlying Dissatisfying SST Encounters

Focusing first on the dissatisfying incidents, the classification process resulted in the emergence of four categories: technology failure, process failure, customer-driven failure, and poor design (see Table 3.1 for sample quotes). When respondents described a dissatisfying encounter, they commonly (43 percent of the dissatisfying incidents) discussed a time when the technology simply did not work. Most of us who use SSTs frequently (or even infrequently) have encountered Web sites that will not log you on or have features that are not functioning, or ATMs that are not operating correctly. Having an SST that is not functioning is a very basic problem, but it is one that seems all too common and memorable to consumers.

Sometimes the SST worked when the customer used it, but there was a breakdown somewhere else in the service-delivery process, leading the customer to get an unexpected negative outcome. For example, one respondent described a time when she placed an order for merchandise online. The order was lost and she was sent the incorrect merchandise twice. These types of process failures represented 17 percent of the dissatisfying incidents in the sample. What is interesting about process failures is that even though the technology itself may have worked perfectly, the customer still blames the SST for the later disappointments in follow-up and delivery.

The term "self-service" means that customers are getting service for themselves. Hence, it is not surprising that, with their expanded role, customers influence the outcome they receive. Though these customer-driven failures made up only a small percent of the overall dissatisfying encounters (4 percent), it was evident that some consumers did recognize (and admit!) that their own actions impacted their outcome. However, even when it is their own fault, customers are still likely to attribute some of the blame

Table 3.1

SST Categories

Dissatisfying incidents

Customers perceive SSTs to be dissatisfying when:

- The technology fails (43%).
"ATM broke down. It kept my card. I had to have the card reissued."

- The service process fails (17%).
"After a month passed from placing my original order, I e-mailed the customer service center with my order confirmation number. They had lost my order. I reordered, only to be sent the incorrect merchandise twice."

- The customer him- or herself messes up (4%).
"I was attempting to get money from an ATM and couldn't remember my PIN number. I was leaving in one hour before the bank opened for mainland Japan, and the machine took my card."

- They are poorly designed (36%).
"I was trying to order books from a book club online. The system was confusing, and I ordered two of the same title without knowing it."

"I did not realize that some [ATM] machines put limits on how much you can get out. The machine did not tell me I went over my limit for the day. It just spit my card back out, so I kept trying different amounts until I was able to get some cash out."

Satisfying incidents

Customers perceive SSTs to be satisfying when:

- They solve an intensified need (11%).
"My ride to work didn't show up, and I had no money in my pocket. I had 20 minutes to get to work. I went to the cash machine and got some cash for the cab ride. . . . I made it to work 10 minutes late instead of not at all."

- They do their job (perform as intended) (21%).
"I needed gas . . . inserting the card, selecting credit, pumping the gas, and then asking for a receipt. I received the gas I needed and wanted, and got a receipt."

- They are better than the interpersonal alternative (68%).
"The Web page's forms were clear and easy to use. I had no difficulty deciding on my purchase and going ahead with the order."

"I was on my way to a friend's house and was low on gas. I was in a huge hurry, so using the pay-at-the-pump saved me a lot of time."

"[I] was having a videotape sent of a house I was interested in putting an offer [on] and was very anxious to get the tape so I could make my decision. [It was] convenient to be able to check on [the] parcel's whereabouts any time of day or night."

Source: Adapted from Meuter et al. 2000.

to the firm, which might lead them to avoid the SST the next time they need a particular service.

The last category, and a particularly large one (36 percent) involved dissatisfying encounters focused on poor design of either the technology or the service. Some of the incidents focused on a time when the technology worked but the respondent did not care for how it worked, leading the user to be unhappy with the encounter. Many respondents discussed automated phone systems that had menu choices that were impossible to understand or Web-site processes that were difficult to figure out. In addition, some respondents were dissatisfied with how the service itself was put together, or there were aspects of the service that they did not like. For example, a respondent discussed an e-retailing site that only let products be shipped to the cardholder's address. This is not very efficient if one is trying to buy a gift for someone who lives elsewhere.

Overall, looking at the results for the dissatisfying encounters, it is clear that dissatisfaction is being driven by failure—different types of failure but failure nonetheless. While technology and process failures, customer-driven failures, and poor design were indicative of dissatisfying encounters, a different set of factors was associated with the satisfying incidents.

Themes Underlying Satisfying SST Encounters

The classification process for the satisfying incidents resulted in three categories: solved an intensified need, did its job, and better than the alternative (see Table 3.1 for sample quotes). Some respondents focused on the fact that the SST was able to bail them out of an emergency situation or help them to deal with an intense need they were experiencing (11 percent of the satisfying incidents). For example, several respondents discussed how an ATM saved the day when they were caught unexpectedly in dire need of cash. A parent with a sleeping child in the car described how he could stay near his sleeping child while using a pay-at-the-pump machine and a drive-up ATM to get gas and money in order to get to work the following morning. With wide accessibility being a characteristic of many SSTs, their ability to help solve customers' problems results in SST interactions' being remembered favorably.

Interestingly, when asked to describe a satisfying encounter, 21 percent simply discussed what the technology enables them to do. The descriptions of these encounters were basically a recounting of the steps the respondent went through using the SST with a focus on the service that was provided. For example, one respondent discussed how he was able to go to a Web site and look for the product he wanted (in this case it was Wisconsin cheese). He found the product, clicked on "Buy," gave his credit card number, and the cheese arrived several days later. These respondents appeared to have a "Wow, it works!" sort of sentiment. Some consumers still seem to be in awe of what SSTs can do. However, this is not likely to remain the case indefinitely as customers gain more experience with these SSTs and begin to have higher expectations for their performance, especially with more basic SSTs.

Finally, the third and by far the largest category (68 percent) involved incidents where the focus was on how the SST was better than an alternate service-delivery method. The respondents highlighted benefits they received from using the SST, such as saving time, having more control (i.e., being able to get the service when or where they wanted), saving money, or being able to avoid service employees. Using the Internet, customers can save time by not having to stand in line and by being able to get information more quickly without having to wait for it to be mailed. Customers can shop for a product online anytime day or night. As one respondent enthusiastically remarked, "The Internet is always open."

Research Conclusions

Looking at the themes underlying the satisfying and dissatisfying encounters, it is clear that different drivers lead to customers' satisfaction versus dissatisfaction with SSTs. This result is in contrast to research on interpersonal services where the causes of satisfaction and dissatisfaction were mirror images of each other (Bitner et al. 1990).

In our SST encounters research, customers were clearly most satisfied when they received unique benefits from the SST that they perceived were not available from traditional interpersonal service-delivery alternatives. From solving an immediate need to simply providing easier, twenty-four-hour access, consumers appear to value the unique benefits of SSTs. These observations highlight the need for companies to provide and communicate unique benefits to customers. Consumers also were very satisfied when things simply worked as expected or as they should. The existence of this prominent theme draws vividly into focus the current state of many SSTs and the significant number of poorly functioning systems.

In contrast, consumers are dissatisfied with failure regardless of the source of the failure, whether it be the technology, the customer him- or herself, or a failure that occurs elsewhere in the service-delivery process. Interestingly, service recovery, a factor consistently noted as important in impacting satisfaction in interpersonal service encounters (Bitner et al. 1990; Bitner et al. 1994; Tax et al. 1998), was noticeably absent in our research on SSTs. All of the failures described in the dissatisfying incidents highlight the lack of recovery that occurs in technology-based encounters. Also, no descriptions of excellent service recovery in the face of a service failure were mentioned as satisfying by our respondents. Clearly there is an opportunity here for firms to prevent failures in the first place, but also to develop effective recovery mechanisms for failures that are inevitable.

Besides recovery, interpersonal service encounter research also emphasizes the importance of customization ("flexibility," "adaptability," and "bending the rules") and spontaneous delight ("special extras") as primary sources of customer satisfaction (Bitner et al. 1990). Neither of these themes was evident in our research involving SSTs. It is interesting to conjecture whether over time customers will come to expect these levels of service from SSTs as well. Given their current state of development, SSTs are clearly not, as a general rule, providing this level of service. Yet, there are benchmark examples of firms that do, suggesting that in the future expectations will change and more will be demanded of successful SSTs (see also Bitner et al. 2000; Rust and Lemon 2001). Internet-based SSTs are particularly suited to the task of providing enhanced personalization and customization that could increase customer satisfaction with the service provided as well as raise the bar in terms of what customers view as excellent service from a technology-based encounter.

Customer Adoption of SSTs

In addition to seeking an understanding of customer dis/satisfaction themes in the context of SSTs, we wanted to explore more broadly the issue of customer acceptance to better understand why some SSTs succeed and others fail. This type of knowledge is essential to answering questions regarding adoption and usage of SSTs. In this section, we first discuss existing research that examines adoption of new innovative technologies and then highlight a recent study we conducted that focuses specifically on factors impacting customer trial of a new SST.

Previous Research

The adoption of new technologies has been a focal point of research during the past decade. Several studies have focused on developing profiles of those likely to use an SST (Bateson 1985; Darian 1987; Donthu and Garcia 1999; Eastlick 1996; Greco and Fields 1991; Langeard et al. 1981; Zeithaml and Gilly 1987). For example, Jean Darian (1987) and Alan Greco and Michael Fields (1991) examined the types of consumers likely to adopt in-home shopping while Valarie Zeithaml and Mary Gilly (1987) studied the reason for acceptance and rejection of technological innovations by the elderly. Research also has highlighted how consumers' feelings and attitudes about technology impact adoption. A. Parasuraman (2000) examined the role of technology readiness and its influence on consumers' predisposition to use new technologies. Technology anxiety, defined as the apprehension or fear that people feel when thinking about using or actually using technology, has been shown to predict SST usage for Internet-based and other types of SSTs (Meuter et al., Forthcoming). Other research has concentrated on consumers' attitude toward using a particular technology (e.g., Dabholkar 1996; Davis 1993). The Technology Adoption Model suggests that actual use of a technology is determined by the individual's attitude toward using it, which in turn is impacted by the perceived usefulness and ease of use of the technology (Davis 1993).

In previous work looking more broadly at the adoption of innovations, both consumer perceptions of innovation characteristics (e.g., relative advantage, compatibility with existing values and needs, complexity: Labay and Kinnear 1981; Rogers 1995; Venkatraman 1991) and individual differences (e.g., age, gender, previous experience: Danko and MacLachlan 1983; Dickerson and Gentry 1983; Globerson and Maggard 1991) have been established as critical determinants of various adoption behaviors. Although there has been support in the literature for these factors influencing adoption, results have often been inconclusive or contradictory. For example, different innovation characteristics have been found to be significant across various types of innovations. Similarly, individual differences such as demographics also have generated inconsistent findings. The conflicting research suggests that we do not yet have a complete understanding of the effect these factors have on adoption and indicates that there may be other important factors that influence adoption that have yet to be identified. It could even be that there are overarching factors that encompass innovation characteristics and individual differences, allowing us to explain adoption behavior more parsimoniously.

Given the conflicting findings in the adoption literature and the limited amount of work examining SST adoption, we wanted to increase our understanding of consumer SST adoption behavior to provide direction for managers developing new SSTs and perhaps, at the same time, provide insights into the inconsistencies in previous research. Specifically, we set out to understand the factors that lead someone to try an SST for the first time. From a managerial perspective, adoption of and commitment to the innovation cannot take place without this initial trial.

Research on SST Trial

We began our investigation by conducting interviews with consumers focused on their SST usage across a wide range of different applications. During in-depth interviews with customers, we asked them to discuss which SSTs they use, which they don't, and why. It became evident through analysis of the transcripts from the interviews that three factors were critical in determining whether or not someone tried an SST. We refer to these three factors together as "consumer-readiness variables" as shown in Figure 3.2. Together the three factors indicate a readiness to engage or try the SST.

The first consumer-readiness factor is role clarity—the customers' understanding of their role and how to use the SST of interest. Many respondents indicated that they did not use SSTs when they were unsure of what to do and they had not been shown how to use them. For example, a consumer discussing online prescription services stated, "I wouldn't use it unless I understood what I was doing. I'd be less likely to even try it if I didn't understand it." Another said, "I would say, to know what is expected of me in terms of what I need to do. To me, that's the whole key of understanding and then using the technology" (discussing whether to try automated hotel checkout).

The second consumer-readiness factor is motivation. This is the customer's perception that he receives some benefit from using the SST compared to other service-delivery alternatives. Evidence of both intrinsic and extrinsic motivation emerged during the interviews. For example, some respondents mentioned that they liked interacting with technology. One stated, "I like anything high tech. I'm a very gadget-y kind of person" (referring to self-scanning of purchases). Other responses highlighted the importance of extrinsic motivation that resulted from benefits they received such as saving time ("It's not that I hate checking out at the [hotel] desk, it's just more the speed . . . it's just in the room, you click it and you're done, but when you go downstairs to check out you have to wait in line") or price savings ("It [online investment transactions] is cheaper. For me, it was cheaper than calling . . . with the fees"). The importance of providing unique benefits was highlighted earlier in terms of their impact on customers' satisfaction with SSTs. It appears that customers' perception of benefits is critical as well in motivating them to try the SST.

The third customer-readiness variable is ability, which refers to customers' self-confidence that they possess the skills and have the necessary resources or equipment to use the SST. Referring to online investment transactions, one consumer responded: "No way, I think when you're talking about serious money and trading and selling stocks and bonds, whoa! I wouldn't want to do the wrong thing with my money, especially in the stock world. I would probably screw it up" (discussing online investments). Another consumer highlighted the resource aspect of ability. When discussing her use of online prescription services, she stated, "I probably would, but I don't have Internet access at home."

Figure 3.2 **Factors Impacting Customer Trial of SSTs**

Consumer-Readiness Variables

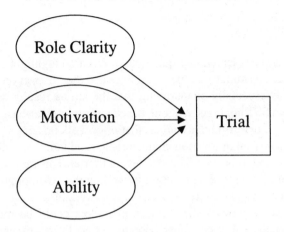

All three of these factors—role clarity, motivation, and ability—figure prominently in the management literature as key factors that impact the effectiveness of employees in performing their role on the job (Vroom 1964) and have been discussed as factors that are required for customers to perform their role effectively in situations where they help to cocreate a service along with the service provider (e.g., Bowen 1986; Schneider and Bowen 1995). Our qualitative research suggests that these factors are important in impacting consumer trial of SSTs as well.

Based on these results, we were interested in quantitatively examining whether these three factors do in fact impact SST trial and how they might relate to other variables tested in previous adoption research. We conducted two large-scale studies of customers (828 completed the first survey and 734 completed the second) of a mail-order business in the pharmaceutical industry. The company we worked with was interested in moving more customers to SST ordering systems and away from interpersonal interactions over the phone. Each study focused on a different SST alternative that the company offered to its customers. The first investigated an automated phone system, and the second examined a newly introduced online ordering option. The goal was to compare those who had tried the SST with those who had not yet tried it in order to better understand factors leading to trial. The results from both surveys showed that all three consumer-readiness factors predicted trial, though role clarity and motivation were the strongest predictors. In fact, across both contexts, the consumer-readiness variables of role clarity, motivation, and ability were more effective predictors of trial than the innovation characteristics or the individual difference variables that have been extensively investigated in previous literature. Basic awareness also emerged as a key predictor (see Meuter et al. 2002 for a complete discussion of this research and results).

Research Conclusions

Both the qualitative research and quantitative research highlight the importance of all three consumer-readiness variables and their impact on SST trial. In addition, it is especially encouraging that the strong results were replicated across two SST contexts: a phone-based and an Internet-based service-delivery system. These findings suggest that prior work on adoption that has focused exclusively on innovation characteristics and individual differences has perhaps ignored important factors relevant to trial. This may account for some of the conflicting findings present in the literature. Although the innovation characteristics and individual differences variables are relevant factors to consider, it appears that service providers could be much more successful in encouraging customer adoption of SSTs by emphasizing the key factors of role clarity, motivation, and ability.

Discussion

Managerial Implications for e-Service

The results emerging from our SST research have important implications for firms that offer service via one or more SSTs, including those that provide e-Service. For example, customer satisfaction/dissatisfaction with technology-based service encounters, including e-Service, appears to be driven by basic requirements rather than bells and whistles. Whether or not customers will try a new SST also depends on basics. The research indicates that to be successful with a new SST or providing e-Service, a firm will need to address some fundamental questions:

Does the SST Work and Work Reliably?

It was evident from our research on customer satisfaction with SSTs that failure with the technology or with the service process was a common occurrence experienced by many consumers. First and foremost, companies should investigate ways to keep their SSTs up and running. Advancements in technology may enable companies to more closely monitor the functioning of the technology interface itself, but that alone will not eliminate sources of failure. Given our findings that a substantial portion of the failures occurred at points other than the initial customer–technology interface, it highlights the importance of focusing on the entire service process from start to finish. In e-retailing, this means looking at the service`from the beginning when a customer first interacts with the site and makes an online purchase to when the product ultimately arrives at his or her door.

Effectively integrating the technology into the service process appears still to be a challenge for companies. A recent GartnerGroup study cited a lack of integration between the enabling technology and the customer experience as a key reason that none of the top e-retailing sites they investigated provided good customer service (Amuso et al. 2000). Similarly, companies also should examine whether or not their SST functions in a way that is satisfying to customers. Given the dissatisfaction associated with poor technology and service design, our research suggests that real benefits may accrue to companies that know their customers and involve them in the design process. An interface that looks absolutely perfect to developers may not take into account different customer goals or experience with technology, leading to dissatisfied customers.

If the SST Fails, Is There a Service-Recovery Plan in Place?

In research involving interpersonal service encounters, excellent service recovery is discussed as essential (Bitner et al. 1990; Bitner et al. 1994; Tax and Brown 1998; Tax et al. 1998). In our research, no firms had customer-oriented systems in place for dealing with service failures in technology-based service encounters.

It is clear that this is an area where vast improvements are needed. Some progress has been made by e-retailers. Advanced features such as live chat can aid in the service-recovery process online. However, these features have been implemented by only a minority of e-Service providers, and there is still much work to be done to develop effective service-recovery systems online as well as for other non-Internet-based SSTs. The importance of service recovery from a managerial perspective cannot be overstated. If customers continue to have negatives experiences using a firm's SST and no service recovery takes place, it is likely to have a detrimental effect not only on customers' willingness to use the technology-based service-delivery channel to get service but also on customers' perceptions of the firm itself.

Do the Customers Understand Their Role and Know What to Do?

Customers are unlikely to try a new SST including a new Internet site if they are uncertain about how it works or what they are supposed to do in order to get the desired outcome. Given these new roles that customers have to learn, firms must devote attention and resources to customer education and make sure that customers have the necessary information. Often CSRs can play a key role in helping to educate customers about how the SST works. This may mean having employees available to walk customers through the process when the SST is first introduced. For example, some Internet sites enable CSRs to control customers' browsers to aid them in navigating through their site (Fister 2000). Easy to read, step-by step instructions to inform customers about their role and what is expected of them can also be an integral part of the customer education process.

Does the Customer Have the Ability to Use the SST?

Customers must possess the self-confidence that they have the skills necessary to use the SST as well as have the needed resources or equipment. When trying to diagnose the reason for low SST usage, it is important first to verify that the customer base of interest has access to the SST. For example, for a company offering an online service, it would be important to know what percentage of its customers have Internet access. A lack of self-confidence is more challenging to identify, but, for services where this condition is likely to be an issue (e.g., online investing), customer education that enhances their confidence in their ability or risk-free trial opportunities can help encourage customer use of the SST.

Are Customers Rewarded for Using the SST?

Customers need to perceive that they get some type of reward or benefit from using the SST versus traditional service-delivery options. Using an SST alters their existing patterns of behavior, so a clear benefit is required before there will be any voluntary behavioral change. These benefits might involve time savings, money savings, or added control and convenience in terms of when or where they get the service. Companies need to make sure not only that benefits rewarding to their customers exist but also that customers are aware of the benefits they will receive using the SST. Part of the customer education process should be devoted to describing these benefits to customers. These are basic marketing tasks that are often overlooked with SSTs. Making sure that customers perceive these benefits is important, especially given that our research indicates that not only are these benefits likely to motivate customers to try a new SST, but they are also a key reason customers are satisfied with an SST once they have tried it. Hence, these benefits likely play a critical role in getting customers to adopt the SST and to commit to using it for all of their service needs.

Based on our research, we believe that positive answers to the above questions will go a long way toward helping firms succeed with new SSTs, including e-Service. However, we also realize that we are operating at the early stages of this development process. As SSTs become more sophisticated and as companies begin to understand more fully how to develop and maintain customer commitment, competition among successful SSTs is likely to escalate. Providing the basics may no longer be enough in a new SST-competitive environment.

Future Research

The growth of e-Service as well as in the number of SSTs in the marketplace clearly conveys the importance of this stream of research and the need for more work focusing on technology-based service encounters. There are many things we do not know about SSTs and customer interactions with these new technologies. Future research can focus on enhancing what we currently know in the areas of customer adoption, customer experiences with SSTs, and various outcomes that may occur from customers using SSTs.

We have begun to explore adoption of SSTs by highlighting the key consumer-readiness variables, but there is still much to be learned. For example, given that customers need to be motivated in order to try an SST, what works best? How can incentives and the timing of those incentives be utilized in the most effective manner? How can we better predict when someone will use an SST versus an interpersonal alternative when both options exist? Is there a pattern in terms of the type of situation or stage in the customer's relationship? Are the adoption issues different in a business-to-business context?

There also is a developing body of knowledge related to SST customer experiences and research to understand online service quality dimensions. However, there are also abundant unanswered questions such as: Do the bases for satisfaction change over time? How can the dimensions of online service quality best be managed? Do customers perceive waiting time any differently in a technology-based environment? Once again, are these issues any different in a business-to-business context?

Finally, for a complete understanding of the impact of these SSTs, it is imperative to understand some of the important outcomes from customer use of SSTs. Although we have seen the development of research in the other two areas, this appears to be a critically important area that has been left largely unexplored. The very nature of SSTs inhibits the development of close interpersonal relationships with customers. How does this impact customer retention and loyalty? With competitors being a click away and with often little or no interpersonal bonds being formed in a technology-based environment, are the costs of switching perceived to be reduced? Alternatively, do these technological tools create a different type of bond with customers that will prevent switching? Do these technological interactions lead to more or less word of mouth and is technological "word of mouse" seen as more or less influential?

It is also important for companies to understand the impact that SST touch points may have on consumers' use of other channels. There has been some research suggesting that though, for example, customers may use online services to get answers to basic questions rather than place a call to a CSR, some service firms have found that the information presented online has not reduced but instead has increased the volume of calls to call centers (Watson and Fenner 2001). More informed customers are calling with more sophisticated questions requiring better trained CSRs with better technical support to address consumers' questions. Hence, rather than reducing costs, in some instances, costs have increased. Firms must be cognizant of possible interchannel dependencies. Future research could examine the nature of the interdependencies that may exist when firms offer multiple channels for service delivery to customers.

Overall, continued work in this area will further our understanding of technology-based encounters, including e-Service. Insights from research along with further technology advancements will hopefully improve customers' experiences using all types of SSTs. This result will take firms a step closer to achieving SST and e-Service excellence that can lead to increased customer satisfaction, loyalty, and profitability.

References

Amuso, C.; J. Bivin; C. Ferrara; D. Fluss; and L. Hager-Duncan. 2000. "E-Tailers' Top-10 Customer Service Mistakes." Research note, GartnerGroup: www.gartnerweb.com.

Bateson, J.E.G. 1985. "Self-Service Consumer: An Exploratory Study." *Journal of Retailing* 61 (fall): 49–76.

Bitner, Mary Jo; Bernard H. Booms; and Mary Stanfield Tetreault. 1990. "The Service Encounter: Diagnosing Favorable and Unfavorable Incidents." *Journal of Marketing* 54 (January): 71–84.

Bitner, Mary Jo; Bernard H. Booms; and Lois A. Mohr. 1994. "Critical Service Encounters: The Employee's View." *Journal of Marketing* 58 (October): 95–106.

Bitner, Mary Jo; Stephen W. Brown; and Matthew L. Meuter. 2000. "Technology Infusion in Service Encounters." *Journal of the Academy of Marketing Science* 28(1): 138–149.

Bowen, David E. 1986. "Managing Customers as Human Resources in Service Organizations." *Human Resource Management* 25 (fall): 371–383.

Dabholkar, Pratibha A. 2000. "Technology in Service Delivery: Implications for Self-Service and Service Support." In *Handbook of Services Marketing and Man-*

agement, ed. Teresa A. Swartz and Dawn Iacobucci. Thousand Oaks, CA: Sage, 103–110.

————. 1996. "Consumer Evaluations in New Technology-Based Self-Service Options: An Investigation of Alternative Models of Service Quality." *International Journal of Research in Marketing* 13(1): 29–51.

————. 1992. "The Role of Prior Behavior and Category-Based Affect in On-Site Service Encounters." In *Diversity in Consumer Behavior,* vol. 19, ed. John F. Sherry and Brian Sternthal. Provo, UT: Association for Consumer Research, 563–569.

Danko, William D., and James M. MacLachlan. 1983. "Research to Accelerate the Diffusion of a New Innovation: The Case of Personal Computers." *Journal of Advertising* 23 (June–July): 39–43.

Darian, Jean C. 1987. "In-Home Shopping: Are There Consumer Segments?" *Journal of Retailing* 63(2): 163–186.

Davis, Fred D. 1993. "User Acceptance of Information Technology: System Characteristics, User Perceptions and Behavioral Impact." *International Journal of Man-Machine Studies* 38: 475–487.

Dickerson, Mary Dee, and James W. Gentry. 1983. "Characteristics of Adopters and Non-Adopters of Home Computers." *Journal of Consumer Research* 10 (September): 225–235.

Donthu, Naveen, and Adriana Garcia. 1999. "The Internet Shopper." *Journal of Advertising Research* (May–June): 52–58.

Eastlick, Mary Ann. 1996. "Consumer Intention to Adopt Interactive Teleshopping." MSI Working paper, Report no. 96–113.

Fister, Sarah. 2000. "E-Commerce Meets E-Service." *Training* 37 (June): 42–46.

Globerson, Shlomo, and Michael J. Maggard. 1991. "A Conceptual Model of Self-Service." *International Journal of Operations & Production Management* 11(4): 33–43.

Greco, Alan J., and D. Michael Fields. 1991. "Profiling Early Triers of Service Innovations: A Look at Interaction Home Video Ordering Services." *Journal of Services Marketing* 5(3): 19–26.

Haubl, Gerald, and Valerie Trifts. 2000. "Consumer Decision Making in Online Shopping Environments: The Effects of Interactive Decision Aids." *Marketing Science* 19(1): 4–21.

Labay, Duncan G., and Thomas C. Kinnear. 1981. "Exploring the Consumer Decision Process in the Adoption of Solar Energy Systems." *Journal of Consumer Research* 8 (December): 271–278.

Langeard, Eric; John E.G. Bateson; Christopher H. Lovelock; and Pierre Eiglier. 1981. "Services Marketing: New Insights from Consumers and Managers." MSI working paper, Report no. 81–104.

Lenhart, Amanda; Lee Rainie; Susannah Fox; John Horrigan; and Tom Spooner. 2000. "Who's Not Online." Pew Internet and American Life Project: www.pewinternet.org.

Meuter, Matthew L.; Mary Jo Bitner; Amy L. Ostrom; and Stephen W. Brown. 2002. "Consumer Adoption of Self-Service Technologies." Working paper.

Meuter, Matthew L.; Amy L. Ostrom; Mary Jo Bitner; and Robert I. Roundtree. Forthcoming. "The Influence of Technology Anxiety on Consumer Use and Experiences with Self-Service Technologies." *Journal of Business Research's,* special issue on e-retailing.

Meuter, Matthew L.; Amy L. Ostrom; Robert I. Roundtree; and Mary Jo Bitner. 2000.

"Self-Service Technologies: Understanding Customer Satisfaction with Technology-Based Service Encounters." *Journal of Marketing* 64 (July): 50–64.

Montoya-Weiss, Mitzi; Glenn B. Voss; and Dhruv Grewal. 2001. "Bricks and Clicks: What Drives Customers' Use of the Online Channel and Overall Satisfaction in a Multichannel Context?" Working paper, North Carolina State University.

Novak, Thomas P.; Donna L. Hoffman; and Yiu-Fai Yung. 2000. "Measuring the Customer Experience in Online Environments: A Structural Modeling Approach." *Marketing Science* 19(1): 22–42.

Parasuraman, A. 2000. "Technology Readiness Index (TRI): A Multiple Item Scale to Measure Readiness to Embrace New Technologies." *Journal of Services Research* 2(4): 307–320.

Pew Internet and American Life Project. 2000. "Daily Internet Activities." Pew Internet and American Life Surveys (March–October): www.pewinternet.org.

Price, Linda L., and Eric J. Arnould. 1999. "Commercial Friendships: Service Provider-Client Relationships in Context." *Journal of Marketing* 63(4): 38–56.

Rogers, Everett. 1995. *Diffusion of Innovations*. 4th ed. New York: Free Press.

Rust, Roland T., and Katherine N. Lemon. 2001. "E-Service and the Consumer." *International Journal of Electronic Commerce* 5(3): 85–101.

Ruyter, Ko de; Martin Wetzels; and Mirella Kleijnen. 2001. "Customer Adoption of E-Service: An Experimental Study." *International Journal of Service Industry Management* 12(2): 184–207.

Schneider, Benjamin, and David E. Bowen. 1995. *Winning the Service Game*. Boston: Harvard Business School Press.

Solomon, Michael R.; Carol F. Surprenant; John A. Czepiel; and Evelyn G. Gutman. 1985. "A Role Theory Perspective on Dyadic Interactions." *Journal of Marketing* 49 (winter): 99–111.

Surprenant, Carol F., and Michael R. Solomon. 1987. "Predictability and Personalization in the Service Encounter." *Journal of Marketing* 51 (April): 73–80.

Szymanski, David M., and Richard T. Hise. 2000. "E-Satisfaction: An Initial Examination." *Journal of Retailing* 76(3): 309–322.

Tax, Stephen S., and Stephen W. Brown. 1998. "Recovering and Learning from Service Failure." *Sloan Management Review* 40(1): 75–88.

Tax, Stephen S.; Stephen W. Brown; and Murali Chandrashekaran. 1998. "Customer Evaluations of Service Complaint Experiences: Implications for Relationship Marketing." *Journal of Marketing* 62 (April): 60–76.

Venkatraman, Meera P. 1991. "The Impact of Innovativeness and Innovation Type on Adoption." *Journal of Retailing* 67(1): 51–67.

Voss, Chris. 2000. "Developing an eService Strategy." *Business Strategy Review* 11(1): 21–33.

Vroom, Victor H. 1964. *Work and Motivation*. New York: Wiley.

Watson James K., Jr., and Joe Fenner. 2001. "The High Price of Self-Service." *Informationweek.com*, January 22.

Zeithaml, Valarie, and Mary C. Gilly. 1987. "Characteristics Affecting the Acceptance of Retailing Technologies: A Comparison of Elderly and Non-Elderly Consumers." *Journal of Retailing* 63(1): 49–68.

Zeithaml, Valarie; A. Parasuraman; and Arvind Malhotra. 2001. "A Conceptual Framework for Understanding e-Service Quality: Implications for Future Research and Managerial Practice." MSI working paper, Report no. 00-115.

4

Robots and Gunslingers

Measuring Customer Satisfaction on the Internet

David Simms

Introduction

e-Service and the Internet

The Internet's influence on culture, buying habits, entertainment, and personal communication cannot possibly be overstated. The revolutionary dimension that the Internet offers business, and marketing especially, is accelerated intimacy with a huge populace. The Internet enhances the ability to tap into a diverse collection of resources, the depth and breadth of which have never before been available to the general population. "E-customers" are driven to the Internet for the convenience, comfort, and control of filling their needs in their own space, whether they are looking for entertainment or information, or perhaps only to buy a new pair of shoes. Their demands for service are many. Their patience and forgiveness for less than real-time, custom response are not long. The Internet is not just a boundless catalog or advertisement or simply a new sales channel. It is an information space, a means of communication, and an opportunity to nearly realize the long-standing ideal of one-on-one customer marketing on a grand scale. The enterprise now has the potential to be closer than ever to the customer. The challenge comes in how the enterprise will capitalize on that prospect by identifying, measuring, and acting on the voice of the e-customer in this rapidly evolving environment.

Robots and Gunslingers

The Internet provides a paradox between impersonal technology and intimate human interaction. On one hand, the Internet gives the ability to stay in closer touch. On the other hand, it adds a quality of distance and anonymity. Service in the e-space becomes a challenge as service providers struggle to understand this new and rapidly evolving medium. In seeking an appropriate analogy, consider a mix of cultural icons—the present melding with the past.

"Robots and gunslingers" seems an appropriate metaphor for e-business satisfaction measurement on the Internet. Cutting-edge tools exist to assist the e-business in understanding and measuring e-customer satisfaction, ranging from robots ("bots") and spiders—bits and bytes of software code that combine sites looking for broken links and poor functional performance—to "pop-up" customer surveys seeking intimate customer opinion. Thousands, even millions, of customer data points can be gleaned from the ever-expanding Internet population in a matter of minutes or hours as opposed to days, weeks, and months. The speed of data gathering can now be measured with a clock as opposed to a calendar. Whether using paid "opt-in" survey takers (gunslingers, in our parlance) or large personal customer lists, monitoring the pulse of the customer has never been easier or more important. The Internet creates an opportunity to interact, collect information, and personalize offerings to a degree never before seen and, as previously stated, approaches the ideal of true mass one-on-one marketing and communication. The Internet is rapidly making us all its customers.

e-Business: A New Interactive Dynamic

How a business leverages the electronic medium to communicate and serve the customer will ultimately dictate the winners and losers in the battle for cyberspace. In some cases the traditional means of superior monetary resources to gain an advantage just will not work in cyberspace. Realizing that the playing field that creates the dynamic between customer and provider is more level than ever is the first step in understanding e-satisfaction. While the Internet has not quite proven to be the "Great Equalizer" (Borland 1998), as once prophesied by early Internet sages, the electronic medium does reduce the impact of several core influences on consumer behavior, including greatly reduced switching costs, and spatial and physical advantages.

Competition is only a click away, and bigger does not always equal to advantage. Technology allows critical elements of location, inventory, and selection to exist as strongly on a $29 set of rented Web pages as on multi-million-dollar Amazon.com. A rapidly growing network of low-margin fulfillment and e-commerce platform providers creates an illusion of grandeur and girth with functional and content parity unequaled in the brick and mortar space. Whether big or small, an e-business must clearly understand its customers' wants, needs, and "delight triggers," and consistently deliver on these demands. To accomplish this, the e-business must establish ways of communicating directly with the customer, initiating a relationship, and continually adjusting its service offering to meet their demands.

Servicing the e-Customer

Purists contend that a customer is a customer. Whether brick and mortar, e-shopper, traditional catalog customer, or some combination thereof, customers are in many ways all the same. Customers have needs for services, entertainment, and information. The interactive environment and the physical or service product both impact satisfaction. Elements such as page-loading speed, ease of navigation, and page design replace location, parking space, queuing, and merchandising as environmental factors. The Web fundamentally changes how customers interact with potential service providers. When customers first use the Internet, they may find the ease of reaching so many potential providers and options absolutely amazing. As the newness of the medium wears off, the euphoria that creates random "wandering" through the first truly global information candy store gives way to the realization of the medium's true benefits: convenience and efficiency. Experienced Internet users do not so much surf the Internet as they *attack* it with purpose.

The e-business must be prepared for the speed with which customers progress through product/service adoption, and the speed with which they can defect. Nonetheless, satisfying the e-customer is brutally simple in concept: find out what they want, and then provide it to them more efficiently, faster, and more consistently than the competition. This is obviously more easily said than done. Aside from existing in a somewhat hidden realm behind the portal/search engine gatekeeper, the customer controls the terms of the engagement: the length, breadth, and depth of the relationship (Jupiter Media Metrix 2001). The strength of this gatekeeping ability increases daily. In this anonymous setting, an early exit from the buying process leaves few clues as to what went wrong. Therefore, a method for collecting information from Web-site visitors, satisfied or not, becomes an essential component of any company's e-business service strategy.

The Psychology of the e-Service Experience

How we allocate our time—our most precious resource—frequently dictates our success or failure. We see this connection clearly in society, where efficiency has become valued as a personal trait. Taking literally the premise that the customers (and that means all of us) value time very highly in their lives, a major component of the value of the Internet becomes clear. The Internet can be the ultimate as a time-saving tool. As the medium evolves, the ability to perform hours, days, even weeks of research in a few keystrokes, to automate time-intensive processes, to have access to global entertainment and shopping resources, without even starting the car, becomes reality. The Internet is capable of improving our self-images by conserving our precious time and thereby convincing us we are being efficient. Consequently, convenience is frequently a main driver of Internet usage. Convenience ultimately results in the conservation of time and processing capacity for things deemed more important. In many polls, convenience dominates as the primary reason for acquisition of goods and services on the Internet. This is not to say that all customers will have the same needs, or that all will necessarily be primarily seeking convenience. What it does mean, however, is that the customer will likely have a discrete goal to fulfill, and little tolerance for an agenda that does not closely mirror that need.

Along those lines, the enterprise must understand that all customers are not created equal. The customer's set of wants runs headlong into the limits imposed by a company's business model and economic resources, both of which must be optimized by the enterprise while keeping the customer in mind. Since no provider of goods or services can be everything to everybody, defining the target customer, mobilizing resources to serve his or her needs properly, and developing a loyal relationship form the basis for e-survival. Customer focus must be more than a buzz phrase; it needs to be woven into the basic fabric of the company culture in order to satisfy the e-customer.

Courting the Customer

Expectations of e-services are frequently formed based on experience in the brick and mortar world. The formation and alteration of expectations and opinion no longer take years to develop. They now develop in real time. With the rapid adoption of the Internet for everything from quick access to weather reports and sports scores to international research and weekly grocery shopping, the impact of simple things such as word of mouth and first impressions wield unusual power. Switching costs literally nothing for the first-time customer. A study by Web partner, a software development and consulting company, offered the following interesting statistics: Only 4 percent of dissatisfied customers will tell you so. The other 96 percent quietly defect, and 91 percent of defectors never come back. These facts are ignored at the online product or service provider's peril.

The Role of Expectations

The customer satisfaction response is a combination of sensory perceptions relating to the performance of a unique experience. It is a summary judgment comparing *expected* experience with the perception of the actual experience. The mental comparison of past summary experiences with a current, unique experience creates an event known as disconfirmation (Oliver 1980). Disconfirmation results when an event does not go as expected. It can be a positively disconfirming event where the performance was better than expected, or a negatively disconfirming event, where the performance does not measure up to the customer's expectation. This disconfirmation, positive or negative, creates a new mental benchmark for future performances, either strengthening current expectations, lowering expectations, or serving to "raise the bar" for future encounters.

Pre-Visit Expectations

There are many factors working both independently and in conjunction with the customer maturation process that create changes in customer expectations. One factor that works in conjunction with the maturation process is pre-visit expectations, which are based upon customers' previous experience, word of mouth, and other cues, including the avenue of discovery.

The Avenue of Discovery

The avenue of discovery is the path that brings the customer to your door. The avenue itself can create expectations. Customers can take a direct path, a path that includes the use of the gatekeeper such as a search engine, or arrive through a link from another Web site. These paths can provide subtle cues that may impact expectation and therefore satisfaction.

Position in search engine rankings can have an impact on pre-experience impressions of provider quality and service. As many as 60 percent of searchers indicated they felt that companies that ranked higher on searches were "top providers" or "market leaders" (IntiMetrix 2001b). On the other hand, some believe the position ranking of search results is actually purchased, where a premium is paid for higher ranking. While the reality is that these ratings can be a result of all or none of the above, annotations for superior service reported by companies such as BizRate and Yahoo, which are typically earned through positive customer feedback, were viewed by a like amount (58 percent) as being "bought" (IntiMetrix 2001a).

As in other media, marketing associations also impact customer impressions, further adding to pre-visit expectations. The baggage of companies associated with the e-business through affiliations and banner ad links must be considered. Therefore, an e-business should exercise caution when choosing partners and outside organizations to participate in its avenue of discovery. E-businesses should link to businesses that possess similar values and demographic customer profiles whenever possible. Since activity on the Internet is becoming highly focused and goal oriented, linking to partners who do not create a synergy and improved outcome for the customer can lead to a frustrating customer experience and, at best, a steady stream of unqualified viewers. Unwanted traffic creates noise in your customer research data, and it derails efforts to better understand the true target market, customers and their behavior, and how to win customer loyalty.

Customer Loyalty

Developing customer loyalty takes time. A recent study showed that after a single visit fewer than 5 percent of visitors considered themselves mentally "loyal customers" of an e-business. After two to four visits over 54 percent considered themselves to be loyal customers. By the time they had visited five or more times, 93 percent considered themselves to be "loyal patrons" (IntiMetrix 2001b). This result indicates that it is critical not only to understand the customer maturation process but also to understand where the customers believe they are in this maturation cycle.

Loyal customers are your company's best customers. For this reason, understanding and studying loyal, mature customers is important. Loyal customers are typically more profitable, give better word of mouth, and are frequently more willing to develop symbiotic partnership-style relationships.

The Evolution of the Customer Relationship

Early Stage Users—"First-Timers"

Understanding this group is important because—to use a fishing bromide—you cannot hook a fish if you cannot attract it. First-time visitors provide clues as to what to use for "customer bait." They are frequently trolling, looking for a solution to their need. They may never evolve into a loyal customer. In fact, once you know more about them demographically and in terms of what they expect, you may not want them. Customers who focus on issues where an advantage cannot be gained strategically, that is, the pure price shopper, may demand an inordinate amount of resources for unacceptable gain.

The first-time user typically comes to you for a trial experience that may or may not end in transaction. In commerce, they may focus on issues that revolve around immediate gratification, such as price. They are acutely aware of functional aspects of the experience, such as page-loading speeds and content organization. With few "strings" attached, their visit may be fleeting.

Repeat Visitors—"Midtermers"

When "first timers" have a successful experience and they come back, we refer to them as "midtermers." This group *may* be willing to develop a relationship. Understanding what brings them back is a key to turning the corner and opening the door to creating a relationship. Although still likely to be concerned with price-related issues in a commerce environment, typically, loyalty programs and increased selection of services begin to take on greater importance in the satisfaction equation. Previous studies indicate that moving a midlevel user to a loyal customer may require from three to five visits (Zemke and Connellan 2001), although the number of experiences to move this customer from uncommitted to midlevel varies based upon the level of involvement and investment on the part of the customer.

Mature Users—The Loyal Customer

This is the prized group. You have succeeded in winning repeat behavior. Understanding what this group likes about you and how to satisfy and "delight" them should be the focus of satisfaction efforts. This group usually accounts for a disproportionate amount of e-business revenue and profits. Pricing issues impacting the satisfaction equation with the first-timers and midtermers are frequently replaced by requests for consistent service, increased access, and loyalty programs. It is with this key group that the benefits of personalization and two-way communication are realized and "one-on-one" marketing is closer to becoming a reality.

What Constitutes Loyalty?

Repeat usage does not necessarily constitute "loyalty." In the physical world, one could argue that for loyalty to exist, it needs to be acknowledged by the customer. It is therefore an intentional affiliation created by forces other than inertia.

The Internet is different. In less competitive marketplaces, the argument could be made that factors such as inertia and geographic location are equally important drivers of repeat purchase and intention to purchase. However, on the Internet, where switching costs are low and the competition is literally a click away, repeat usage and intention to repurchase are potentially better indicators of loyalty. Satisfying the customer is not always enough to keep him or her (Reichheld 1996), so understanding the drivers of retention, specifically, is sometimes more important than even understanding satisfaction itself.

Frequently, a loyal customer is a more profitable customer. One retail study showed a strong correlation among satisfaction, purchase frequency, and increases in size of purchase.

As Figure 4.1 illustrates, the customer who has five or more unique customer engagements spends on average five times more per transaction than a first-time customer. These more experienced customers also report a 60 percent increase in intention to repurchase versus those with only one to three experiences (IntiMetrix 2001b). This loyal group reported an increase of over 200 percent in the total percent of requirements filled from the e-business (IntiMetrix 2001b). The loyal customer is also more likely to give quality commentary and share in the responsibility for creating the optimal suite of services to meet and exceed their needs. They are really stakeholders in your success. Serving and satisfying the loyal customer should be the overriding goal of the e-business.

The Customer-Centered Culture

A customer-centered mindset dictates that the provider design the company around the current and future needs of the customer. As in the brick and mortar world, achieving customer satisfaction is the process of understanding, meeting, and exceeding the wants, needs, and desires of the customer. To consistently do this, a provider must develop a "customer-centric" mindset that consistently focuses on the needs of its customers, aspires to meet those needs, and sometimes surpasses their expectations. Exceeding expectations, creating "delight" or pleasant surprise, is a proven way to keep customers coming back for more (Rust et al. 1996). A product-service focus is not enough. The formation of the customer-centric mindset is a broader task, requiring nurturing a culture that brings the customer voice into the basic fabric of the organization. The customer voice should be driven through the organization starting at the executive level and influencing everything from systems design and human resources to communication systems.

The Customer Is Always Right, Right?

First and foremost, it is the customer's opinion that counts. The gold standard for measuring customer satisfaction and loyalty is customer opinion. Although it is important to measure and benchmark technical performance,

Figure 4.1 **Spending by Experience: 2001 Online Retail Study**

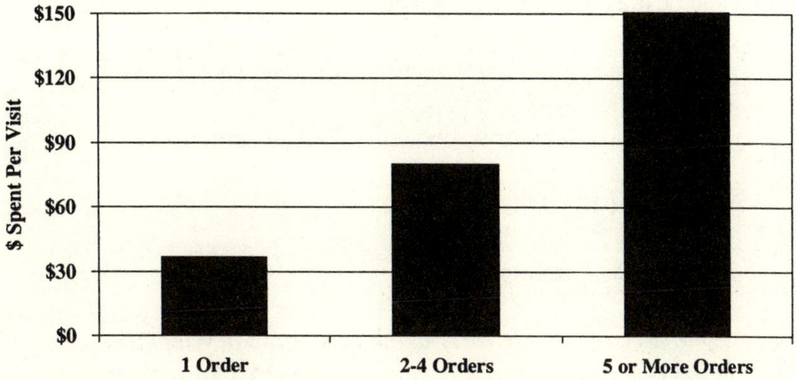

Source: IntiMetrix 2001b.

these measures are not useful if not linked to the customer's perception. For example, a two-second page-load speed means nothing if the customer feels it takes too long. If two seconds is considered too long by the customer, he or she is likely to be dissatisfied, regardless of the status of this concrete performance measurement. It is the customer's perception of the performance that is important.

A customer focus is not to be confused with the mindset that "the customer is always right." That approach does not consider the financial accountability issues at the core of any successful business. Customer focus entails knowing more than what customers want. You must learn *what they can afford to pay and what they are willing to pay for.*

Remember the loyal customer. Straying too far from the capabilities of your organization to meet the needs of a noncore customer can result in both damage to your core group and the acquisition of a less loyal and potentially more demanding customer, perhaps one you cannot satisfy. A true customer-provider relationship is symbiotic. The balance between satisfying customer needs and making the business prosperous is delicate.

Not surprisingly, many freewheeling Internet pioneers now provide exceptional postmortem case studies in how *not* to start and run a successful business, where ordinary measures of success were apparently ignored. The rate of company failure on the Internet is staggering, with estimates of well over 1,000 failed companies in 2000 and another 200 corpses floating in the e-dead pool by the end of May 2001 (Flop Tracker 2000). In the early stages of the Internet, market entry was relatively easy. With unprecedented access to huge amounts of venture capital to test business models, many large, well-funded companies failed to capture the critical mass of customers predicted.

This result was partly a result of these companies' failure to understand the needs and desires of their target markets.

> *With the launch of the e-commerce site, bbq.com will be to barbecue what Amazon is to books.*
> —Anthony Johndrow, bbq.com CEO and cofounder

Born: April 10, 2000
Died: June 27, 2000
Burned: $1.68 million

> *Some decisions made early in the company's development, combined with current market conditions, prevented Kozmo from overcoming the challenges associated with conquering the last mile.*
> —Gerry Burdo, Kozmo.com president and chief executive

Born: 1997
Died: April 12, 2001
Burned: Roughly $280 million

Satisfying the customer will not always save a flawed business model. Lessons from the first wave of Internet failures and successes are driving a second and third wave of more focused and efficient companies. Many current Internet companies are opting for the old model of "granular" growth, adding capacity and resources as a business grows. This reversal replaces the popular mid-1990s *Field of Dreams* model, where the hope was "If you build it, they will come." Long-term viability of the enterprise and a pathway to profitability should be built into the business model from the start. Any financially stable operating structure needs to be based upon a fundamental understanding and ability to satisfy the needs of the customer.

Measuring Customer Satisfaction

Why Measure Customer Satisfaction?

The simple answer is that any business exists to serve the needs of its customers. Theodore Leavitt, Professor Emeritus of the Harvard Business School, sums it up nicely: "The purpose of a business is to create and keep a customer."

Business offerings and processes should be a function of customer needs, using the voice of the customer to fuel the business. Research has clearly established the critical link between customer satisfaction and customer retention (Rust et al. 1996). Since it is something of common knowledge that finding a new customer can be ten times more expensive (or more) as retaining an existing one, developing a loyal customer base is paramount to success, regardless of the business channel or medium.

The Internet has special perks for those who can retain their customers at a superior rate. Efficiencies relating to customer service, customer profiling, communication, and administration may make it less expensive to create and maintain a loyal Internet customer, resulting in higher profits for the successful enterprise.

Every company with a presence on the Internet needs a formal system for collecting customer satisfaction feedback. The reason should be obvious. Your business is customer service. Regardless of what you produce, hard goods or pure services, you are a service company, and the voice of the customer should drive your actions. Many companies make the mistake of developing a view of their customers' needs by reflecting on how *they* feel their customers view the world (Johnson and Gustafsson 2000). This creates a flawed, if not distorted, view of "customer reality," and provides a golden opportunity for internal politics and agendas to corrupt the process of developing customer intimacy.

Survey Development and Data Collection

The art of survey development relies heavily on the survey developers' ability to relate potential actions to a particular question. Conscious focus on maintaining an actionable relationship between question and response keeps the survey on task and controls survey length. Fighting the urge to include "nice to know" questions greatly increases the odds of keeping the customer engaged, allowing the customer to see the potential personal benefit of survey completion. This link to personal benefit is important. Be prepared to act upon the results, because if a customer provides feedback and sees no results, the backlash can result in poor future response rates and a negative attitude toward the company (Johnson and Gustafsson 2000).

When you solicit feedback, you are asking your customer to allocate their valuable time to you, so be respectful of it. A good rule of thumb is to collect only truly necessary data and use it only for its stated purpose. This is both ethical and legal. The business will likely get better data if it sticks to asking questions that are relevant and not arbitrarily personal.

Privacy Issues

The ability to collect data, including personal information, has been simplified through the proliferation of information-grabbing robots, cookies, and other seemingly innocuous forms. A recent case of unauthorized capture and cross reference of personal information spawned a rash of privacy initiatives, including federal legislation aimed at full disclosure of data collected and usage guidelines ("Real Networks" 1999). However, the legalese cloaking some privacy policies makes disclosure and enforcement into complex issues. It is important to have a clear privacy statement posted on your Web site, and to abide by it at all costs. Your company's reputation depends on it.

What Data to Collect

Although there are various methods of gaining customer feedback, direct questioning usually works best. Focus groups and one-on-one interviews are excellent ways to connect with the customer. However, time, expense, and customer convenience make standard surveys a very appealing avenue for collecting customer-satisfaction information, especially in the automated world of the Internet. Because of the convenience and cost efficiencies found in e-survey systems, we will focus our discussion primarily on surveys as a form of data collection.

Survey Design

Rule number one in developing a customer survey is to keep it simple. Basically there are three types of information that every customer satisfaction survey should have: (1) demographics, (2) product/service performance, (3) overall measures.

Measuring satisfaction starts with asking the right questions. This involves doing the proper preliminary research to understand the different processes of interaction between you and your customers. Creating actionable surveys starts with properly mapping the process and subprocess framework. This is the process of breaking down the customer interaction into fundamental actionable elements. Although several sources of literature exist on this technique, the endnotes direct the reader to a particularly relevant example (Rust et al. 1994).

Measuring the Internet Experience

Basic Framework of e-Customer Interaction

The customer-provider interaction is a complex combination of physical performance and transactional factors. Customer interaction with a Web site is grounded in simple fundamentals of design and functionality. If a commerce component is involved, issues related to standard transactional experience—

product availability, selection, and price—also play a role. Given that the Internet (at this time) provides experience only in two senses—sight and sound—the interactive experience has somewhat standard elements.

Critical Metrics

Below are the basics of the Web-site experiences, common elements of any company's Web presence. These elements are fundamental attributes that significantly impact satisfaction:

- Navigability/"ease of use"
- Content
- Aesthetics/visual attractiveness of site
- Customer service
- Buying experience (if a commerce site): selection; availability; pricing

Site Navigation

Ease of Finding Site. Much like a brick and mortar customer experiencing confusing directions en route to a store, if customers have a hard time finding you, they can bring a negative emotional state to the experience before they even open the "door" to your site. Understanding the path that customers take to your site can make a significant difference in how you structure your entry and how you promote your site. Products such as WebTrends allow you to track the points of entry of your site. This type of forensic analysis can be a powerful marketing tool as well as a useful diagnostic in the quest to provide the best possible customer experience.

Time Spent Waiting for Pages to Load. Time spent waiting is a cornerstone satisfaction issue. Load speed is usually a combination of both "uncontrollable" and "controllable" issues, including Web server performance and architecture sufficiency, server Internet connection performance, and Web-site design (graphics quantity and sizes). This is no small issue. One market research company estimates that potentially several billion dollars are lost annually due to poor page-loading speeds and corresponding visitor bailout. E-Marketer estimates that 95 percent of Web-site visitors leave if page-load speed extends beyond thirty seconds. Therefore, making sure your site is designed properly, supported by the proper server architecture and connected with the proper size link to the Internet is critical to ensuring flawless performance. Internet service providers such as Keynote Systems, which measures page-load speeds from various locations and on various Internet backbone providers, can be a helpful tool to pinpoint potential trouble spots.

General Site Organization. If a customers cannot find what they need, they burn time and have a frustrating experience. Making sure your site contains easy-to-understand intuitive hierarchies is a cornerstone to satisfying your customers. Many companies offer site-testing programs with proprietary browser-based tracking of clickstream information. These companies frequently recruit panelists, armed with modified browsers, to perform a series of basic site functions and tasks. Custom browsers track their successes and failures, creating electronic trails to monitor the ease with which a panelist achieves a predetermined goal on the tested site. The resulting analysis allows for an understanding of how easily customers are able to achieve the goals they set out to perform on your site. This information can lead to reductions in customer support calls and shopping cart abandonment, and increases in customer satisfaction and ultimately to increased revenue.

Ease of Ordering. This is a critical component of the buying process, and many companies fail to address it with the proper amount of attention. Just as any successful retailer is mindful of making sure customers can easily make purchases by providing superior store organization, speedy point of sale (POS) computer systems, and even personal shoppers, the company's Web store should reflect this same thoughtful consideration. The functionality of the checkout process must be *flawless*, easy, and as reassuring as possible. Many customers still fear transacting over the Web, suspicious that their private financial and personal information will be stolen. Adding functionality that allows for the secure storage of credit card and other commerce-enabling information is becoming increasingly commonplace and adds to the ease of completing the process. Sensitive information such as credit card numbers and other personal data *must* be treated with the utmost care. The element of trust is crucial in online commerce, and how a company goes about building trust is as important as any other element of the Internet presence.

Content Information

Proper Quantity of Information. The proper quantity of information necessary varies according to the customer's needs. Customers' perceived importance of their buying decision, the consequences of their acting without having enough information, and the amount of knowledge customers bring with them to the site are each important drivers of the need for information. The value of having the right content and enough content cannot be overstated (Glazer 1991). If a potential customer does not have enough information to effect a decision or accomplish the goal, he or she will probably look elsewhere and therefore not be satisfied with the site. This visitor will probably not return.

Current, Up-to-Date, Accurate Content. Customers need the latest, most accurate information available. If your customers cannot trust that the information they gather on your site is correct, they will look elsewhere. Since a part of relationship development is building trust (Zemke and Connellan 2001), accurate information is crucial. If your content, or aspects of your content, are ancillary to your core offering, you may want to consider purchasing content from a secondary provider. However, be particularly discerning in all outsourcing activities, and make certain that the provider's sources are accurate. You will not get the chance to point the finger elsewhere in cyberspace. How often do you need to update your content? Some sites are hit continuously all day. News services need to push out new content in real time. If you have a newsletter, how frequently is there relevant new information to deliver? This may require "asking" your customer, so go ahead, ask!

Interesting. What is interesting varies from person to person. The importance and meaning of "interesting" can vary wildly depending upon the goal of your customer. The Web-site visit must provide the customer with a memorable experience. Thus, even with the most time-sensitive of operations, a little flair goes a long way.

Visual Attractiveness. The Internet is a visual medium. Much like a dynamic picture, the visuals must be attractive and appealing, but not overbearing. Proper choice of graphics should be based upon the character and nature of your product or service. Although the site should be appealing, the main satisfaction factor of graphics tends to be whether they are relevant and whether they negatively impact the physical performance of the Web site. A general rule of thumb for creating an overall more satisfying experience is that "less is more." Use graphics to make a point or provide visual information (product pictures, and so on). An examination of customer demographics can provide clues as what type of graphics your site can support. If a particular customer group is dominated by users with high-speed, broadband, or dedicated connections, then a graphics-heavy site may be acceptable. However, if your customer base is composed of a high percentage of users on dial-up or low-speed modems, pay particular attention to the quantity and size of graphics, as they will tend to impact the performance of the Web site. The best option is to strive to make your Web site accessible to everyone. Unless there is a technical issue related to your "core customer" group, consider having a parallel site that has fewer graphics. Customers with lower connection speeds will appreciate the consideration.

- Colors—Color choice has as much to do with aesthetics as it does common sense. Colors should be a reflection of the emotion you are trying to convey, should accurately reflect your offline branding efforts (if any), and should also be used to provide ease of reading.

- Easy-to-Read Text—Font style and size can be important drivers of satisfaction. If a site is perceived as being cluttered, or the font is too small, making reading difficult, or if the fonts are difficult to distinguish from the page background (example: dark font on a dark background) customers may leave for an easier-on-the-eyes experience.
- Clutter—Similarly, too much information can negatively impact the interactive experience. Poorly organized information can make for a confusing and frequently unsatisfying experience. The Web is filled with clutter. Your customer is seeking organization and ease of use. Trying to do too much in too little space is self-defeating.

Customer Service

Customer Support. Volumes have been written on the importance of customer support. Keeping with the theme of efficiency, the first thing to realize is that regardless how well you build and add "poka-yoke" (mistake proof) devices to your site-management process, there will be service issues. Arming your service-support hierarchy (level one, level two, and so on) with tools to solve customer problems with the minimum number of escalations to different levels is an important driver of customer satisfaction. In addition, offering support anytime your customer needs it (24/7) via multiple channels can greatly increase measured customer-satisfaction levels for customer support. According to a study of the Web hosting industry, customers reported a 73 percent higher level of satisfaction with their hosting providers who provide online chat as a supplement to their existing e-mail and telephone-based customer service support, see Figure 4.2 (IntiMetrix 2001b).

Buying Experience—Selection, Availability, Accessibility of Desired Product. Related somewhat to ease of navigation, this issue could be measured by how many searches are required for a user to isolate the desired information, or at least know definitively the solution is not available at this site. Easy, intuitive search hierarchies are critical. This also means ensuring that if your customer clicks on men's shoes, he is not directed to women's shoes (or forced to search through them), building confidence in the site and its owners.

Competitiveness of Pricing. Competitiveness, while not necessarily having the lowest price, is critical. Since the Internet facilitates price comparison, the wise company must clearly understand customer sentiment concerning price. However, building your competitive advantage based upon price creates a house of cards, especially if the pricing strategy exists at the expense of fewer service options.

Overall Measures. In addition to overall satisfaction, two other variables that can play a key part in understanding the customer satisfaction

Figure 4.2 **Overall Satisfaction with Customer Service with Support Services**

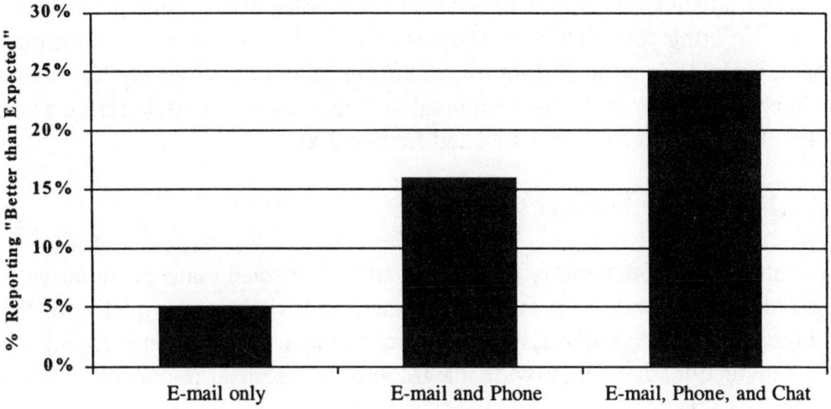

Source: IntiMetrix 2001b.

response are intention to revisit/repurchase and willingness to recommend. These measures provide valuable ways to calculate the financial
impact of customer satisfaction as it relates to repurchase and positive
word of mouth.

Intention to Revisit/Repurchase

Though frequently left out of surveys, intention to repurchase/revisit is a
critical factor in getting the most out of your customer-satisfaction information. Intention to revisit allows you to put a "hard" number to your satisfaction rating. If analyzed properly, this metric gives the provider the ability to
understand the incremental value in increasing levels of satisfaction, bringing to life the concept of the lifetime value of the customer.

The Lifetime Value of the Customer

Understanding the lifetime value of the customer is a key concept. It is a fact
that a company cannot be everything to everyone, so the enterprise needs to
focus on satisfaction as a tool for developing relationships with the customers it wants to keep. The lifetime value of the customer is a relatively simple
calculation.

Lifetime Customer Value = NPV value of a customer per transaction ×
number of transactions during the "appropriate customer lifetime."[1]

Examining the difference in intention to repurchase at each level of reported overall satisfaction could vividly display the incremental value of satisfying and delighting your customers. This concept of the lifetime value of the customer also plays an important role in the concept of customer equity—a key element in determining the overall value of the customer and therefore a key driver of a firm's strategy (Rust and Lemon 2001).

Likelihood of Recommending

Intention to recommend is also a frequently neglected concept. Intuitively, people are reluctant to provide recommendations where the quality of the interaction is at risk. Thus, this is another element, when statistically related to satisfaction, that can provide insight into the financial impact of satisfaction.

Positive word of mouth is an important driver of trial. In the case of a major Web retailer, recommendation by friends was the number one reported reason for trial (IntiMetrix 2001a). When quantitatively measured against the overall satisfaction variable, this can be another powerful tool in understanding the value of achieving higher levels of satisfaction.

Types of Data Collection

Survey Links

Survey links allow your customers to provide feedback at the point of opportunity or issue, in practice becoming a form of "critical incident" collector. The critical incident (Bitner 1990) is an experience that inordinately impacts the poles of the customer satisfaction measurement. Customers can frequently recall pleasant or terrible experiences that happened years before and that have shaped their product preferences ever since. These are critical incidents. Immediate collection of critical incidents gives management the ability to address issues in a timely manner, adjusting (hopefully) in advance of permanent damage to the customer relationship.

Page buttons as links to surveys are a great way to collect responses in case of a problem, particularly if this includes a mechanism to quickly report issues to management. The problem with a casual link to a regular survey is the issue of "selection bias," similar to the issues inherent in restaurant comment cards. Patrons who fill out a self-selecting comment card typically rest on the ends of the spectrum. While this self-selected feedback can help identify immediate issues or particular "critical incidents," these issues can be aberrations. If this is the only information available, management may get an unrepresentative view of the customer experience and allow these few incidents to overshadow the vast majority of other everyday experiences that characterize the regular flow of business. Thus, the survey as a link to the site is a great way to collect unsolicited response, but it has its limitations in understanding the majority of everyday interaction and satisfaction in general.

The E-mail Invitation Survey

E-mail invitations soliciting survey participation have become very popular. In this application, a Web-based survey typically sits behind a link that a targeted e-mail recipient clicks to then complete the survey. E-mail invitations are both easily developed and easily administered. Several commercially available software programs can handle the administration of mass mailings, including the ability to mass personalize, much like a conventional mail-merge option. This touch is important. Personalization lends itself to making the survey respondent feel more important, it drives more commitment, and it may result in better response rates and higher-quality data.

E-mail delivery provides the respondent with the ability to easily opt out of the survey by deleting or ignoring the message. This method also allows for either pre-segmentation or profiling of respondents. To get the most out of this vehicle, timing is critical. It is recommended that the survey be delivered as close to the time of service consumption as possible. In the case of retail, postdelivery surveys allow for the documentation of other key satisfaction indicators, including delivery performance to commitments (timing). Internet satisfaction rating service Bizrate tags postpurchase customer satisfaction surveys and automatically delivers a follow-up survey to check on the fulfillment. This allows them to keep track of the important postpurchase aspect of the shopping experience.

"Pop-up" Intervention Survey

The pop-up (JavaScript-based) survey invitation allows for intervention at critical points in the customer experience, such as the performance of certain tasks (i.e., at checkout or upon site exit). This type of data collection provides real-time feedback closest to the point of performance.

Some providers use clever theme-based screens or compensation banners as incentive to complete a survey. This intervention method has pros and cons. On the positive side, recall error is diminished because the event is fresh in the mind of the consumer. Response rates vary, but one site reports that about 30 percent accept the survey invitation, and of those, as many as 80 percent follow through and complete the survey. (SurveySite 2001).

Pop-ups (interventions) have their issues. Aside from the self-selection bias noted previously, a major concern is the fear of the unknown. Intervention into the customer experience should be carefully considered before being executed. Since the customer can exit an experience or transaction at the press of a button, to add an annoyance or distraction is not wise. While pop-ups create a window for taking the survey that does not take the customer from the Web site, it is a disruption to the customer's planned activity. This disruption may lead to an early exit and make the customer less likely to return. This technique should only be employed after completion of the desired action, or upon exit from the Web site, and should include a clear opportunity for the customer to gracefully and quickly opt out.

So what is the best method of survey delivery? A recent survey showed that visitors were 60 percent more likely to take a survey on their own time as opposed to being confronted with a pop-up (IntiMetrix 1999–2001). If your strategy calls for multiple points of collection, a combination of e-mail and on-site collection is advised. This allows you to collect a random sample, and still allows an opportunity to collect critical-incident information at the time of the event. A continuous feedback system, such as IntiMetrix's CustomerMeter, that combines critical-incident collection capability (via open-end questions) along with standardized Internet interaction questions provides a solid base for an ongoing customer-satisfaction measurement system.

Alternate Methods of Data Collection

Several alternate ways to collect customer-satisfaction data exist. Data collection on the Internet is currently a hot topic, and it is subject to some debate as interesting thoughts concerning the future of data collection emerge (Miller and Dickson 2001). One method that has recently gained popularity is the *satisfaction community* model. Segment leader Bizrate pioneered this model. The concept involves creation of a ranking system utilizing customer-provided postpurchase survey feedback. Upon completion of a sale or predetermined conclusive action, a customer is invited to participate in a survey. Merchants and service providers are provided summary charts and graphs of the data as a perk of membership in the satisfaction community.

Although lacking in much "actionable" information, these reports can assist management in understanding general issues. The ratings are then used to create a categorical ranking between segment companies. The decision to participate in a satisfaction community becomes an issue of corporate philosophy regarding the exchange of sensitive data. All customer exchanges between customer and company should be considered confidential, proprietary information. Although the satisfaction community model is a useful tool for consumers, its value to the company is somewhat suspect. In an environment where most avenues of competitive advantage are short-lived, why level the playing field by giving the competition an opportunity to see what your customers think of you? For this reason, think twice before exposing potential weaknesses in public.

Another way to collect feedback is through a *site-evaluation service*. In this model a provider company may recruit demographically similar groups to proxy for actual customers. This model is great for pretesting a site or for gaining outside opinion, but no matter how close the match in demographic or other profiling, the customer experience is dependent upon the individual set of circumstances that surround the interaction. It is a moment in time that cannot be re-created or "mocked up." Factors such as timing, convenience, and other environmental "uncontrollables" play a role in a unique customer experience; thus, it cannot truly be replicated in the controlled environment of the site-evaluation model.

Currently popular evaluation services such as Vividence track actual paths through the customer experience and provide feedback to poka-yoke the customer's path to accomplishing core tasks. While this approach can be useful to reinforce service processes and identify bigger issues, it cannot take the place of the real-time feedback from a customer under the unique set of circumstances that surround a particular customer/provider interaction.

"Build your own" survey software is also readily available. Anyone who wishes can download software or subscribe to a Web survey application, and then create their own surveys. Many do. The ability to author your own surveys is exciting and sometimes an overwhelming temptation. Many providers offer pretested templates to aid in design and in some cases will offer the option to administer and host your survey. This provides an easy way to gain input from your customer. Unfortunately, this technique may violate one of the fundamental rules of good market research: proper question design. Most organizations do not have the internal resources either to craft an actionable survey or to properly analyze the gathered data. The result, while a great opportunity for the amateur researcher, can be poor data quality; unstructured, difficult-to-use feedback for the company; and a nightmare for the customer.

Collecting Data

As discussed earlier, the sample can be collected in several ways. As with all good research, the key is to survey a truly representative sample of your customers. The best way to ensure this outcome is random sampling. A random sample will give you the best opportunity to get an accurate view of the feelings of your customer population.

Use Your Customers Whenever Possible

Panels can be great tools for pretesting your Web site, but remember that your customers are yours for a reason, even if the reasons are environmental or circumstantial. Their profile is not accurately reproducible, and therefore to accurately hear the voice of your customers, you must ask *your customers*.

Capturing and Addressing Complaints

Capturing a complaint is in many ways more valuable than getting a compliment. Complaints are exponentially valuable since, as reported, as low as 4 percent of customers impacted by an issue make the effort to complain, leaving the other 96 percent to quietly defect. Hence, it becomes vital to effectively elicit and address complaints in a timely manner.

One powerful way to accomplish this is to collect negative critical incidents with well-worded and well-placed questions. An open-response question such as "What was the worst thing you experienced on our Web site today?" creates an opportunity both to gather previously unarticulated issues and to turn a customer's negative experience into a positive one through resolution. However, once you solicit a complaint, you must be prepared to act.

Never ignore a complaint. The customers must be convinced that the time they have spent in providing feedback derives benefit for them and helps the business. When you ask for feedback, it is critical that you respond directly and swiftly to the complainant. Ignoring complaints can lead to poor word of mouth, which is inherently viral in nature and potentially disastrous. This is not to say that every complaint can be resolved or acted upon—resolving them might be impractical, financially unfeasible, or even silly. Complaints or suggestions should be *acknowledged* in any case, thanking respondents for their input.

With the amount of data collected by the properly equipped e-company, it may be impossible for you to personally respond to all those who provide feedback, and in fact many sites that request feedback carry clear messages regarding this issue. Single complaints can reflect an underlying, underexposed problem. Statistics show that unexpressed complaints outnumbered complaints received by as many as twenty to one (TARP 1979). To best understand the gravity of a single complaint, think of the sentiment of an angry mob of twenty, carrying torches and defecting to your competition.

Frequency of Data Collection

Data collection should be continuous. Simply put, continuous collection is important because the customer needs change. With the relative ease of reaching customers through e-mail, Web buttons, and pop-ups (interventions), customers can get overwhelmed. Oversurveying can lead to survey burnout and a degradation of data quality. When faced with a limited time and willingness to respond, sticking to a tight agenda may make the difference in completion versus a busy customer filing the survey in the circular e-file.

The Evolution of Customer Satisfaction Tools

Most impediments related to collecting customer satisfaction data are rapidly vanishing. Today, a plethora of companies exist that can quickly and relatively painlessly provide survey and data collection services. With this in mind, the issue turns not to how to collect customer satisfaction information, but to what to do with it once collected.

"Smart tools" are tools that lead the e-business past the "data dump" stage of satisfaction data analysis, providing various automated and semi-automated analytical components to the service. As these tools evolve, they should open the door for expanded participation in market research at the midsize to small company level, as the top reasons frequently given for businesses not performing customer satisfaction research are expense and lack of internal expertise to perform needed work (IntiMetrix 1999–2001).

The Internet allows the researcher the ability to generate volumes of data, and that can be equally dangerous. Misrepresentation of data is rampant. Misunderstood or improperly used data can cause more damage than the benefits that might be derived from quality information analysis. Smart tools— fully automated products that provide basic analysis—will be a catalyst for creating rapid adoption of customer satisfaction tools. The opportunity for every Web site to collect quality information and emerge with a clear understanding of their customers' wants and needs is nearly reality. This development will benefit customer and business alike.

Excelling at Customer Satisfaction

Today's e-business needs to seek every opportunity to distinguish and endear itself to the customer. Unless the e-business takes an active role in setting the standard for understanding and satisfying the customer, it runs the risk of blending into the scenery. In a medium where the battle lines for customer loyalty and equity are being drawn and redrawn in real time, only truly customer-service–focused organizations will survive.

Notes

The author would like to recognize the contributions of Perry Mykleby and David Cristofaro, without whose assistance and support this work would not have been possible. Also, heartfelt thanks to my family—Taylor, Devon, Victoria, Mom, Dad, Sheila, Melissa, and Skip.

1. "Appropriate" is a judgment call based upon what you know about your customers. A fifteen-year-old may use your site only to purchase video games until he is twenty-two (seven years); however an eighteen-year-old may purchase music until she is sixty (forty-two years).

References

Bitner, Mary Jo. 1990."Evaluating Service Encounters: The Effects of Physical Surroundings and Employee Responses." *Journal of Marketing* 54 (April): 69–82.

Borland, Jim. 1998. "Move Over, Megamalls, Cyberspace Is the Great Retail Equalizer." *Knight–Ridder/Tribune Business News*, April 13, p. 11.

Flop Tracker. 2000. *The Industry Standard* (May). [Flop Tracker was the name of a column that tracked companies that "flopped"/went bankrupt. *The Industry Standard* was a (now defunct) online and hardcopy publication.]

Glazer, Rashi. 1991."Marketing in an Information-Intensive Environment: Strategic Implications of Knowledge as an Asset." *Journal of Marketing* 55 (November): 1–19.

IntiMetrix. 2001a. Study of the Web hosting industry, Spring.

———. 2001b. Spring customer satisfaction study (Web van), April.

———. 1999–2001. Various statistics pulled from internal and proprietary research.

Johnson, Michael D., and Anders Gustafsson. 2000. *Improving Customer Satisfaction, Loyalty and Profit*. San Francisco: Jossey-Bass.

Jupiter Media Metrix. 2001. www.mediametrix.com (June).

Miller, Thomas W., and Dickson, Peter R. 2001."Online Market Research." *International Journal of Electronic Commerce* 5(3) (spring): 139–168.

Oliver, Richard L. 1980."A Cognitive Model of the Antecedents and Consequences of Satisfaction Decisions." *Journal of Marketing Research* 17 (November): 460–469.

Pastore, Michael. 1998."Convenience Draws Online Shoppers." CyberAtlas: www.cyberatlas.com (December 23).

"Real Networks Hit with Privacy Lawsuit." 1999. *Internet News* (November): 5–16.

Reichheld, Frederick F. 1996."Learning from Customer Defections." *Harvard Business Review* (April): 56–69.

Rust, R., and K. Lemon. 2001."E-service and the Consumer." *International Journal of Electronic Commerce* 5(3) (spring): 85–101.

Rust, Roland T.; Anthony J. Zahorik; and Timothy L. Keiningham. 1996. *Service*

Rust, Roland T.; Anthony J. Zahorik; and Timothy L. Keiningham. 1996. *Service Marketing*. New York: HarperCollins.

———. 1994. *Return on Quality: Measuring the Financial Impact of Your Company's Quest for Quality*. Chicago: Probus.

TARP. 1979. *Consumer Complaint Handling in America: Final Report*. Washington, DC: Office of Consumer Affairs.

SurveySite. 2001. www.surveysite.com.

Zemke, Ron, and Tom Connellan. 2001. *E-Service: 24 Ways to Keep Your Customers When the Competition Is Just a Click Away*. New York: AMACOM, American Management Association.

5

"In Web We Trust"

Establishing Strategic Trust Among Online Customers

Irina Ceaparu, Dina Demner, Edward Hung,
Haixia Zhao, and Ben Shneiderman

Introduction

Establishing trust between customers and companies through Web interfaces, a key component of successful e-Service, is not as easy as through human–buyer–human-seller interaction (Morgan and Hunt 1994; Doney and Cannon 1997; Rust and Lemon 2001). The risks associated with e-commerce can be broadly classified into the following categories:

- *Business practices.* Whether a company will carry out its orders for products and services as it claims and whether there are product guarantees.
- *Information protection.* Customers seek assurances that they have reached a properly identified World Wide Web site, and that the company will protect private customer information.
- *Transaction integrity.* Customers involved in e-commerce seek assurance that the company has effective transaction integrity controls. Trusted companies have a history of processing transactions accurately, completely, and promptly, and of appropriately billing its customers.

A number of experiments have been conducted to determine the factors that influence customers' trust in online businesses. J. Lee et al. found that comprehensive information about the products, values shared with other customers, and diverse means of communication can effectively increase trust, which in turn can increase customer loyalty (Lee et al. 2000).

According to F.N. Egger's research (Egger 1999; Egger and de Groot 2000), trustworthiness often depends upon the strength of a brand name, that is, its reputation. In addition, consumers should be informed about the vendor's privacy policy—for example, why vendors might require unusual personal details and what happens to confidential information after the transaction. Customers' judgment of trustworthiness can also be aided by the involvement of independent parties. Moreover, a valid legal framework that supports the transaction may also be a determinant of customers' trust.

In 1998, AT&T Laboratories conducted an experiment (ATT 1999) to determine the nature of online privacy concerns. They established that privacy seals, policies, and the type of information disclosed are important factors in online trust. Their study, which covered a sample of 381 Internet users, had these major findings:

- Internet users are more likely to provide information when they are not identified.
- Some types of data are more sensitive than others.
- Internet users dislike automatic data transfer.
- A joint program of privacy policies and privacy seals seemingly provides a level of user confidence comparable to that provided by privacy laws.

The study by Cheskin Research (1999) determines the elements that communicate trust in e-commerce sites, based on customers' and experts' feedback. The six fundamental forms for communicating trust are: brand, navigation, fulfillment, presentation, up-to-date technology, and seals of approval. A second study by Cheskin Research (2000) investigates which are the most recognizable and trusted symbols of online security and identifies the most trusted Web sites.

A report by the Nielsen-Norman Group (Nielsen et al. 2000), based on usability testing with sixty-four customers, found that they expect:

- succinct and readily accessible information about the company;
- fair pricing, fully revealed;
- sufficient and balanced product information;
- correct, timely, professional site design;
- clear and customer-friendly policies;
- appropriate use of personal information;
- trustworthy security; and
- access to helpful people.

P. Kollock points out that trustworthiness of the Web site is essential for the success of a business transaction separated in space and time (Kollock 1999).

B.J. Fogg et al. (2000) conducted an online study in which more than 1,400 people answered questions concerning credibility of Web sites. This study found trustworthiness to be one of the five key components of general credibility of Web sites. It advises Web designers to honestly represent the nature of the Web site.

These issues are helpful, but they need to be converted into specific design guidelines. Based on F. Fukuyama's (1995) political concepts and E. Uslaner's (Forthcoming) study of the linkage between Internet usage and trust, B. Shneiderman (2000) defines e-commerce trust as a "positive expectation about the future based on past performance and truthful guarantees." His proposed design guidelines to establish trust in e-commerce include:

- Provide clear guarantee with compensation.
- Get certificates from third parties.
- Provide and enforce privacy and security policy.
- Disclose patterns of past performance.
- Provide references from past and current users.
- Support dispute resolution and mediation services.

These guidelines are merely conjectures, which are the basis for experimental studies such as this one.

The importance of certificates of trust from third parties has generated activity for several organizations (Urban et al. 2000). They provide certificates of trust and seals of approval for e-commerce Web sites:

- TRUSTe (www.truste.org) is an independent nonprofit organization dedicated to building consumer trust and confidence in the Internet. Its privacy seal program is an online branded seal that is awarded only to sites that adhere to the TRUSTe set of privacy principles for disclosure, access, and security.
- BBBOnline (www.bbbonline.org) is a subsidiary of the Council of Better Business Bureaus. Its mission is to promote trust on the Internet through the BBBOnline Reliability and Privacy Seal programs. The first confirms that the company follows good customer-service practices, and the second confirms that the company stands behind its online privacy policy and has met the program requirements regarding the handling of personal information.
- VeriSign (www.verisign.com) provides through its site trust services a

seal of assurance for e-commerce sites that meet disclosure, integrity, and protection criteria.

- WebTrust (www.cpawebtrust.org) is a set of principles and criteria for business-to-consumer e-commerce, developed by the public accounting profession. The WebTrust seal of assurance is a symbolic representation of a practitioner's objective report.
- Chamber Seal (www.chamberseal.com) provides an online trust seal issued by the U.S. Chamber of Commerce. It assures that the holder of the seal is a real and legitimate business with a physical presence at an identifiable location and that this information has been verified by a trusted third party—the local chamber of commerce.

Critics point out that these attempts at voluntary regulation are flawed because the enforcement is weak. The value of a certificate of trust may grow if these organizations review and publicly disseminate their findings of improper activities. Also they can serve a positive role by promoting best practices and encouraging truthful reporting.

Experiment

Introduction and Hypothesis

Our experiment is designed to determine what features are important in inducing strategic trust among online customers, which factors will most likely make a business-to-customer e-commerce Web site trustable and persuasive to the extent that customers will purchase from the Web site. We hypothesize that in addition to standard usability issues, these three issues will influence trust: extensive customer service, external testimonials, and graphical representation of security and privacy policies.

According to our hypothesis the most trusted page is the one containing an external testimonial, a detailed customer service statement with contact information, and graphic seals.

Variables

We chose three common strategic trust-inducing features from real Web sites that were not thoroughly studied in previous experiments, but are considered to be important for an e-commerce site's trustworthiness. We changed one independent variable according to the pilot study results. The amount of personal information that was initially selected as one of the independent variables was not a factor in a Web page's trustworthiness. All subjects said they can always give fake personal information, except for the necessary shipping and billing information. The final independent and dependent variables are as follows:

Independent Variables

Customer service (two treatments; see Figure 5.1)
- *Limited contact information.* Only an e-mail address is provided.
- *Extensive contact information.* E-mail address, telephone numbers, real store addresses are provided.

Testimonial (two treatments; see Figure 5.2)
- *Self-testimonial.* The Web site provides self-testimonial.
- *External testimonial.* The Web site has external testimonial from some well-known magazines and a feedback forum.

Security features representation (two treatments; see Figure 5.3)
- *Graphics.* We used real seals from Web sites that provide external testimonials and verify sites' security, and designed seals for self-testimonials and privacy policy.
- *Text.* The testimonial is represented as text.

We designed $2 \times 2 \times 2 = 8$ Web pages with different combinations of treatments of the three independent variables, as shown in Appendix 1–8, described in Table 5.1.

Dependent Variables

Relative rank of trustworthiness: each subject estimated trustworthiness of each of the eight Web pages on a scale from one (least trustworthy) to nine (most trustworthy). Subjects were asked to rate the pages according to their readiness to buy from the site and provide their personal information and credit card number. The pages were presented to the subjects in a random sequence, but the subjects could revisit each page. Subjects were timed and observed during the evaluation.

Subjects

We chose subjects who are comfortable with computers and had been Internet users before the experiment. Six undergraduate and forty-six graduate students from the University of Maryland participated in our study. Our subjects consisted of thirty-four males and eighteen females between the ages of

Table 5.1

Combinations of Features in the Web Pages

Page #	Customer service	Testimonial	Seals
1	Extensive	External	Graphic
2	Extensive	External	Text
3	Extensive	Self	Text
4	Limited	External	Text
5	Extensive	Self	Graphic
6	Limited	External	Graphic
7	Limited	Self	Graphic
8	Limited	Self	Text

twenty and thirty-seven. The majority of the subjects are computer science majors. There were also physics, economics, art history, library science, electrical engineering, mathematics, mechanical engineering, French, and biochemistry majors.

We conducted a within-subjects experiment. No training was required. Prior to the experiment, our subjects were given instructions about the purpose of the experiment, their tasks, and the procedure of the experiment.

Materials

The following materials were used to conduct the experiment:

- The simulation of eight commercial Web sites based on a WinNT server. The results of the evaluation were automatically entered into the Microsoft SQL database.
- Postexperimental questionnaire.
- Written and oral instructions.

Procedures and Problems

Subjects were presented with the experimental interface that is divided into two frames (see Figure 5.4). The left frame contains links to the eight Web pages. Initially the right frame contains the instructions. The order of the eight Web pages linked to the eight buttons is randomly initialized when the first page is loaded. When the buttons are clicked, the Web page corresponding to the button is shown in the right frame. The subjects clicked the eight buttons to browse the eight Web pages, and gave each page a relative trust rank on a scale from one (least trustable) to nine (most trustable) by clicking the radio button in the left frame.

Figure 5.1 **Limited and Extensive Customer Information**

Customer care	Customer care
We guarantee your satisfaction with our services and products! E-mail us: service@chz.com	We guarantee your satisfaction with our services and products! To find a nearby CHZ store or contact our Sales, Customer Service, or General Inquiries by phone, call 1-800-CHZ-COMP (1-800-123-4567). For Technical Support, call 301-123-6789. Phones are staffed 9 AM to 5 PM, Monday–Friday. E-mail us: service@chz.com

They could click the eight buttons in any order they wanted, and could jump back and forward to make changes of ranks. The experiment software recorded the time that subjects took to finish ranking, which was from the moment the index page was loaded to the moment the subjects clicked the submit button to indicate they had finished ranking. On submission, the ranks were recorded by the software. Then a short questionnaire asking about the subject's background and opinion about e-commerce Web site trustable features was displayed. The subjects answered all the questions and clicked the submit button. The software recorded their answers to the questionnaire and brought up an acknowledgment page. The subjects were observed and asked some questions by the observer about their answers to the questionnaire at the end of the experiment.

Results

Our program collected the results of evaluations and the answers to the postexperiment questionnaires into two tables in the SQL database. The average time to carry out the rankings was 5 minutes, with the maximum time being 11.5 minutes.

The means-of-trustworthiness ranks and standard deviations for all pages reveal the strong differences in user perceptions (Table 5.2 and Figure 5.5).

The results of the three-way repeated Analysis of Variance, using degree

Figure 5.2 **Self- and External Testimonials**

Our services are second to none. We provide the best possible service and the lowest prices!	Our services are second to none. We repeatedly earn high ratings for our technical services in magazine reviews, customer comments, and indepedent surveys. See the latest review in the March issue of *Good Housekeeping* magazine. Check out our Feedback Forum.

of trust as the dependent variable, indicate that all three main effects of customer service, testimonials, and graphical representation were highly ($p < .001$) statistically significantly different (see Table 5.3). There were no statistically significant interaction effects.

Questionnaire Results

Out of fifty-two subjects, eleven buy online more than ten times a year, twenty-three buy three to ten times, fifteen buy one to three times, and three students never bought anything online. Only two students are online at least two to three times a week; the rest are online every day. Twenty of fifty-two people spend more than three hours online; twenty-nine spend one to three hours, and only three students spend less than an hour.

The majority (thirty-seven people) consider security to be a significant factor in their decision. Three of these students never bought anything online. Only one student does not take the security of the site into consideration while making his three to ten online purchases a year. Fourteen people list the security feature as a small factor in their decision. We added an average degree of trust for each person obtained in the experiment to the questionnaire results as a dependent variable for statistical analysis. The analysis showed that some of the factors we predicted to be

Figure 5.3 **Seals and Their Textual Equivalents**

Privacy   Our   VeriSign
policy   testimonial   Secure site

important in establishing trust are indeed important. The two-sample *t*-test confirmed the importance of the following features (*t*-critical two-tail = 2.7): security and privacy seals; contact number available; clearly stated return policy; possibility of returning a purchase at a nearby store; discount or special offers; ease of use of the Web site; privacy statements. There was no statistically significant difference for other factors, such as the question about merchandise type, which proved to be misleading since many subjects believed it referred to the company name used in this study (see Table 5.3).

Discussion

The goal of our experiment was to establish which features that appear on commercial Web sites are trust-inducing. Previous studies determined that elements like brand, navigation, fulfillment, presentation, up-to-date technology, and seals of approval communicate trust in e-commerce Web sites. Our study produced remarkably strong results indicating the importance of all three features: customer service (extensive and limited), testimonial (self and third party), and security feature representation (graphics and text).

Three-way analysis shows that there is interaction between three tested features. Interaction between testimonials and their graphical representation and testimonials and customer service is significant. The analysis of the customer service feature showed that extensive customer service is very important. The pages that have extended customer service scored on average two points higher than the pages that contained only the e-mail address of the online store. This outcome is supported by the postexperimental question-

Figure 5.4 **The Experimental Web Site**

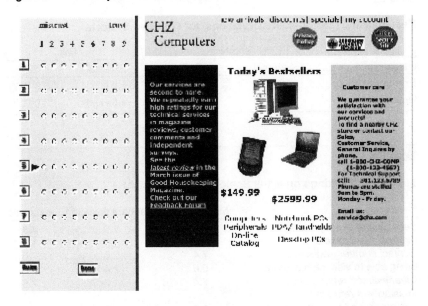

naire results. These results showed that information like contact address plus phone number and a clearly stated return policy are major concerns for customers. These two features scored highest among all decision factors for online purchases.

The analysis of self- and third-party testimonials showed that the presence of an external testimonial also contributes to building up trust. Although this proved to be statistically significant in the experiment, in the questionnaire it was not considered to be that significant. Sixteen out of fifty-two subjects never heard of the third parties presented in our pages. So there may be other reasons that contribute to this significant difference. According to subjects' feedback, one of the reasons may be the amount of information customers see on the front page of the Web site—the longer text may be visually more convincing.

The analysis of security feature representation showed that graphic seals of approval and graphic security seals induce more trust as opposed to the same information represented textually. The reason may be that visual memory triggers trust without analysis of content.

The questionnaire the subjects filled out after the experiment contributed to our understanding. Our expectation was that mentioning the physical store adds to the credibility of the Web site. The subjects' feedback shows that they do not consider the online store to be an extension of the physical store,

Table 5.2

Mean Ranking (and Standard Deviations) for Fifty-Two Subjects

Seals	Graphic		Text	
testimonial	External	Self	External	Self
Extensive service	7.9 (1.1)	6.2 (1.5)	6.4 (1.7)	5.3 (1.7)
Limited service	5.3 (1.7)	4.0 (1.7)	4.5 (1.7)	3.0 (1.7)

Table 5.3

Subjective Rankings on a 1–9 Scale (1 = low, 9 = high)

Factor	Mean value	Standard deviation	t-statistic
Security and privacy seals	6.7	1.9	4.8
External testimonials	5.8	1.7	1.6
Contact number available	7.4	2.0	7.0
Being able to visit the real store	5.6	2.4	0.8
Clearly stated return policy	7.4	1.8	7.6
Possibility of returning a purchase at a nearby store	6.4	2.5	3.2
Privacy statements	6.2	2.1	3.0
Merchandise type	6.1	2.2	2.6
Discount or special offers	6.6	2.2	4.0
Professional design of the Web site	5.7	2.2	1.2
Ease of use of the Web site	6.3	2.0	3.4

Note: Factors that were statistically significant at the *p* <0.05 are shown in italic.

but rather its convenient replacement. Therefore, details about the real store proved to be unimportant.

The strong results are striking, but they should be followed up with validation studies that use real Web sites and customers. Such a longitudinal study would measure variables that matter to merchants, such as percent of customers making purchases and returning to make second purchases.

Conclusions

Impact for Practitioners

Our experiment shows that all three features we tested are important in establishing strategic trust among online customers. Web site designers should

Figure 5.5 **Mean and Standard Deviation Bars for Trustworthiness Rankings from Fifty-Two Subjects**

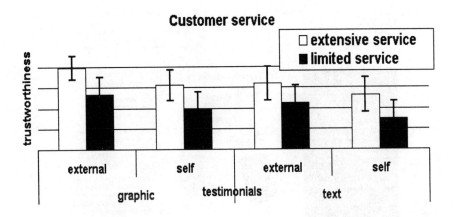

include extensive customer service information, provide phone numbers for technical support, clearly state the return policy, and provide an address for merchandise return. Graphic seals should be included as well as external testimonials, if available.

Suggestions for Future Research

Our study can be considered as a preliminary investigation into a very interesting topic of online trust. Future research should take into consideration the following issues that we came across when running our experiment:

- We were very careful about the visual impact of colors, size of tables, but we did not take into consideration the length of text.
- The source of the external testimonial has to be meaningful to the subjects.
- The questionnaire should be more specific about the kind of information requested.
- Because the dependent variable of the experiment is subjective, the number of subjects should be greater, and they should belong to different population groups.

Appendix

Figure A5.1 **Extensive Customer Service, External Testimonial, and Graphic Seals**

Figure A5.2 **Extensive Customer Service, External Testimonial, and Text Seals**

Figure A5.3 **Extensive Customer Service, Self-Testimonial, and Text Seals**

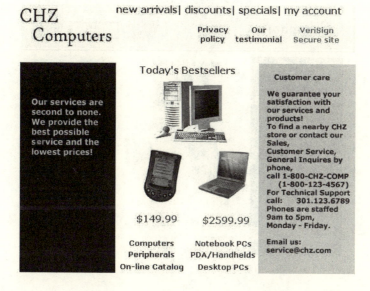

Figure A5.4 **Limited Customer Service, External Testimonial, and Text Seals**

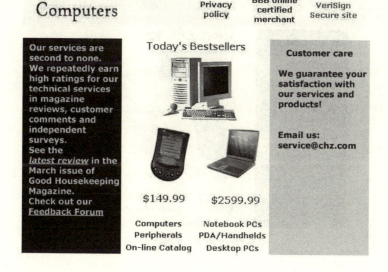

Figure A5.5 **Extensive Customer Service, Self-Testimonial, and Graphic Seals**

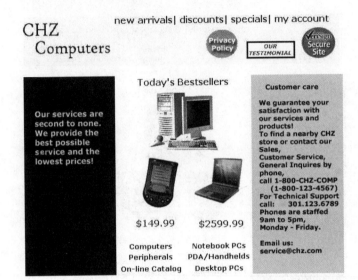

Figure A5.6 **Limited Customer Service, External Testimonial, and Graphic Seals**

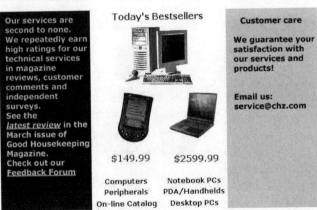

Figure A5.7 **Limited Customer Service, Self-Testimonial, and Graphic Seals**

Figure A5.8 **Limited Customer Service, Self-Testimonial, and Text Seals**

Note

We thank Dr. Eric Uslaner from the Department of Government and Politics, University of Maryland at College Park, for his advice and review of the experiment materials. We thank Daniel W. "Chip" Denman, assistant director for Research Programs, Office of Information Technology, University of Maryland at College Park, for his advice on statistical methods and Dr. Kent Norman and Tim Pleskac, Department of Psychology, University of Maryland at College Park, for directing us to the VassarStats software. We thank all of our subjects for participating in the experiment during their busy schedule. We appreciate constructive suggestions made on an early draft by Carolyn Snyder.

References

AT&T Labs. 1999. "Beyond Concern: Understanding Net Users Attitudes About Online Privacy Research Technical Report." www.research.att.com/library/trs/TRs/99/99.4/.

Cheskin Research and Studio Archetype. 1999. "E-commerce Trust Study." www.studioarchetype.com/cheskin/index.html.

Cheskin Research. 2000. "Trust in the Wired Americas." www.cheskin.com/think/studies/trust2.html.

Doney, P.M., and J.P. Cannon. 1997. "An Examination of the Nature of Trust in Buyer-Seller Relationships." *Journal of Marketing* 61(2) (April): 35–51.

Egger, F.N. 1999. "Human Factors in Electronic Commerce: Making Systems Appealing, Usable and Trustworthy." *Proceedings of Twelfth Bled International E-Commerce Conference,* Bled, Slovenia, June: www.ipo.tue.nl/homepages/fegger/bled99.htm.

Egger, F.N., and B. de Groot. 2000. "Developing a Model of Trust for Electronic Commerce: An Application to a Permissive Marketing Web Site." *Proceedings of the Ninth International World Wide Web Conference,* Amsterdam, The Netherlands, May 15–19: www.ipo.tue.nl/homepages/fegger/WWW9.htm.

Fogg, B.J.; J. Marshall; O. Laraki; A. Osipovich; C. Varma; N. Fang; P. Jyoti; A. Rangnekar; J. Shon; P. Swani; and M. Treinen. 2000. "What Makes Web Sites Credible? A Report on a Large Quantitative Study." *Proceedings of CHI 2000.* New York: ACM Press, 61–68.

Fukuyama, F. 1995. *Trust: The Social Virtues and the Creation of Prosperity.* New York: Free Press.

Kollock, P. 1999. "The Production of Trust in Online Markets." *Advances in Group Processes* 16: www.sscnet.ucla.edu/soc/faculty/kollock/papers/online_trust.htm.

Lee, J.; J. Kim; and J.Y. Moon. 2000. "What Makes Internet Users Visit Cyber Stores Again? Key Design Factors for Customer Loyalty User Experience in E-Commerce." *Proceedings of CHI 2000.* New York: ACM Press, 305–312: www.acm.org/pubs/articles/proceedings/chi/332040/p305-lee/p305-lee.pdf.

Morgan R.M., and S.D. Hunt. 1994. "The Commitment-Trust Theory of Relationship Marketing." *Journal of Marketing* 58(3) (July): 20–38.

Nielsen, J.; R. Molich; C. Snyder; and S. Farrell. 2000. "E-Commerce User Experience." Nielsen Norman Group: www.nngroup.com/reports/ecommerce.

Rust, R.T., and K.N. Lemon. 2001. "E-Service and the Consumer." *International Journal of Electronic Commerce* 5(3) (spring): 85–101.

Shneiderman, B. 2000. "Designing Web Sites to Enhance Online Trust." *Communications of the ACM* 43(12) (December): 81–83.

Urban, G.L.; F. Sultan; and W.J. Qualls. 2000. "Placing Trust at the Center of Your Internet Strategy." *Sloan Management Review* 42(1) (fall): 39–48.

Uslaner, E. Forthcoming.. *The Moral Foundations of Trust.* Cambridge: Cambridge University Press: www.bsos.umd.edu/gvpt/uslaner/research.htm.

6

e-Service Environment

Impacts of Web Interface Characteristics on Consumers' Online Shopping Behavior

Weiyin Hong, Kar Yan Tam, and Chi Kin (Bennett) Yim

Introduction

With the proliferation of electronic commerce, more and more businesses are trying to conduct transactions with their customers on the Internet. According to Forrester Research, the online retail market is predicted to reach U.S.$184 billion by the year 2004. However, these e-businesses are realizing that their successes are less determined by a traditional business model (e.g., low prices) than by delivering top-notch, repeatable service that creates satisfied customers (Zemke and Connellan 2000). As the novelty of the Internet continues to wear off, e-businesses that want to maintain a sustainable advantage in the virtual world must try to differentiate by emphasizing superior or "knock-your-socks-off" e-Service (Zeithaml et al. 2000).

The Web site is particularly important for e-Service companies because very often the only contact that customers and suppliers have with these firms is through their Web sites on the Internet. No wonder we see an increasing number of e-Service firms, particularly e-tailers, employing Web analytics (i.e., the technology of monitoring and summarizing Web site use patterns) to evaluate how the Web interface design could impact the use patterns, and thus, the profitability of their sites (Jarvis 2001). As stated in the introduction of this book, the Web site or, more specifically, the Web interface represents the e-Service environment, which is one of the three founding components of e-Service. Just like the physical design and spatial arrangement of products in a physical outlet affects the shopping process, the user interface of an online store will have a significant impact on the information search and browsing process of online customers. A recent exploratory study by V.A. Zeithaml et al. (2000) revealed that consumers consider eleven dimensions when they evaluate e-Service quality. Among these dimensions are ease of site navigation, reliability, and site aesthetics, all of which are related to Web interface design. Web design as a critical element of the delivery of superior e-Service is, thus, unquestionable. Another reason Web interface design is important to e-Service is that the interface design of most Web sites is problematic. According to reviews by several magazines, less than 40 percent of Web sites are usable in the sense that customers can actually find what they are looking for (Smith 2000). A study conducted by the International Customer Service Association (ICSA) and e-Satisfy.com (2000) also revealed that only 35 percent of e-customers are satisfied with their online purchase experience. These are serious warning signs that e-Service providers must improve their e-Service environment through gaining a better understanding of how Web interface characteristics affect consumers' online experience.

It is important to note that unlike traditional information systems (such as decision support systems or information retrieval systems), e-commerce systems bear the characteristics of both an information system and a marketing channel. Building on the platform of the Internet and computers, an e-commerce system is a service provided by servers on the network and accessed by users via the Internet browsers. Meanwhile, an e-commerce system also serves as a marketing channel where product information can be displayed and transactions can be performed. Therefore, in studying the e-Service environment and reviewing its impact on consumer online shopping behavior, we must examine pieces of evidence from both the information system (IS) and marketing research perspectives and integrate them with findings from existing e-commerce studies. The main purpose of this chapter is to summarize the state-of-the-art understanding of the impacts of Web interface characteristics on consumers' online shopping behavior, with a focus on the information presentation (from the IS perspective) and display of product information (from the marketing perspective). We focus on the information environment of the Web interface because interactive information service is critical to understanding the role of e-Service (Rust and Lemon 2000). We will also present managerial implications that come out of the literature review as well as an agenda for future research in this area.

In the next section, we will first examine evidence on information presentation from the IS literature and discuss its implications. Then, research on the display of product information from the marketing perspective is reviewed.

Insights from research on Web interface design in the e-commerce literature are then discussed to present managerial implications. Finally, we will present an agenda for future research on the topic.

Research on Information Presentation from the Information System Literature

Although research on information presentation exists for various types of information systems, such as information retrieval systems (e.g., Hu et al. 1999) and online public-access catalogs (see Yee 1991 for a review), the majority of the research effort centers around the use of graphics versus tables on decision support systems (DSS). Moreover, most of the prior research on information presentation was conducted in the managerial decision-making context, which is quite different from the online shopping environment. For example, for managerial decision tasks, accuracy and efficiency are the foremost concerns, while for the online shopping tasks, there are usually no right or wrong answers, and consumers' experience becomes critical. Nevertheless, a review of the IS literature can provide a useful starting point to understand the effects of information presentation on online shopping systems as they bear the basic characteristics of information systems.

The Effects of Graphics Versus Tables

Early research on the use of graphics in DSS made it simple to compare different information presentation formats on decision-making performance. W. Remus (1984) compared graphical and tabular displays as decision aids for a production scheduling problem and found that tabular display of information leads to lower cost than the graphical display. N.S. Umanath and R.W. Scamell (1988) examined the influence of tabular versus graphical display (bar chart) on users' recall performance and found that graphical display results in better recall of data pattern than the tabular display. D.B. Mackay (1987) compared traditional tabular displays of multivariate financial data with a new graphical display technique (facial display). The results suggest that the relative advantage of graphical display to tabular display on decision-making depends on both the individual differences and the problem characteristics. G.W. Dickson et al. (1986) compared tables with bar charts and line plots on several performance criteria, including interpretation accuracy, quality decision, and ability to convey a message to decision-makers. Superiority of graphic presentation is not supported by a set of cumulative experiments, suggesting that the effectiveness of the data display format is largely a function of the task at hand.

A clear focus of these early studies on graphical information presentation was to compare its effectiveness in supporting decision-making with that of tabular information presentation. The inconsistent findings of these studies inspired reflections on the research of computer graphics, which gave rise to some review and research direction papers. G. DeSanctis (1984) reviewed research on graphical information presentation from a large number of disciplines, including statistics, human factors engineering, cartography, psychology, educational communication, and marketing. She proposed a framework to conduct research on the use of graphics as decision aids with user characteristics and decision context (such as task) as major interacting variables. S.L. Jarvenpaa and G.W. Dickson (1988) reviewed previous studies on computer graphics in terms of the presentation formats (table versus graphic), the type of tasks, and the user experience. J.H. Coll and R. Coll (1993) further classified sixteen variables that are related to the efficacy and choice of information presentation formats. Two pertinent variables that had been consistently identified in these reviews are characteristics of the task and users. The effectiveness of computer graphics in aiding decision-making seems to depend on both the tasks they intend to support and the individual differences of system users. In the following subsections, we will review research covering this interaction effect between information presentation format and task and user characteristics.

Role of Task on the Effectiveness of Information Presentation Formats

A large number of the following studies have included the decision-making task as an interaction with information presentation formats in affecting decision performance (e.g., Coll et al. 1994; Jarvenpaa 1989). Specifically, it was found that while tables are better at data retrieval tasks, graphics are more congenial to trend detection and prediction. Efforts have also been made to build theories in explaining the interaction between tasks and information presentation formats, including the cognitive fit theory (Vessey 1991; Umanath and Vessey 1994), the cost-benefit paradigm (Jarvenpaa 1989; Vessey 1994), the componential analysis of cognitive effort (Kennedy et al. 1998), and the anchoring characteristics (Tan and Benbasat 1990, 1993).

Among the various theoretical explanations, the cognitive fit theory has received the greatest attention (Vessey 1991). It basically argues that the different information presentation formats, such as tables (symbolic representation) and graphics (spatial representation), and different problem-solving tasks, such as trend detection (spatial task) and data value retrieval (symbolic task), emphasize different types of information and problem-solving processes. When both the information presentation format and the task emphasize the same type of information and processes, a cognitive fit will occur that produces a consistent mental representation for problem-solving, and subsequently leads to a faster and more accurate performance in decision-making. However, when there is a mismatch between the information format and the task, cognitive fit will not take place. Problem-solvers will then need to transform some of the mental representation that induces additional effort and results in relatively lower performance than if there is a cognitive fit. The theory of cognitive fit has been empirically validated in a variety of problem domains, such as programming (Sinha and Vessey 1992) and object-oriented modeling (Agarwal et al. 1996), and other data representation variations, such as multi-attribute data (Umanath and Vessey 1994), multimedia (Hubona 1998), and maps (Dennis and Carte 1998; Mennecke et al. 2000; Smelcer and Carmel 1997). We would expect that the effectiveness of various information presentation formats in an e-Service environment will likely be affected by the task that the online consumer would want to perform coming to the site. For example, a consumer who looks to compare prices would probably prefer to see that items in the same product category are ranked in order by price.

Individual Differences and Information Presentation Effectiveness

Another major factor that might moderate the effects of graphical information presentation on decision-making performance is individual differences. S.L. Loy (1991) examined three individual thinking skills (verbal skill, logical-reasoning skill, and visual thinking skill) and found that when doing problem structuring, high visual thinkers benefit more from the use of graphics-based DSS than the low visual thinkers do. Similarly, Umanath et al. (1990) compared two screen/report display formats (tables versus graphics) in an information recall context, with individual imagery orientation (verbalizer versus visualizer) as a moderating variable. The findings suggest that the graphical information presentation enhances the pattern recall performance of the visualizers, but not the verbalizers or the mixed type. Another individual difference variable that has been examined is cognitive ability (field dependent versus field independent). In general, users with high cognitive ability (field independents) benefit more from graphical-based information presentation than those with low cognitive ability (field dependents) (Benbasat and Dexter 1985; Pracht and Courtney 1988).

Recent research on computer graphics introduces other types of graphics on information systems and includes other aspects of individual differences. The major type of computer graphics under investigation in recent IS studies is map-based presentation on geographical information systems (Dennis and Carte 1998; Smelcer and Carmel 1997). It reveals a trend that, with the increasingly more powerful publishing technologies, more sophisticated information presentation formats will become the focus of IS research. Recent research can also be found that goes beyond the traditional individual differences variables to incorporate users' objectives (for oneself versus for others) into the understanding of their preferences for different information presentation formats (2D, 2.5D, or 3D bar graph) (Tractinsky and Meyer 1999). Again, these are more sophisticated forms of computer graphics that are enabled by the development of information technologies.

Table 6.1 summarizes the empirical studies on computer graphics, with a focus on the comparison between graphical and tabular information presentation in a decision-making context. Independent variables in these studies are classified into three major types: information presentation, task, and user. The rest of the independent variables are included in the "Others" category. Two major dependent variables adopted in these studies are decision time and decision quality, which reflect the efficiency and the effectiveness of information presentation in supporting decision-making tasks respectively. In the "Results" column, we report only significant interaction effects between information presentation and task/or user, because they are of major relevance to the Web interface characteristics research.

Implications for Web Interface Research

As the above studies collectively suggest that the effect of information presentation may interact with the characteristics of both the tasks and the users, studying information presentation in isolation will not be fruitful. In the domain of e-commerce, the message presented here is that in order to examine the Web interface characteristics, it is important to take consumers' shopping tasks or individual differences into consideration. While consumers' individual differences are relatively difficult to collect in the online shopping environment, due to privacy considerations, among others, studying the effects of consumers' shopping tasks together with the Web interface characteristics becomes critical in research on Web interface design. Consumers' shopping tasks can be captured either by the pattern of their clickstream data, or by explicit solicitation of their responses through online interaction (e.g., type in a keyword search).

Table 6.1

Summary of IS Studies on Information Presentation

Studies	Independent variables				Dependent variables	Results (interaction effects* only)
	Information presentation	Task	User	Others		
Remus (1984)	Tabular; graphical.	N/A	N/A	N/A	Actual cost; individual decision rules; composite decision rules.	N/A
Benbasat and Dexter (1985)	Tabular; graphical.	N/A	Cognitive ability (field dependent/ independent).	Color.	Decision time; decision quality; user perceptions of information systems attributes.	Cognitive ability.
Benbasat and Dexter (1986)	Tabular; graphical; combined tabular and graphical.	N/A	N/A	Color; time constraint.	Profit performance; decision time; satisfaction.	N/A
Dickson et al. (1986)	Table; graphics (bar charts, line plots, graphics).	N/A	N/A	N/A	Interpretation accuracy; decision quality; task difficulty; report reliability.	N/A
Pracht and Courtney (1988)	Graphical interactive structural modeling.	N/A	Cognitive ability (field dependent/ Independent).	N/A	Problem structural comprehension.	Cognitive ability.
Umanath and Scamell (1988)	Table; graphics (bar chart).	N/A	N/A	N/A	Recall (specific value, direction, pattern).	N/A
Jarvenpaa (1989)	Attribute bar chart; alternative bar chart; grouped bar chart.	Linear; conjunctive; majority of confirming; elimination-by-aspect.	N/A	N/A	Acquisition direction; evaluation direction; decision time; decision quality.	Task.

Study	Presentation format	Task	Individual difference	Other factor	Dependent variables	Interaction*
Umanath et al. (1990)	Tabular; graphical.	N/A	Individual imagery orientation.	Order of presentation.	Recall (point and pattern).	Individual imagery orientation
Loy (1991)	Graphic-based problem-structuring aid.	N/A	Individual thinking skill (visual, verbal, logical reasoning).	N/A	Effectiveness of understanding problems.	Visual thinking skill.
Vessey and Galletta (1991)	Table; graph.	Spatial task; symbolic task.	Problem-solving skill.	Order of problem presentation.	Time; accuracy.	Task; problem-solving skills.
Tan and Benbasat (1993)	Bar chart; symbol plots; lines graphs.	High or low y-value anchoring tasks.	N/A	Time period; data sets.	Time; accuracy.	Task.
Umanath and Vessey (1994)	Table; graphs; schematic faces.	N/A	N/A	Information load.	Time; accuracy.	N/A
Smelcer and Carmel (1997)	Table; map.	Task difficulty.	Cognitive skill.	Graphical relationships.	Time; accuracy.	Task.
Dennis and Carte (1998)	Table; map.	Geographic containment task; geographic adjacency task.	N/A	N/A	Decision process; accuracy; time.	Task.
Kennedy et al. (1998)	Table; graphics (line graph, bar chart).	Value extraction; comparison; trend detection.	N/A	Data	Strategy composition; efficiency; accuracy; strategy formulation time; uniformity.	Task.
Tractinsky and Meyer (1999)	2D bar graph; 2.5D bar graph; 3D bar graph.	Decision oneself; decision others; impress others.	N/A	Content desirability.	Choice of presentation format; suitability of presentation format.	Task.

*Interaction with the information presentation formats on one or several of the dependent variables.

Research on Display of Product Information from the Marketing Literature

The question of how the display of product information influences consumer behavior has been extensively investigated in marketing research. A number of useful theories and empirical findings have been accumulated that are potentially applicable for studying e-commerce as a new marketing channel. However, as noted by R.A. Peterson et al. (1997):

> Because the Internet possessed certain unique characteristics that have no counterparts in conventional retailing, it might also be necessary to construct specialized theories that would explain the mechanics and consequences of marketing to consumers through the Internet. (p. 333)

Nevertheless, a review of the marketing literature will help to locate existing theories as well as identify important interface variables to be examined in the online environment.

Research on product information display in the marketing literature manifests two focuses. The first focus is on the information format, which is the overall arrangement and organization of product information either in physical retail stores or in a simulated consumer decision-making environment. For example, product information can either be organized by brands or by attributes. The second stream of this research focuses on the specific display characteristics evolving around the design of advertisements. The display characteristics that are usually examined in these studies include sequential order, size, and color.

We will first discuss findings related to the format of information display. Then, we present research findings derived from the design of advertisements.

Findings on Information Format

Information format refers to the presentation and organization of information about the available alternatives and their attributes (Cooper-Martin 1993). The alternatives could be different brands of either physical products (e.g., Coca-Cola and Pepsi for soft drink) or other types of consumer goods (e.g., selection of an apartment). Each alternative usually has a set of attributes based on which consumers are going to make their purchase or selection decisions. Marketing researchers as well as social psychologists strongly believe that information format has a major impact on consumers' information search-and-decision process (Abelson and Levi 1985; Bettman et al. 1991). For example, J.R. Bettman and P. Kakkar (1977) presented subjects with information about eleven brands of breakfast cereal, with thirteen attributes for each alternative. It was found that in an alternative-centered information format, where each alternative was described in a separate booklet, subjects processed product information by alternatives. On the other hand, in an attribute-centered information format where information about each attribute was given in a separate booklet, subjects processed information by attributes.

The effects of product information display on consumers' decision process can be understood via the cost-benefit framework. First, there was empirical evidence that the availability of certain product information increases the use of that information (Muller 1985; Russo 1977; Russo et al. 1986). For example, J.E. Russo (1977) showed that consumers become more price-sensitive when unit price information of various brands of a grocery product was presented to shoppers in a sorted list. Similarly, T.E. Muller (1985) found that when consumers were provided with nutrition information in a brand-by-nutrient matrix on a point-of-purchase sign, sales would shift toward the nutritionally higher-ranked brands. The rationale embedded in these findings is that when consumers are provided with displays where certain product information becomes more readily available, they are more likely to process that piece of information because the cost to use it becomes lower.

Second, organizing product information either by alternative or by attribute affects consumers' decision process by varying the cost associated with different information *acquisition* strategies. Generally, it is easier to retrieve information of an attribute in a by-attribute information format, and to retrieve information of a brand in a by-alternative information format. However, it also depends on the cost to access one type of information over another type of information format (e.g., how difficult it is to make an attribute-oriented search in a by-alternative format). For example, in J.R. Bettman and P. Kakkar's (1977) experiment, different alternatives or different attributes were organized in separate booklets. Hence, the cost to retrieve information of a certain attribute across different brands becomes very high for the by-alternative information format. However, when all information is simultaneously presented in the by-alternative format, D.A. Schkade and D.N. Kleinmuntz (1994) observed an attribute-based acquisition (rather than alternative-based), probably because the related cost is lower when all information is available simultaneously. Hence, consumers tend to select their information acquisition strategies based on the cost associated with them.

Finally, information format will affect the decision process by varying the cost to perform different *decision* strategies. Facing a set of alternatives, each described on several attributes, consumers may adopt several heuristics (i.e., decision strategies), such as elimination-by-aspects heuristic, lexicographic heuristic, and equal-weight heuristic, to simplify their choice tasks (see Bettman et al. 1991 for a review). When a particular information format lowers the cost of performing a certain heuristic, consumers are more likely to adopt that heuristic for decision-making. For example, R. Sethuraman et al. (1994) presented an analytical framework showing that information format (by alternative or by attribute) determines optimal cut-off strategies for screening alternative tasks. More compelling evidence could be found when computer-assisted decision aids are provided to decision-makers (Todd and Benbasat 1991, 1992, 1994; Winding and Talarzyk 1993). For example, a cutoff format, which allows consumers to specify the cutoff value of attributes, should support the elimination-by-aspect heuristic, where alternatives with any attribute lower than the cutoff value will be dropped from further consideration. Therefore, consumers are likely to select a decision strategy consistent with the information format in order to reduce their effort.

Implications for Web Interface Design

A common finding in these studies is that consumers seem to put more emphasis on the cost (i.e., effort) rather than on the benefit (i.e., accuracy) when making purchase decisions based on product information. When facing a tradeoff between effort and accuracy, they tend to select the information acquisition-and-decision strategy that can minimize their effort with acceptable accuracy. In the e-Service domain, consumers are likely to become more effort-sensitive due to the dual impact of a greater amount of information available and consumers' seeking effort reduction on the Web. Therefore, the design of Web sites should put more emphasis on the effort-reducing interface characteristics (e.g., price-sorting tools) than on the accuracy-increasing interface characteristics (e.g., tools to calculate weighted average of brands based on consumers' rating on each product attribute), as they are more likely to be adopted by online consumers. Also, online retailers can direct consumers' attention to some of the attributes or alternatives by manipulating the cost of accessing this information on the Web sites (such as putting the brand on promotion at the top of the Web page).

Findings from the Design of Advertisements

Another stream of research in marketing related to Web interface design is on the design of advertisements. Various display characteristics have been examined and found to significantly influence consumers' attention to the advertisement, and their recall and preference of the advertisements (see

Table 6.2 for a summary). Although reading is significantly different in the printed media versus the electronic media (Muter and Maurutto 1991; Wright and Lickorish 1983), a review of display characteristics in the traditional printed media can help to identify potential interface characteristics on the Web. To a certain extent, an e-Service Web site bears the characteristics of electronic advertisements, where product information is presented and designed to capture consumers' attention. Furthermore, the Web is often suggested as an alternative advertising medium (Dréze and Zufryden 1997; Ducoffe 1996). In the following subsections, we will focus on three display characteristics that have been found to be important in advertisement studies—color, size, and position—and discuss their potential implications for e-Service research.

Color

Color was found to be useful to attract consumers' attention in traditional advertising media, such as magazines and yellow advertisements (Hornik 1980; Lohse 1997; Twedt 1952; Valiente 1973). Illustrations with color are more likely to attract attention than the black-and-white displays. This variable was traditionally of interest in the printed media due to the cost involved in providing colorful prints. However, in the online environment, product information can very easily be presented in color with almost no additional cost, as the Web, by its nature, is a colorful environment. Therefore, color itself may not be of major interest to researchers working on the Web interface characteristics. However, instead of simply attracting attention, color may have a more profound impact on consumers' online shopping behavior. For example, N. Mandel and E.J. Johnson (1999) found that the background color of Web pages can manipulate salient features of products and subsequently influence consumers' final choices. Hence, it is suggested that while the effects of color may not be obvious on the Web in its traditional sense, it could have a major impact on consumers' online shopping behavior from a new perspective.

Size

Size is another important display characteristic in printed media. The direct relationship between the size of advertisements and consumers' attention and preference has been well documented (Hoque and Lohse 1999; Hornik 1980; Lohse 1997; Rhodes et al. 1979; Twedt 1952; Valiente 1973; Yamanaka 1962). Usually, the bigger the size of an advertisement, the larger the chance that it is going to attract consumers' attention. There are reasons to believe

Table 6.2

Summary of Advertising Research on Display Characteristics

Studies	Context	Independent variables*	Dependent variables
Yamanaka (1962)	Newspaper	*Size, page number, position* on the page, *type* of illustration.	Readership score.
Twedt (1952)	Magazine	Pictorial and *color, size,* typographic size, information, field, ad schedule.	Readership score.
Valiente (1973)	Magazine	*Color, size* of illustration, copy size, pictorial information, number of words and colors, similar ads, previous schedule.	Reader's attention (noted reader score), reader's interest (read most score).
Rhodes et al. (1979)	Yellow-page advertisement	*Size* of the brand name, *position* on the page, headline *typeface.*	Correct identification (recall of brand name and headline).
Hornik (1980)	Printed advertisement	*Size* of illustration, *color, position* of illustration, style of product design, perceived usability of product, elements (single vs. multiple, price, beauty, quality of photography, special offers, emotional appeal).	Preference of ads.
Lohse (1997)	Yellow-page advertisement	*Color, size,* availability of *graphics, position* on the page, *bold font,* number of types of information in the ad.	View time (fixation), ordinal number of each fixation on a page, choice.
Hoque and Lohse (1999)	Electronic Yellow-page advertisement	Serial *position, travel distance,* display advertisement (*size*).	View time (fixation), ordinal number of each fixation on a page, choice.

* Important independent variables are displayed in italics.

that size will remain important in the electronic environment because other things being equal, the larger an object is, the more attention it is likely to get. However, A.Y. Hoque and G.L. Lohse (1999) questioned whether the size of an advertisement will have a positive effect in the online environment because due to the limited screen size, a big advertisement will no longer have the same advantage online as it does in the printed media.

In an experiment on electronic yellow pages, they found that consumers are actually less likely to choose a graphical advertisement due to the difficulty of viewing a large advertisement online. Therefore, the potential for display size to influence online consumers' attention is limited by the screen size of the computer.

Position

The position of an advertisement on printed media also determines the attention that it is likely to receive from the consumers. Advertisements placed near the headline or listed on the top of a list have a higher chance of being attended to or being selected by consumers (Hornik 1980; Lohse 1997; Rhodes et al. 1979; Yamanaka 1962). The position effect was also found for electronic yellow pages even when there is no obvious reason to expect any difference due to the serial position in a list (Hoque and Lohse 1999). Because of the large amount of information available online and the cost it involves in scrolling for information in the lower part of the Web pages, consumers may terminate a search before the complete listing was scanned, emphasizing the position effect. The importance of this effect of serial order in interface design has also been recognized in research in IS (Marshall et al. 1987; Umanath et al. 1990).

Implications for e-Service Environment

The review of advertising literature suggests that the display characteristics found to be important in traditional printed media may or may not be as important in the online environment. The special characteristics of the electronic media need to be analyzed and compared with the traditional media before we can directly apply prior findings to the new e-Service environment. The Web also contains unique features that the printed media is not capable of providing. For example, different forms of animation, such as flash, pop-outs, and moving texts, can be found online, but is unimaginable in the printed media. Therefore, more research is needed to examine these new interface characteristics and see how they affect consumers' online shopping behavior.

Research on Web Interface Design from the e-Commerce Literature

Survey research on Web interface design usually includes a large number of design variables that have the potential to affect online consumer behavior (Dholakia and Rego 1998; Gehrke and Turban 1999; Lohse and Spiller 1998a, 1998b). For example, G.L. Lohse and P. Spiller (1998b) classified Web interface design features into five categories—interface variables, merchandise, service, promotion, and convenience—and successfully predicted the store traffic and sales with these variables. Taking hit-rate as an indication of the effectiveness of Web page design, U.M. Dholakia and L.L. Rego (1998) surveyed 300 home pages of commercial Web sites and found that both the information content (e.g., number of quarterly changes to home page) and the design features of the Web pages (e.g., number of clickable pictures and use of animation) are important to the popularity of the Web site. Taking a different approach, D. Gehrke and E. Turban (1999) reviewed forty-seven papers about Web design and found five major focuses of these studies: page-loading speed, business content, navigation efficiency, security, and marketing. One thing in common among these studies is that they mix the effect of Web interface characteristics with that of other related variables, such as information content and page-loading speed.

More focused research on Web interface design can be found at both the structure level (Baty and Lee 1995; Westland and Au 1997/98) and the individual feature level (Chau et al. 2000; Kim and Yoo 2000; Sears et al. 2000). At the structure level, the emphasis is on the overall design of the Web site structure rather than on some specific design features. For example, J.C. Westland and G. Au (1997/98) conducted an experiment to compare consumers' shopping experiences across three digital retailing interfaces—catalog search, bundling, and virtual reality storefront. J.B. Baty and R.M. Lee (1995) proposed a functional architecture for electronic shopping infrastructures to improve vendor representation and customer navigation, with a focus on product differentiation and comparability. At the individual feature level, researchers usually put their focus on the effects of specific design features on the Web pages, such as add-on hyperlinks (Kim and Yoo 2000), presentation mode (image versus text) (Chau et al. 2000), and high-end graphical enhancements (Sears et al. 2000). While some of the interface variables examined in these studies have been studied in traditional IS research (e.g., graphics), the other interface variables under investigation are unique to the online environment (e.g., hyperlinks).

A more direct manipulation of the Web interface is the provision of decision aids on the Web site. Exploiting the unique capability of the Web to provide interactive tools, e-commerce researchers have examined the impact of various decision aids on online consumer behavior (Häubl and Trifts 2000; Pereira 2000). For example, G. Häubl and V. Trifts (2000) noticed that in a highly complex decision environment such as the Web, interactive tools can be particularly valuable in supporting consumers' screening of available products and in-depth comparison of selected products before making the actual purchase decision. They found that two interactive decision tools, a recommendation agent (a tool for screening alternatives) and a comparison agent (a tool for organizing product information), have substantial impact on consumers' extent of product information search as well as the quality of their purchase decision. Similarly, Pereira (2000) compared four online decision tools (elimination by aspects, weighted average method, profile building, and simple hypertext design), with each of them supporting a different search strategy. It was found that online consumers tend to prefer some decision tools to others depending on their product class knowledge and amount of information provided.

Future Research on Web Interface Design

Existing empirical research on Web interface design has examined a great variety of topics, in terms of the selection of interface variables, the focus of the study, and the functionalities examined. Future studies on the Web interface design should first decide on the level of the research: will it be focusing on the overall design of Web site structure, or focusing on some specific design features. If the focus is on the individual feature level, there are roughly three categories of interface variables to be studied from the earlier reviews of the IS and marketing literature. The first category deals with information content on the Web site, such as product information (e.g., number of products, number of attributes, and promotions), business information (e.g., contact information and FAQ section), and frequency of information updates. The second category is related to functionalities provided on the Web site, such as interactive decision aids and software agents. The last category resembles the concept of information presentation in traditional IS research. It may include the size of images, number of pictures, use of animations, background color, serial position on the Web page, and so forth. Together, this set of variables could be referred to as Web interface characteristics. We note that a clear focus in defining the scope of research is needed to provide more accurate understanding of the variables under investigation.

Given the multidisciplinary nature of e-commerce research, it turns out to be both useful and crucial to understand the relevant issues from various research angles. As information systems, the efficiency and the effectiveness of e-commerce systems are wanted features. However, while consumers may like an e-Service to be provided and completed quickly, online retailers may want to retain consumers as long as possible on their Web sites to convey more Web site information to the consumers. Future research can be conducted to find out whether there are some ways to achieve the seemingly contradictory objects of both sides by manipulating the Web interface design characteristics. There are some preliminary research results that suggest that it is possible to reach the dual goal simultaneously (Hong et al. 2001).

Meanwhile, it is also important to look at e-Service from the marketing perspective, which emphasizes consumers' experience. An enjoyable experience depends to a great extent upon the quality of the service. The topic of service quality has been widely examined in the traditional marketing area. In contrast, knowledge on how customers assess electronic service quality is very limited. An exception is a recent exploratory study conducted by V.A. Zeithaml et al. (2000). They reported that consumers consider eleven dimensions when they evaluate e-Service quality: access, ease of navigation, efficiency, flexibility, reliability, personalization, security/privacy, responsiveness, assurance/trust, site aesthetics, and price knowledge. Since most of these dimensions are comprised of perceptual attributes, future research that focuses on linking objective Web interface characteristics to these perceptual attributes is needed before a high-quality e-Service environment can be developed.

References

Abelson, R.P., and A. Levi. 1985. "Decision Making and Decision Theory." In *Handbook of Social Psychology: Theory and Method*, vol. 1, ed. G. Lindzey and E. Aronson. New York: Random House, 231–309.

Agarwal, R.; A.P. Sinha; and M. Tanniru. 1996. "The Role of Prior Experience and Task Characteristics in Object-Oriented Modeling: An Empirical Study." *International Journal of Human-Computer Studies* 45: 639–667.

Baty, J.B., and R.M. Lee. 1995. "InterShop: Enhancing the Vendor/Customer Dialectic in Electronic Shopping." *Journal of Management Information Systems* 11(4): 9–31.

Benbasat, I., and A.S. Dexter. 1985. "An Experimental Evaluation of Graphical and Color-Enhanced Information Presentation." *Management Science* 31(1): 1348–1364.

———. 1986. "An Investigation of the Effectiveness of Color and Graphical Information Presentation Under Varying Time Constraints." *MIS Quarterly* 10(1): 9–81.

Bettman, J.R., and P. Kakkar. 1977. "Effects of Information Presentation Format on Consumer Information Acquisition Strategies." *Journal of Consumer Research* 3 (March): 233–240.

Bettman, J.R.; E.J. Johnson; and J.W. Payne. 1991. "Consumer Decision Making." In *Handbook of Consumer Behavior,* ed. T.S. Robertson and H.H. Kassarjian. Englewood Cliffs, NJ: Prentice-Hall, 50–84.

Chau, P.Y.K.; G. Au; and K.Y. Tam. 2000. "Impact of Information Presentation Modes on Online Shopping: An Empirical Evaluation of a Broadband Interactive Shopping Service." *Journal of Organizational Computing and Electronic Commerce* 10(1): 1–22.

Coll, J.H., and R. Coll. 1993. "Tables and Graphs: A Classification Scheme for Display Presentation Variables and a Framework for Research in This Area." *Information Processing and Management* 29(6): 745–750.

Coll, R.A.; J.H. Coll; and G. Thakur. 1994. "Graphs and Tables: A Four-Factor Experiment." *Communications of the ACM* 37(4): 77–86.

Cooper-Martin, E. 1993. "Effects of Information Format and Similarity Among Alternatives on Consumer Choice Processes." *Journal of the Academy of Marketing Science* 21(3): 239–246.

Dennis, A.R., and T.A. Carte. 1998. "Using Geographical Information Systems for Decision Making: Extending Cognitive Fit Theory to Map-Based Presentation." *Information Systems Research* 9(2): 194–203.

DeSanctis, G. 1984. "Computer Graphics as Decision Aids: Directions for Research." *Decision Sciences* 15: 463–487.

Dholakia, U.M., and L.L. Rego. 1998. "What Makes Commercial Web Pages Popular? An Empirical Investigation of Web Page Effectiveness." *European Journal of Marketing* 32(7/8): 724–736.

Dickson, G.W.; G. DeSanctis; and D.J. McBride. 1986. "Understanding the Effectiveness of Computer Graphics for Decision Support: A Cumulative Experimental Approach." *Communications of the ACM* 29(1): 40–47.

Dréze, X., and E. Zufryden. 1997. "Testing Web Site Design and Promotional Content." *Journal of Advertising Research* 37(2): 77–91.

Ducoffe, R.H. 1996. "Advertising Value and Advertising on the Web." *Journal of Advertising Research* 36(5): 21–35.

Gehrke, D., and E. Turban. 1999. "Determinants of Successful Website Design: Relative Importance and Recommendations for Effectiveness." *Proceedings of the 32nd Hawaii International Conference on System Sciences*, Maui, Hawaii, January 5–8, 1999.

Häubl, G., and V. Trifts. 2000. "Consumer Decision Making in Online Shopping Environments: The Effects of Interactive Decision Aids." *Marketing Science* 19(1): 4–21.

Hong, Weiyin; J.Y.L. Thong; and K.Y. Tam. 2001. "The Effects of Information Format and Shopping Task on Consumers' Online Shopping Behavior." Working paper, Hong Kong University of Science and Technology.

Hoque, A.Y., and G.L. Lohse. 1999. "An Information Search Cost Perspective for Designing Interfaces for Electronic Commerce." *Journal of Marketing Research* 36 (August): 387–394.

Hornik, J. 1980. "Quantitative Analysis of Visual Perception of Printed Advertisements." *Journal of Advertising Research* 20 (December): 41–48.

Hu, P.J.-H.; P.-C. Ma; and P.Y.K. Chau. 1999. "Evaluation of User Interface Designs for Information Retrieval Systems: A Computer-Based Experiment." *Decision Support Systems* [Special Issue: From Information Retrieval to Knowledge Management: Enabling Technologies and Best Practices] 27(1/2) (November): 125–143.

Hubona, G.S. 1998. "Mental Representation of Spatial Language." *International Journal of Human-Computer Studies* 48(6): 705–728.

International Customer Service Association (ICSA) and e-Satisfy.com. 2000. http://sellitontheWeb.com/ezine/news0382.shtml.

Jarvenpaa, S.L. 1989. "The Effect of Task Demands and Graphical Format on Information Processing Strategies." *Management Science* 35(3): 285–303.

Jarvenpaa, S.L., and G.W. Dickson. 1988. "Graphics and Managerial Decision-Making: Research-Based Guidelines." *Communications of the ACM* 31(6): 764–774.

Jarvis, S. 2001."Follow the Money." *Marketing News* 35(21): 1, 10.

Kennedy, M.; D. Te'eni; and J.B. Treleven. 1998. "Impacts of Decision Task, Data and Display on Strategies for Extracting Information." *International Journal of Human-Computer Studies* 48: 159–180.

Kim, J., and B. Yoo. 2000. "Toward the Optimal Link Structure of the Cyber Shopping Mall." *International Journal of Human-Computer Studies* 52(3): 531–551.

Lohse, G.L. 1997. "Consumer Eye Movement Patterns on Yellow Pages Advertising." *Journal of Advertising* 27(1): 61–73.

Lohse, G.L., and P. Spiller. 1998a. "Electronic Shopping." *Communications of the ACM* 41(7): 81–87.

———. 1998b. "Quantifying the Effect of User Interface Design Features on Cyberstore Traffic and Sales." In *CHI'98 Conference Proceedings*, Los Angeles, April 18–23. Los Alamitos, CA: ACM Press, 162–174.

Loy, S.L. 1991. "The Interaction Effects Between General Thinking Skills and an Interactive Graphics-Based DSS to Support Problem Structuring." *Decision Sciences* 22: 846–868.

MacKay, D.B. 1987. "Performance Differences in the Use of Graphic and Tabular Displays of Multivariate Data." *Decision Sciences* 18: 535–546.

Mandel, N., and E.J. Johnson. 1999. "Constructing Preferences Online: Can Web Pages Change What You Want?" Working paper, E-Commerce Research Forum, February: http://fourps.wharton.upenn.edu/~naomi/construct.htm.

Marshall, C.; C. Nelson; and M.M. Gardiner. 1987. "Design Guidelines." In *Applying Cognitive Psychology to User-Interface Design*, ed. M.M. Gardiner and B. Christie. New York: Wiley.

Mennecke, B.E.; M.D. Crossland; and B.L. Killingsworth. 2000. "Is a Map More Than a Picture? The Role of SDSS Technology, Subject Characteristics, and Problem Complexity on Map Reading and Problem Solving." *MIS Quarterly* 24(4): 601–629.

Muller, T.E.. 1985. "Structural Information Factors Which Stimulate the Use of Nutrition Information: A Field Experiment." *Journal of Marketing Research* 22(May): 143–157.

Muter, P., and P. Maurutto. 1991. "Reading and Skimming from Computer Screens and Books: The Paperless Office Revisited?" *Behaviour and Information Technology* 10(4): 257–266.

Pereira, R.E. 2000. "Optimizing Human-Computer Interaction for the Electronic Commerce Environment." *Journal of Electronic Commerce Research* 1(1): 11–20.

Peterson, R.A.; S. Balasubramanian; and B.J. Bronnenberg. 1997. "Exploring the Implications of the Internet for Consumer Marketing." *Journal of the Academy of Marketing Science* 25(4): 329–346.

Pracht, W.E., and J.F. Courtney. 1988. "The Effects of an Interactive Graphics-Based DSS to Support Problem Structuring." *Decision Sciences* 19(3): 598–621.

Remus, W. 1984. "An Empirical Investigation of the Impact of Graphical and Tabular Data Presentations on Decision Making." *Management Science* 30(5): 533–542.

Rhodes, E.W.; N.B. Leferman; E. Cook; and D. Schwartz. 1979. "T-Scope Tests of Yellow-pages Advertising." *Journal of Advertising Research* 28(4): 429–440.

Russo, J.E. 1977. "The Value of Unit Price Information." *Journal of Marketing Research* 14(2): 193–201.

Russo, J.E.; R. Staelin; C.A. Nolan; G.J. Russell; and B.L. Metcalf. 1986. "Nutrition Information in the Supermarket." *Journal of Consumer Research* 13 (June): 48–70.

Rust, R.T., and K.N. Lemon. 2000. "E-Service and the Consumer." *International Journal of Electronic Commerce* 5(3): 85–102.

Schkade, D.A., and D.N. Kleinmuntz. 1994. "Information Displays and Choice Processes: Differential Effects of Organization, Form, and Sequence." *Organizational Behavior and Human Decision Processes* 57(3): 319–337.

Sears, A.; J.A. Jacko; and E.M. Dubach. 2000. "International Aspects of World Wide Web Usability and the Role of High-End Graphical Enhancements." *International Journal of Human-Computer Interaction* 12(2): 241–261.

Sethuraman, R.; C. Cole; and D. Jain. 1994. "Analyzing the Effects of Information Format and Task on Cutoff Search Strategies." *Journal of Consumer Psychology* 3(2): 103–136.

Sinha, A.P., and I. Vessey. 1992. "Cognitive Fit: An Empirical Study of Recursion and Iteration." *IEEE Transactions on Software Engineering* 18(5): 368–379.

Smelcer, J.B., and E. Carmel. 1997. "The Effectiveness of Different Representations for Managerial Problem Solving: Comparing Tables and Maps." *Decision Sciences* 28(2): 391–420.

Smith, E.R. 2000. *e-Loyalty*. New York: Harper Business.

Tan, J.K.H., and I. Benbasat. 1990. "Processing of Graphical Information: A Decomposition Taxonomy to Match Data Extraction Tasks and Graphical Representations." *Information Systems Research* 1(4): 416–439.

———. 1993. "The Effectiveness of Graphical Presentation for Information Extraction: A Cumulative Experimental Approach." *Decision Sciences* 24(1): 67–191.

Todd, P., and I. Benbasat. 1991. "An Experimental Investigation of the Impact of Computer-Based Decision Aids on Decision Making Strategies." *Information Systems Research* 2(2): 87–115.

———. 1992. "The Use of Information in Decision Making: An Experimental Investigation of the Impact of Computer-Based Decision Aids." *MIS Quarterly* 16(3): 373–393.

———. 1994. "The Influence of Decision Aids on Choice Strategies: An Experimental Analysis of the Role of Cognitive Effort." *Organizational Behavior and Human Decision Processes* 60(1): 36–74.

Tractinsky, N., and J. Meyer. 1999. "Chartjunk or Goldgraph? Effects of Presentation Objectives and Content Desirability on Information Presentation." *MIS Quarterly* 23(3): 397–420.

Twedt, D.W. 1952. "A Multiple Factor Analysis of Advertising Readership." *Journal of Applied Psychology* 37: 207–215.

Umanath, N.S., and R.W. Scamell. 1988. "An Experimental Evaluation of the Impact of Data Display Format on Recall Performance." *Communications of the ACM* 31(5): 562–570.

Umanath, N.S.; R.W. Scamell; and S.R. Das. 1990. "An Examination of Two Screen/Report Design Variables in an Information Recall Context." *Decision Sciences* 21(1): 216–240.

Umanath, N.S., and I. Vessey. 1994. "Multiattribute Data Presentation and Human Judgment: A Cognitive Fit Perspective." *Decision Sciences* 25(5/6): 795–824.

Valiente, R. 1973. "Mechanical Correlates of Ad Recognition." *Journal of Advertising Research* 13 (March): 13–18.

Vessey, I. 1991. "Cognitive Fit: A Theory-Based Analysis of the Graphs versus Tables Literature." *Decision Sciences* 22: 219–240.

———. 1994. "The Effect of Information Presentation on Decision Making: A Cost-Benefit Analysis." *Information and Management* 27: 103–119.

Vessey, I., and D. Galletta. 1991. "Cognitive Fit: An Empirical Study of Information Acquisition." *Information Systems Research* 2(1): 63–85.

Westland, J.C., and G. Au. 1997/98. "A Comparison of Shopping Experiences Across Three Competing Digital Retailing Interfaces." *International Journal of Electronic Commerce* 2(2): 57–69.

Winding R.E., II, and W.W. Talarzyk. 1993. "Electronic Information Systems for Consumers: An Evaluation of Computer-Assisted Formats in Multiple Decision Environments." *Journal of Marketing Research* 30 (May): 125–141.

Wright, P., and A. Lickorish. 1983. "Proof-reading Texts on Screen and Paper." *Behaviour and Information Technology* 2(3): 227–235.

Yamanaka, J. 1962. "The Prediction of Ad Readership Scores." *Journal of Advertising Research* 2(1): 18–23.

Yee, M.M. 1991. "System Design and Cataloging Meeting the User: User Interfaces to Line Public Access Catalogs." *Journal of the American Society for Information Science* 42(2): 78–98.

Zeithaml, V.A.; A. Parasuraman; and A. Malhotra. 2000. "A Conceptual Framework for Understanding e-Service Quality: Implications for Future Research and Managerial Practice." Working paper, Marketing Science Institute.

Zemke, R., and T. Connellan. 2000. *E-Service: 24 Ways to Keep Your Customers When the Competition Is Just a Click Away.* New York: American Management Association.

Part II

Business Opportunities and Strategies

7

Smart Versus Dumb Service Strategies

A Framework for e-Business Intensity

Rashi Glazer

Introduction

E-Services are "smart" services—that is, they are offerings that have intelligence or computational ability built into them, and therefore they adapt or respond to changes in the environment as the consumer interacts (or uses) them. More generally, e-Services are a component of "smart markets"—markets defined by frequent turnovers in the general stock of knowledge or information embodied in products and services and possessed by customers and competitors. In contrast to traditional "dumb" services (or "dumb markets")—which are static, fixed, and basically information-poor—smart services and markets are dynamic, turbulent, and information-rich.

At first glance, it would appear that all services are "smart," since, along with the lack of inventory, the defining characteristic of a service (as opposed to a "product") is that it does not "exist" in the absence of use by (or interaction with) the consumer. However, a more careful analysis reveals the extent to which, in fact, most service offerings (at least in the advanced industrial economies of the twentieth century) have been "dumbed down" to remove all intelligence and possibilities for adaptation as they are used. Taking advantage of the industrial-age (dumb) technology of the assembly line—in the interests of efficiency, predictability, and, ultimately, cost-minimization—the objective of most service businesses has been to standardize and "productize" their offerings; and the "holy grail" of the service industry has ultimately been to have customers without ever having to interact with them!

However viable and profitable the traditional dumb strategies have been, the new economy and the emergence of smart, flexible technology allow—indeed, require—a new perspective. This is the essence of e-Services in smart markets. What is emerging is a set of smart, or "information-intensive," strategies that represent an appropriate evolutionary response to the emergence of information-intensive, "smart" markets. While all individual business functions and the discipline of strategy itself are being reshaped by both the need and the ability to incorporate higher levels of information processing into their activities, many of the most important developments are in the area of marketing—typically the activity (if not formal organizational function) charged with managing the relationships between the firm and its customers.

To begin, we can identify several key consequences of the "information-intensive" environment in which the e-Services firm of the future will compete:

• The appearance of what may be accurately described as a new stage in the history of market development—that of "differentiated offerings in decentralized markets" (Blattberg et al. 1994). This is replacing the current era—that of "differentiated offerings in centralized markets"—in which the identification of differences in buyers' tastes gave rise to "brand" competition and target marketing based on segmentation and positioning. By contrast, the new phase is characterized by the ability to identify individual buyers (who continually provide information about their preferences) and then develop and deliver specific products and services to them.

• The widespread breaking down of boundaries where once there were well-defined roles or discrete categories: (a) Boundaries between products are breaking down (in particular, the boundary between products and services!). (b) Boundaries between the firm and the external world are breaking down: between the firm and its customers, as customers participate in the design of their own products and communications becomes more interactive and two-way; and between the firm and its competitors, as firms realize they need to partner in order to put in place the infrastructure issues necessary for the sale of their own products. (c) Within the firm, boundaries between departments are breaking down, as no department or area has all the information necessary (and the flow of information between departments is not fast enough) to respond to customer requests before the competition does.

• The transformation of the firm's orientation toward what might be called a sense-and-respond mode (as opposed to "make and sell" [Haeckel 1994]—that is, the ability to identify and ultimately anticipate customer needs and satisfy customer requests as quickly as possible. Coincident with this ability is the belief that value-added resides in processes and people ("the way we do things around here") as opposed to things.

• An orientation to customer rather than product—including customer rather than product management systems and new metrics for performance rooted in customer-based accounting systems (e.g., lifetime value of customer rather than profit and loss by product, and customer "share of wallet" rather than market share by product). Identifying the customer as an asset means that the focus of attention shifts away from service offerings *per se* and that the customer, and not the product, is viewed as the real generator of wealth for the company. The source of competitive advantage is seen less in terms of having unique or superior products and more with respect to having special *relationships* with customers based on collecting and processing information about them from continual interactions with them.

Smart Service Strategies

By observing the activities of firms that have taken the lead in trying to exploit their information about customers as the basis for competitive advantage, a picture is emerging of information-intensive or "smart" decision-making at both the strategic and tactical or marketing-mix programmatic levels. The goal is to develop a "taxonomy" or categorization scheme of generic strategies (notable because of the degree to which they have been replicated across a variety of seemingly different situations) that can be used to compare and contrast them. The result is a preliminary "theory" of information-intensive strategy, paralleling that of the more traditional strategic framework, which has guided management practice in typical "dumb" markets (Glazer 1999). Among the smart service strategies that have been observed to date are:

• *Mass customization* (Pine 1992)—being able to tailor individual offerings to customers without adding additional costs (getting the best of both worlds between the traditional generic strategies of mass production and niche or target marketing). Mass customization takes advantage of developments in both flexible operations and flexible marketing methods.

• *Yield management*—maximizing the total return to a fixed asset through price discrimination by capitalizing on differential customer price sensitivity (particularly with respect to time). Yield management is primarily used in industries where there are high initial fixed costs, but very low variable costs.

• *Capture the customer*—also known as one-to-one marketing, affinity marketing, customer intimacy, event-oriented prospecting, cross-selling, and so forth, the ultimate objective is to realize as high a share as possible of a customer's total (lifetime) purchases in a given (often expanding) set of categories.

- *Virtual company/extended organization*—taking on the value-added activities of a firm's partners in the supply chain through integrated database management; in effect dissolving the functional boundaries between the two (technically distinct) organizations.
- *Manage by wire* (Haeckel and Nolan 1993)—developing an "informational representation" of the way the firm makes decisions ("how we do things around here"), thus allowing the organization to automate the increasing level of interactions with customers that are the keys to competitive success. Manage by wire draws on the CIF and other databases, as well as a set of appropriate "expert systems" and other decision tools, with the goal of modeling the enterprise and "committing to code" as much as possible the procedures that form the basis of managerial decision-making.

e-Business Intensity

What (if anything) can be said about the path of evolution or transformations within industries and individual firms toward adopting the smart services orientation? To address this issue, we introduce the notion of "e-business intensity." In the most general sense, a firm can be thought of as a set of value-added activities and processes as well as the functions developed around these activities and processes—what is commonly called the value chain (e.g., Porter 1980, 1985). In particular, the value chain operationalizes the two core concepts traditionally used to discuss firm behavior—strategy and structure (Chandler 1972; Abell and Hammond 1979; Miles and Snow 1978). A firm or industry is e-business intensive to the degree that its value-chain activities, strategies, and structures have been influenced or transformed by e-business.

The goal of the research project that underlies the present discussion is to understand the factors that would lead us to conclude that a given service organization or industry is more or less e-business intensive than another. The output of the analysis is an "e-Service Intensity Score" (ESIS) that quantifies the level of e-business adaptation and allows any individual firm or industry to compare its own level of e-business adoption—the extent to which it is a "smart" service—with that of its peers.

Preliminary research (primarily in-depth interviews and focus groups with managers across a wide sector of industries) suggested that the notion of e-business intensity has three components—that is, an organization can be thought to have a high ESIS score to the degree it: (a) perceives e-business as critical to its success; (b) has a well-defined e-business strategy; (c) is an e-business strategy leader in its industry.

Component (a) is the *motivator* guiding (b), the firm's *intention* to move in the direction of e-business processes, leading to (c) the *achievement* of its e-business initiatives. The focus of the research described was to identify a set of specific factors or "key drivers" that explain the extent to which a given organization perceives e-business as critical to its success, has a well-defined e-business strategy, or is an e-business strategy leader in its industry. Thus, in a formal sense, the objective was to develop and test the validity of the "model"

$$ESIS = f(key\ drivers),$$

where the three components (perceptions of e-business criticality, well-defined e-business strategy, e-business strategy leadership) are the dependent or criterion variables, and the key drivers are the independent or predictor variables.

Methodology and Data

The research to be described proceeded in two stages. First, a wide-ranging series of "qualitative" focus groups and in-depth one-on-one interviews were conducted with mid-high-level managers from a cross section of industrial sectors and with varying functional responsibility within their organizations (general management, marketing, finance, sales, MIS, human resources, and so on). The purpose of this first phase was to test, in a preliminary sense, some generic hypotheses (rooted in prior theory) as to the possible evolution of e-business and the potential key drivers that might account for the variance in evolution across firms and industry sectors.

The output of this qualitative data became the basis for the second phase of the research, a detailed quantitative survey comprising 80 items (from an initial list of more than 200), which were believed to be the set of key drivers associated with e-business intensity. These items can be conceptualized as testable research hypotheses as to the antecedents of ESIS. For each item, respondents indicated their level of agreement (on a one-to-one "agree/disagree" scale) with a statement—where agreement could be interpreted as "support" of the particular hypotheses represented by that item. Respondents also provided additional information as to the industry sector in which they operated and (for a specific product category) information regarding their firm's product-market objectives, market share, and product category growth rates. The questionnaire (which yielded 600 responses) was administered to a cross section of managers with varying functional responsibility across a wide range of firms and industry sectors. Among the specific service-related industrial sectors included in the study are communications, financial services, insurance, distribution services (including retailing), professional services (such as accounting, management consulting, and information technology), and public-sector services.

A Theoretical Framework for e-Business Intensity and ESIS

As noted above, a firm is essentially a "strategy" and a "structure"—and any individual firm can be defined in terms of the particular set of value-chain activities and functions through which strategy and structure are operationalized. A firm's strategy represents the fit between its own internal resources or "core competencies" and the demands of the external environment—that is, customers and competitors—and is reflected in a set of "product management" decisions. A firm's organizational structure represents the particular functional areas and processes designed to facilitate the implementation of strategy.

Consequently, any theory or conceptual framework wishing to understand changes in strategy and structure (whether occasioned by e-business or any other phenomena) might profitably begin by identifying four general categories of variables: those associated with customers, competitors, product management, and organizational structure. Such was the case with the current research. In particular, what guides the study is the notion that e-business will transform the firm (and ultimately the industry) by influencing in predictable ways (i.e., through the "key drivers") the value-chain activities and functions related to any and all of these four general categories.

Value-chain activities (whether intra- or interfirm) essentially involve processes of exchange (i.e., the typical economic exchange of goods and services for money and the more general exchange of information) (Glazer 1989, 1991). E-Business influences and transforms the value chain to the extent that it changes the fundamentals of the exchange process—that is, the who, what, when, where, how, and why of exchange (Cherry 1966)—that essentially form the basis of market behavior.

Who?

Economic theory is rooted in the notion that individual "agents" specialize in the roles of producers and consumers (or firms and customers) for any particular good or service. Based on the notion of "consumer sovereignty," the fundamental assumption of market behavior is that the purpose of the firm is to satisfy and respond to the needs of customers and that the role of "supply" is to meet "demand." The penetration of e-business is influencing our basic understanding of firms and consumers in several interesting and important ways. First, the concept of consumer sovereignty and the absolute necessity for firms to satisfy customer needs is at last becoming a reality and not just an idealization too often characteristic of textbook accounts rather than actual marketplace behavior (Seybold 1998; Tapscott et al.1998). At the same time, however a second major development is the breakdown in the specialized economic roles of producers and consumers and the emergence of a system in which firms and customers increasingly interact and participate together in the design and delivery of offerings (Glazer 1991, 1999). Finally, as a consequence of both the process of interactivity and the development of smart or information-intensive goods (as described below under the "what" of exchange), firms are being forced to treat consumers as individuals (or "markets of one") and not as parts of larger aggregates or segments. Notions of "customer intimacy," "customer relationship management," "one-on-one marketing," and, ultimately, the concept of the customer as opposed to the product as being the "new asset" of the organization and the real carrier of value become paramount (Blattberg et al. 1994; Glazer 1999; Peppers and Rogers 1993).

The exchange process between a firm and consumer takes place in the context of competitors (other firms that also exchange with the consumer) and, here too, e-business is having a profound effect on the definition of marketplace roles. On one hand (as discussed below under the "why" of exchange and consumer behavior), the rapidly changing nature of information or technology-intensive products and services, combined with the desire of customers for convenience and one-stop shopping occasioned by e-business, are leading firms from historically distinct industries to compete with one another (Glazer 1991; Tapscott et al. 1998). Consequently, as firms with perhaps different technologies offer alternative solutions to the same underlying customer problems, industry definitions are increasingly in terms of markets (or customers) and not products—the phenomenon of "convergence." The result is "hypercompetition" (accelerated by globalization), which, somewhat paradoxically, leads to a focus on strategic alliances and partners—a sense that "I cannot go it alone or do it all myself" and an emphasis on "who can I cooperate with" rather than "who do I compete with." In short, the boundary between competing firms is also dissolving, and, in many markets, a competitor today is a customer (or value-added partner) tomorrow and vice versa.

What?

E-business is a powerful enabler for perhaps the most dramatic change in the business environment—one that has been developing for at least two decades—that is, the emergence of information-intensive or smart products and services as the primary sector of the economy (Glazer 1999; Shapiro and Varian 1999). Smart products are products that incorporate intelligence into them and therefore change or adapt as they interact with the user/consumer of the good. Increasingly what is being exchanged is information—and, indeed, the major value-added even for traditional matter- and energy-based products and services is either the information they contain or the information about the exchange itself. Since smart services are based on the interactions between firms and consumers, they are both the cause and effect of the trend toward customization or personalization of offerings. At the same time, information-intensive goods differ in fundamental ways from typical matter- and energy-based goods: they are "non-appropriable" (i.e., "I can give them away without giving them up"); they demonstrate increasing (rather than decreasing) returns to use and therefore do not depreciate in the normal sense; they have a short shelf life (information's quality as "news") and, therefore, depreciate with time (Porat 1976). As a consequence, information goods have short product life cycles (Qualls et al. 1981), while, at the same time, they are subject to so-called "network externalities"—that is, the utility that any one consumer derives from the good is dependent on the number of other consumers who have the good—and therefore what is important is access and use rather than ownership and control (Glazer 1999; Shapiro and Varian 1999).

When/Where/How?

Perhaps the most immediate and obvious effect of e-business is with respect to the "physics" of the exchange process—that is, its temporal and spatial components. E-business and the "network" break down the boundaries of time and space that traditionally define the dimensions within which commerce can be conducted. In one sense, of course, the Internet is just another in a long line of communications and information-processing technologies that have transformed time and space interactions (Innis 1951; McLuhan 1964; Cherry 1966). However, whereas previous media have reduced the importance of time and space, their influence has not been complete, and many boundaries have remained intact. If there is something qualitatively different about the Internet with respect to the historical trend of increased time-space compression, it is that the boundaries erected by time and space have not just been reduced, they have been eliminated once and for all. At least in theory, it is now possible to conduct business with anyone at any time and in any place. As a consequence, any value-chain activity or function that has depended on its particular position in time or space for its raison d'être is in jeopardy of "disintermediation."

Why?

The why of the exchange process addresses the basic motivations for customers to engage in exchange—the so-called "value proposition" that is at the heart of our understanding of consumer behavior. In keeping with the previous discussion of the ways in which the other dimensions (who, what, when, where, how) of exchange are being transformed, e-business is having a profound effect on the generic value propositions associated with most product offerings. Perhaps first and foremost is the changing nature of customer expectations. Consumers expect what must be considered historically unprecedented levels of freedom of choice and, as noted above, to be treated as individuals and to have their idiosyncratic needs satisfied—in other words, they are motivated by a desire for customization or personalization (Blattberg and Deighton 1991; Pine 1992; Peppers and Rogers 1993). This is a direct consequence of smart or information-intensive services. Furthermore, as noted above, smart services imply that this customization will be achieved through high levels of participation or interaction—a continual "dialog" between the firm and consumer. Increasingly, e-business requires that firms, as part of their value proposition, understand the importance to the consumer of the "experience" or process of product/service delivery as well as the product or outcome of the exchange process. This is at the heart of the notion of "customer-relationship management" that is emerging as a key component of e-business activity.

At the same time, with the freedom of choice brought on by smart products comes the requirement to process high levels of information and, ultimately, the burden of information overload. In the information age, information is the abundant resource, while the attention of the information processor (e.g., the consumer) is the scarce resource (Simon 1957, 1972; Glazer 1998). Perhaps more than anything else, consumers are motivated by a desire to conserve their attention with respect to any one particular problem (e.g., product choice), and, consequently, there is the increasing expectation of help on the part of the firm with respect to tasks associated with information processing involving product choice.

Predictors of e-Business Intensity (ESIS): Key Drivers

The outlined theoretical framework formed the basis for an attempt to identify a specific set of value-chain activities that might contribute in a significant way to the development of an ESIS metric. From an initial list of more than 200 variables, 80 "value-chain" factors or key drivers were ultimately identified as potential meaningful predictors of e-business intensity and included in the study as working hypotheses. Of the 80 initial factors, 40 were found to be meaningful predictors of one or all of the three dependent variables (perceptions of e-business criticality; well-defined e-business strategy; e-business strategy leadership). The remainder were found to be unrelated to the differences in ESIS or e-business intensity—either in a fundamental sense (i.e., they are uncorrelated with the various dependent variables) or because they showed little if any variance among themselves with respect to respondents' beliefs (e.g., everyone agreed or disagreed with the statement in question). Those that emerged as key drivers from the original set are those that display relatively high levels of variance on their respective scales and are correlated with the dependent measures of e-business intensity.

The following is a list of the forty variables that were significant predictors of e-business intensity. As discussed above, each value-chain variable or key driver can meaningfully be placed in one of the four categories—customers, competitors, product management, and organizational structure—which were operationalized as Customer Orientation (CO), Competitive Strategy (CS), Organizational Structure (OS), and Product Management (PM).

Customer Orientation

CO1: We share information about customers rapidly throughout the organization.
CO2: Our customers willingly and frequently provide information about themselves electronically.*
CO3: We are an industry leader in the use of the Internet for interacting with customers.*
CO4: We have a highly interactive Internet site compared to other sites.*
CO5: Our customers will, within five years, frequently use intelligent online electronic agents.*
CO6: We believe it is important to filter data to prevent customer information overload.

---

* Indicates the variable is specifically associated with the Internet or an electronic network.

Competitive Strategy

CS1: We share information about competitors rapidly throughout the organization.

CS2: We have more competitors than in the past.

CS3: We worry about nontraditional competitors.

CS4: We are in a strong competitive position relative to others.

CS5: We make use of scenario planning as part of our strategic planning process.

CS6: We are in an attractive business environment relative to other industries.

Organizational Structure

OS1: We place a higher value on hiring employees with good learning skills than those with a specific skill set.

OS2: We use more on-the-job training than in the past.

OS3: Our employees are under more stress as a result of changes in the business environment.

OS4: We are experiencing a breakdown in separation between functions and departments and diminished organizational silos.

OS5: We are paying increased attention to the management of intangible assets.

OS6: We use internal start-ups, outside of usual organizations and processes, to develop and commercialize new products.

OS7: The Internet is changing recruitment and assessment of potential employees.*

OS8: Our MIS/IT function increasingly plays a strategic role in the organization.*

OS9: We are an industry leader in the use of information technology.*

OS10: The information we have online is greater than that of the most knowledgeable person in the organization.*

OS11: Our management of information systems is highly centralized.*

Product Management

PM1: We are placing increased importance on innovation.

PM2: We are placing less importance on being able to forecast product demand.

---

* Indicates the variable is specifically associated with the Internet or an electronic network.

PM3: We are increasingly willing to license ideas and patents from other firms.

PM4: Our customers participate actively in idea generation, product design, and product testing.

PM5: The boundary between our own products and those in other product categories is blurring.

PM6: We offer mass customization of products.

PM7: We are moving from product/brand management to customer management systems.

PM8: We account for P&L by customer rather than by product.

PM9: We are increasingly offering subsequent "generations" of our basic underlying product family.

PM10: We are experiencing dramatic decreases in product life cycles.

PM11: We are placing increasing importance on being a market pioneer.

PM12: We practice "whole life cycle" (cradle-to-grave) product management.

PM13: We see a blurring of the boundary between product and price (price is a more important part of the product itself).

PM14: We see our relationships with logistics' suppliers (FedEx, UPS) as a major source of competitive advantage.

PM15: We see a shift in communication program objectives to behavioral (rather than attitudinal) measures.

PM16: We are narrowing our communications and tailoring them more to individual customers.

PM17: We use the Internet for test marketing.*

Note that these factors, while expressed in terms of "product management," are equally applicable to service organizations.

Models

The specific models analyzed are as follows:

M1: E-Business Critical to Success (Today) = f(key drivers)
M2: E-Business Critical to Success (Three Years)= f(key drivers)
M3: E-Business Critical to Success (Five Years) = f(key drivers)
M4: Well-Defined e-Business Strategy = f(key drivers)
M5: E-Business Strategy Leadership = f(key drivers)

---

* Indicates the variable is specifically associated with the Internet or an electronic network.

The models were analyzed using a stepwise regression procedure with forward selection. Since with analyses of this type multicollinearity is always a concern, prior to the formal econometric analysis, the interitem correlations of the variables were studied to assess the degree of correlation among specific sets of variables. In certain cases, individual variables were eliminated from the analysis in an attempt to handle multicollinearity concerns. What follows are the results of the formal analysis, indicating the key drivers in order of importance for the various "models" under investigation:

(M1) Predictors of "e-Business Critical to Success (Today)" (see Figure 7.1)

$$\text{e-Business Critical to Success Today} = a + b_1CO5 + b_2OS7 + b_3CO1 + b_4CS6 + b_5OS9 + b_6CS3 + b_7PM14 + b_8OS3 + b_9OS2 + b_{10}CO2 + b_{11}PM8 + b_{12}PM17$$

CO5: Our customers will, within five years, frequently use intelligent online electronic agents.

OS7: The Internet is changing our recruitment and assessment of potential employees.

CO1: We share information about customers rapidly throughout the organization.

CS6: We are in an attractive business environment relative to other industries.

OS9: We are an industry leader in the use of information technology.

CS3: We worry about nontraditional competitors.

PM14: We see our relationships with logistics' suppliers (FedEx, UPS) as a major source of competitive advantage.

OS3: Our employees are under more stress as a result of changes in the business environment.

OS2: We use more on-the-job training than in the past [-].

CO2: Our customers willingly and frequently provide information about themselves electronically.

PM8: We account for P&L by customer rather than by product [-].

PM17: We use the Internet for test marketing.

In the list presented (and in those to follow), a negative [-] next to a particular variable indicates that the driver is negatively correlated with the dependent variable. These results are counter to the hypothesized direction and thus remain the subject of future research.

Figure 7.1 **Predictors of "e-Business Critical to Success (Today)" in Order of Importance**

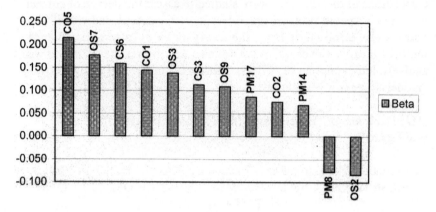

(M2) Predictors of "e-Business Critical to Success (Three Years)" (see Figure 7.2)

E-Business Critical to Success Three Years = $a + b_1CO1 + b_2CO5 + b_3OS3 + b_4CS4 + b_5CS1 + b_6PM1 + b_7CS3 + b_8OS4 + b_9CS6 + b_{10}OS2 + b_{11}PM8 + b_{12}OS8$

CO1: We share information about customers rapidly throughout the organization

CO5: Our customers will, within five years, frequently use intelligent online electronic agents.

OS3: Our employees are under more stress as a result of changes in the business environment.

CS4: We are in a strong competitive position relative to others.

CS1: We share information about competitors rapidly throughout the organization.

PM1: We are placing increased importance on innovation.

CS3: We worry about nontraditional competitors.

OS4: We are experiencing a breakdown in separations between functions and departments and diminished organizational silos.

CS6: We are in an attractive business environment relative to other industries.

OS2: We use more on-the-job training than in the past [-].

PM8: We account for P&L by customer rather than by product [-].

OS8: Our MIS/IT function is increasingly playing a strategic role in the organization.

Figure 7.2 **Predictors of "e-Business Critical to Success (Three Years)"**

Adjusted R^2 = .605

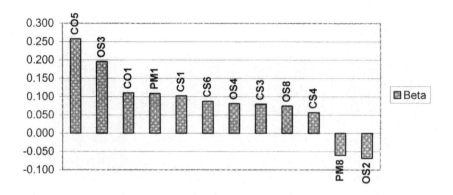

(M3) Predictors of "e-Business Critical to Success (Five Years)" (see Figure 7.3)

e-Business Critical to Success Five Years = $a + b_1CO1 + b_2OS3 + b_3CO5 + b_4CS4 + b_5CO6 + b_6CS1 + b_7PM1 + b_8OS8 + b_9CO4 + b_{10}OS4 + b_{11}PM7 + b_{12}OS1 + b_{13}PM13 + b_{14}OS11$

CO1: We share information about customers rapidly throughout the organization.

OS3: Our employees are under more stress as a result of changes in the business environment.

CO5: Our customers will, within five years, frequently use intelligent online electronic agents.

CS4: We are in a strong competitive position relative to others.

CO6: We believe it is important to filter data to prevent customer information overload.

CS1: We share information about competitors rapidly throughout the organization.

PM1: We are placing increased importance on innovation.

OS8: Our MIS/IT function is increasingly playing a strategic role in the organization.

CO4: We have a highly interactive Internet site compared to other sites [-].

OS4: We are experiencing a breakdown in separations between functions and departments and diminished organizational silos.

Figure 7.3 **Predictors of "e-Business Critical to Success (Five Years)"**

Adjusted R^2 = .696

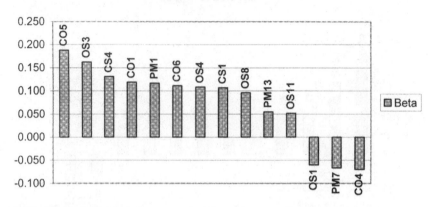

PM7: We are moving from product/brand management to customer management systems [-].

OS1: We place a higher value on hiring employees with good learning skills than those with a specific skill set [-].

PM13: We see a blurring of the boundary between product and price (price is a more important part of the product itself).

OS11: Our management of information systems is highly centralized.

(M4) Predictors of Well-Defined e-Business Strategy (see Figure 7.4)

Well-defined e-Business Strategy = $a + b_1OS9 + b_2CO3 + b_3OS6 + b_4PM8 + b_5PM15 + b_6OS10 + b_7PM17 + b_8CS4 + b_9OS3$

OS9: We are an industry leader in the use of information technology.

CO3: We are an industry leader in the use of the Internet for interacting with customers.

OS6: We use internal start-ups, outside of usual organizations and processes, to develop and commercialize new products.

PM8: We account for P&L by customer rather than by product.

PM15: We see a shift in communication program objectives to behavioral (rather than attitudinal) measures.

OS10: The information we have online is greater than that of the most knowledgeable person in the organization.

PM17: We use the Internet for test marketing.

Figure 7.4 Predictors of Well-Defined e-Business Strategy

Adjusted R^2 = .552

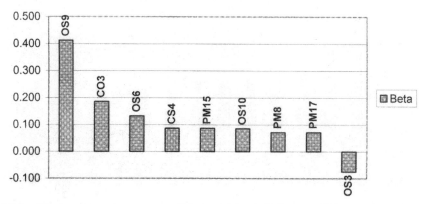

CS4: We are in a strong competitive position relative to others.

OS3: Our employees are under stress as a result of changes in the business environment [-].

(M5) Predictors of e-Business Strategy Leadership (see Figure 7.5)

e-Business Strategy Leadership = $a + b_1 OS9 + b_2 CO3 + b_3 OS4 + b_4 CS6 + b_5 CO4 + b_6 CS5 + b_7 PM8 + b_8 CS4 + b_9 PM2 + b_{10} PM13 + b_{11} PM9 + b_{12} PM10$

OS9: We are an industry leader in the use of information technology.

CO3: We are an industry leader in the use of the Internet for interacting with customers.

OS4: We are experiencing a breakdown in separations between functions and departments and diminished organizational silos [-].

CS6: We are in an attractive business environment relative to other industries.

CO4: We have a highly interactive Internet site compared to other sites.

CS5: We make use of scenario planning as part of our strategic planning process.

PM8: We account for P&L by customer rather than by product.

CS4: We are in a strong competitive position relative to others.

PM2: We are placing less importance on being able to forecast product demand.

PM13: We see a blurring of the boundary between product and price (price is a more important part of the product itself) [-].

PM9: We are increasingly offering subsequent "generations" of our basic underlying product family.

PM10: We are experiencing dramatic decreases in product life cycles [-].

Figure 7.5 **Predictors of e-Business Strategy Leadership**

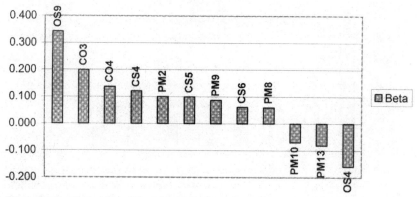

Adjusted R^2 = .516

Hypothesized Factors That Are Not Key Drivers

As noted above, of the eighty original hypothesized predictors, forty were found to be insignificant contributors to the ESIS metric (i.e., unrelated to the differences in e-business intensity)—either because they are uncorrelated with the dependent measures of interest or because they showed little if any variance among themselves with respect to respondents' beliefs (e.g., everyone agreed with the statement). It is instructive to examine those factors for which the respondents were either in general agreement with the underlying statement or were relatively neutral with regard to the statement (neither agreed or disagreed) and therefore did not distinguish among firms.

Factors with high levels of agreement that are not key drivers (do not differentiate among organizations):

1. Customer Orientation
    a. Gathering intelligence about our customers is the responsibility of every department in the organization.
    b. We believe a highly interactive Internet site is one that acts as much as possible like a live salesperson.
    c. We believe our Internet site should be able to answer any question that a customer or supplier has about us.
2. Competitive Strategy
    a. Our planning horizons are much shorter than in the past.
    b. Our strategic planning has become more connected to daily business decisions.

3. Organizational Structure
   a. Employee retention has become a strategic issue for our company.
   b. We are working more with partners outside the company than in the past.
4. Product Management
   a. We believe it is increasingly important to offer multiple versions of our product to the market.
   b. We feel it is important to offer "smart" products (products/services that incorporate information).
   c. We are experiencing dramatically shorter new-product-development cycles.
   d. Our profits may decline because customers have more opportunities to compare prices.
   e. We are focusing more attention on distribution issues for our products than in the past.
   f. We believe that the Internet can help us get closer to our customers.
   g. The boundary between our products and communications is blurring, that is, communication is becoming an important part of the product itself.
   h. We have changed our communication programs to be more "two way," that is, getting information from our customers as well.
   i. Public relations has become more important to us relative to paid advertising.

What is important about these factors is that most respondents agree with them and therefore they are consistent with the general theoretical framework of the movement toward e-business being advanced. However, they do not serve to distinguish among firms with respect to the level of e-business intensity and therefore are not key drivers with respect to understanding what particular factors might lead an organization to be an earlier adopter of e-business value-chain activities or functions (i.e., score high on the ESIS metric).

By contrast, the following factors resulted in a neutral response. These factors are hypothesized to characterize e-business activity; but, across the sample as a whole, firms in meaningful numbers do not appear to be adopting the practices or processes associated with them. While the exact reasons remain a subject for future research, one potentially important implication is that (if the theoretical framework that underlies the specific hypotheses is correct), the areas represented by these particular items are fertile ground for improvement on the part of organizations wishing to become more e-business intensive.

1. Customer Orientation
   Our customers experience more frustration as we employ automated service and support systems.
2. Competitive Strategy
   a. We focus as much on the "cooperative environment" (which companies we can partner with) as on the competitive environment.
   b. We use lifetime value of a customer, share of wallet, and other measures beyond simple market share as performance metrics.
   c. We are doing more decentralized and "real-time" strategic planning than in the past.
3. Product Management
   a. The boundary between actually delivering the product offering and collecting intelligence about our customers is blurring.
   b. It is increasingly difficult to generate ideas for new products.
   c. We increasingly rely on test marketing before full-scale commercialization.
   d. We believe it is better to "throw a product" into the market and see what happens rather than engage in formal test marketing.
   e. We "kill" products faster or more frequently than in the past.
   f. We place increasing importance on setting prices according to value to our customers, not so much according to our costs.
   g. We believe we will see more use of options and futures contracts as part of the pricing mechanisms in our industry.
   h. Our industry is moving toward more of a flat-rate pricing model.
   i. New channels of distribution have created stress with our long-time channel partners.
   j. We believe that retailers will enjoy higher profits than will manufacturers in the future.
   k. We are concerned about being "disintermediated" as a result of the Internet.
   l. We believe that consumer-buying groups will be an important factor in our industry.

Conclusion

The research program at the base of the current discussion revealed in a meaningful (i.e., statistically significant) way that:

1. Individual firms and industries differ with respect to their level of e-business intensity (or ESIS).
2. It is possible to model formally—and therefore predict and understand—

the specific value-chain factors or key drivers that are associated with different levels of e-business intensity or ESIS.

3. Certain industry sectors displayed higher levels of predictive power than others—that is, the models do a better job of linking key drivers (independent variables) to dependent criteria variables—suggesting that, as of now, it is "easier" to understand the hypothesized "reasons" for greater or lesser degrees of e-business intensity in these industries when compared with the others.

However, above and beyond the "content" of any specific findings (i.e., the identification of the particular key drivers for a particular aspect of e-business intensity for a particular industry), what would appear to be most important in evaluating the current study is an appreciation for the process that informed the research. This is especially the case since it is highly probable that, in the fast-moving environment that characterizes the evolution of e-business, any given finding reported here that is "true" today might not necessarily be true in the future.

At the same time, while actual results vary across the individual industry sectors (and while the major contribution of the study is less with respect to the specific findings than in demonstrating the viability of a systematic process or methodology to model the relationship between e-business intensity and value-chain factors), the evidence in general suggests that the key to successful e-business adoption—to become a smart e-Services firm—is the ability to use information technology in general and the Internet in particular *to share information about* and *interact with* customers! Thus, for example, when looking across both the whole sample and the individual sectors as well as across the various dimensions of e-business intensity (the dependent variables), four variables stand out as being key drivers:

O1: We share information about customers rapidly throughout the organization.

CO3: We are an industry leader in the use of the Internet for interacting with customers.

CO4: We have a highly interactive Internet site compared to other sites.

OS9: We are an industry leader in the use of information technology.

Indeed, despite the fact that, of the four classes of variables, the highest number fall under the "product management" category, these variables in general did not emerge as key drivers (except with respect to "strategy leadership"). In relative terms, the highest percentage of key drivers fall within the "customer orientation" dimension. This suggests that organizations that appear to be ahead of the curve with respect to successful e-Services adoption are those that, as a pre-condition, have put in place a strong information technology infrastructure, and devote their resources to developing a strong customer orientation. Alternatively, those firms that wish to improve their e-Services position would do well to examine their value-chain activities to understand the degree to which they have put in place processes that allow for a strong customer orientation and, given the inevitable need to make hard choices with regard to resource allocation, devote less attention to specific "product management" programs and tactics. While in the rapidly changing world of e-business (and e-Services in particular) it is imprudent to point to specific success or failure stories, a scan of the environment reveals quite clearly the degree to which too many firms have rushed to put in place specific e-Service programmatic initiatives without having first attended to the more fundamental issues associated with building a viable and sustainable customer orientation supported by the necessary information technology infrastructure.

More generally, of course, someone with an interest in the e-Services activities of a given firm in a particular industry sector (e.g., a manager, consultant to, or analyst of that sector) would use the results reported both diagnostically and prescriptively within the overall framework of a "call to action." The specific key drivers identified as being important for an industry are precisely those factors to which attention needs to be paid—in that the leverage from devoting resources to these areas is most likely to result in successful e-business adoption. Conversely, those variables that do not emerge as key drivers for an industry (although they are perhaps of significance in another industry) are factors that should command less attention and resource expenditure.

Note

The author wishes to acknowledge the generous support of IBM's Global Consulting Services, the substantial intellectual contributions of David Partridge and Charles Rigger of IBM, and the assistance of Nicholas Lurie, Jonathan Becker, and Hannah Rothman.

References

Abell, Derek F., and John S. Hammond. 1979. *Strategic Market Planning: Problems and Analytical Approaches*. Englewood Cliffs, NJ: Prentice Hall.

Blattberg, Robert C., and John Deighton. 1991. "Interactive Marketing: Exploiting the Age of Addressability." *Sloan Management Review:* 5–14.

Blattberg, Robert C.; Rashi Glazer; and John D.C. Little. 1994. *The Marketing Information Revolution*. Boston: Harvard Business School Press.

Chandler, Alfred D., Jr. 1972. *Strategy and Structure: Chapters in the History of the Industrial Enterprise*. Cambridge: MIT Press.

Cherry, Collin. 1966. *On Human Communication*. Cambridge: MIT Press.

Glazer, Rashi. 1989. "Marketing and the Changing Information Environment: Implications for Strategy, Structure and the Marketing Mix." Marketing Science Institute Research Report no. 89–108.

———. 1991. "Marketing in Information-Intensive Environments: Strategic Implications of Knowledge as an Asset." *Journal of Marketing* 55: 1–19.

———. 1998. "Measuring the Knower." *California Management Review* 40(3) 175–194.

———. 1999. "Winning in Smart Markets." *Sloan Management Review* 40(4) 59–69.

Haeckel, Stephan. 1994. "Managing the Information-Intensive Firm of 2001." In *The Marketing Information Revolution*, ed. Robert C. Blattberg, Rashi Glazer, and John D.C. Little. Boston: Harvard Business School Press.

Haeckel, Stephan, and Richard L. Nolan. 1993. "Managing by Wire." *Harvard Business Review* (September–October) 122–132.

Innis, Harold. 1951. *The Bias of Communication*. Toronto: University of Toronto Press.

McLuhan, Marshall. 1964. *Understanding Media: The Extensions of Man*. New York: McGraw Hill.

Miles, Raymond, and Charles Snow. 1978. *Organizational Strategy, Structure, and Process*. New York: McGraw Hill.

Peppers, Don, and Martha Rogers. 1993. *The One to One Future*. New York: Doubleday.

Pine, Joseph B., II. 1992. *Mass Customization*. Boston: Harvard Business School Press.

Porat, Marc U. 1976. "The Information Economy and the Economics of Information: A Literature Survey." Program in Information Technology and Telecommunications Center for Interdisciplinary Research, Stanford University.

Porter, Michael E. 1980. *Competitive Strategy: Techniques for Analyzing Industries and Competitors*. New York: Free Press.

———. 1985. *Competitive Advantage: Creating and Sustaining Superior Performance*. New York: Free Press.

Qualls, William; Richard W. Olshavsky; and Ronald E. Michaels. 1981. "Shortening of the PLC—An Empirical Test." *Journal of Marketing* 45 (fall): 76–80.

Seybold, Patricia B. 1998. *Customers.com: How to Create a Profitable Business Strategy for the Internet and Beyond*. New York: Times Books.

Shapiro, Carl, and Hal R. Varian. 1999. *Information Rules*. Boston: Harvard Business School Press.

Simon, Herbert A. 1957. *Models of Man*. New York: Wiley.

———. 1972. "Theories of Bounded Rationality." In *Decision and Organization*, ed. C.B. Radner and R. Radner. Amsterdam: North Holland.

Tapscott, Don; Alex Lowy; and David Ticoll. 1998. *Blueprint to the Digital Economy*. New York: McGraw Hill.

8

Real-Time Marketing in e-Services

Sajeev Varki

Introduction

The age of interactivity ushered in by the Internet and World Wide Web is forcing marketers to take into account strategies that harness the power of interactivity to satisfy customer needs better and more profitably. In this context, service researchers have begun to explore how to use the interactivity engendered by the Internet and World Wide Web to improve service delivery. Rust (2001) defines e-Service as the delivery of services by electronic means, the predominant means being the Internet, and makes the call for more e-Service-related research.

This call to e-Service research is timely, given the spread and adoption of the Internet by businesses and consumers, which has acted as a catalyst in the personalization of products and services. This is because the Web enables direct contact between the buyer and seller in an environment capable of one-on-one interaction between the seller with a host of buyers or customers simultaneously in near real time (Rust and Varki 1996). Hoffman and Novak (1996) appropriately label this environment as "computer-mediated." This description captures the essence of the Internet, since computer-mediated interaction brings the power of computation and storage, the twin hallmarks of computerization, to the interaction, thus empowering the interaction.

Further, this call to e-Service-related research is consistent with the established link between technology and marketing practice. Marketers have always sought to employ extant technological advances in their attempts to satisfy customer needs more profitably (Varki and Rust 1998). As Varki and Rust (1998) show in their study of the effects of technology on marketing practice, technological innovations in manufacture, transportation, storage, and communication have influenced the cost and demand structure of markets such that marketers find it increasingly feasible to address customer needs at the individual level profitably.

It is befitting, therefore, that in this chapter we explore how real-time marketing, a strategy that espouses the concept of catering to the individual needs of customers *through time*, can be applied to the context of e-Service. Broadly, we examine how real-time marketing concepts can leverage the interactivity and personalization offered by the Internet and World Wide Web to potentially transform the manner in which traditional services are delivered. Specifically, we first examine how the information content of the service delivery process can be manipulated in real time to enhance the service experience related to delivery. Within this context, we illustrate how customer relationship management (CRM) fits within our framework of real-time marketing in services. Second, we examine how real-time marketing concepts can be applied to enhance the service offering itself. We then look at the opportunities and challenges to applying real-time marketing concepts to e-Service and conclude with discussions about issues in the implementation of real-time marketing in e-Services and possible future research in the area.

Concept of Real-Time Marketing

It is the ability of the Web—the ability that allows customers and marketers to interact in near real time across the boundaries of space—that allows marketers to take advantage of the concept of real-time marketing. The term "real-time marketing" was first introduced by McKenna (1995), the central idea being that advances in information technology such as the Internet enable marketers and consumers to engage in real time, which could be employed to build relationships as well as to customize products and services. This concept was later extended by Oliver, Rust, and Varki (1998), who incorporated an element of dynamism to the relationship with customers by articulating the need not only to cater to the differing needs of customers (or cross-sectional heterogeneity) as in mass customization, but also to embed in products and services the intelligence needed to cater to the changing needs of individual customers (or temporal heterogeneity). Oliver, Rust, and Varki (pp. 31–32) define real-time marketing as "the marketing approach in which personally customized goods or services continuously update themselves to continuously track changing consumer needs, without intervention by corporate personnel, often without conscious or overt input from the customer."

In the world of goods (as opposed to services), the concept of real-time marketing is best illustrated by means of customized cars whose performance is adapted based on the driving style of their owner. Thus, we have the initial customization based on initial sets of preferences, and then we have intelligence embedded in the vehicle via microchips that empower the vehicle to adapt to changing contexts. As we speak, marketers are approaching this ideal. Toyota is experimenting with mass customization and Mitsubishi has begun production of cars with transmissions that adapt to the braking pattern of the driver.

The concept of real-time marketing is not necessarily restricted to big, expensive consumer durables like cars. The concept can be extended even to ordinary consumer products. For example, let us consider nicotine patches that are currently offered as standardized products. A typical segmentation approach would suggest that design alternatives for heavy, medium, and light smokers be examined. Such a segmentation approach, namely a usage-based approach, would be typical. However, there would still be individual deviations around the "average" profile in each of the three categories. Assume that even this individual variation is catered to by "mass customization." The problem still remains that an individual smoker kicking the habit would experience the need for differing levels of nicotine as a function of the stress and anxiety levels that he/she experiences during the day (or over a week). Thus, mass customization, as a managerial orientation, falls short of the ideal by failing to account for the temporal variation in individual needs. If, however, the nicotine patch had a stress "sensor" that regulated the flow of nicotine into the bloodstream, the product could be designed to adapt to the changing needs of the customer, consistent with the tenets of real-time marketing.

Real-Time Marketing in e-Services

In the world of services, a pure example of real-time marketing is the electronic newspaper. In the instance of electronic newspapers, newspaper publishers send the news electronically to the individual subscriber's computer. Most major newspapers provide this service. Typically, the electronic version is customized to individual preferences based on input from the subscriber via direct elicitation. However, the adaptive element comes when an intelligent program adapts the composition of the newspaper (based on the reading patterns of the individual) to better reflect the reading preferences of the subscriber. As one can see, this example of Web-enabled real-time marketing of an information service is not unlike the exemplar of an "intelligent" car used to illustrate the application of real-time marketing in the world of physical goods.

However, the term "service" covers a wide range of services such as medical service, education, car repair, and so on, which differ greatly both in the nature of service and the manner of delivery, and each of which impacts the application of real-time marketing in services. In subsequent sections, we delineate services as comprising support services and the service outcome, and discuss the application of real-time marketing to each of the service components. Heim and Sinha (2001) define "service outcomes" as the service product (e.g., the haircut at a hairdresser's, the meal at a restaurant), and we define "support services" as all those services that facilitate the delivery, installation, and use of a product or service.

Real-Time Marketing Vis-à-Vis Support Services

Support services are an ubiquitous phenomenon since they are present even when physical goods are bought and sold. Thus, a car dealership that deals with a physical good like a car is also involved in services such as answering customer queries, handling customers' paperwork, and honoring warranties/ guarantees, just as an orthodontist's office is involved in answering customer queries, handling customer paperwork in terms of insurance claims and appointments, and guaranteeing its handiwork.

It is clear that the Internet has a role to play in streamlining the delivery of physical goods and services. For example, Web sites that detail the information routinely sought out by customers and help facilitate initial paperwork (preprocess information), update consumers about the progress of their job (in-process information), and provide means for consumers to post feedback (postprocess information) would constitute transference of the service delivery aspects to the Web, consistent with the theme of e-Service, the delivery of service over electronic means such as the Web (Rust 2001). As one can see, it is the information content related to service operations that is amenable to Web-enabled delivery. Since the Web supports computer-mediated one-on-one interactivity, the information exchange can be personalized to individual needs (Rust and Lemon 2001).

For real-time marketing concepts to apply in the context of service delivery, it would be necessary for information exchanges to be anticipated based on previous exchanges, so that the information desired by a consumer is there even before it is articulated. It is in this context that it becomes relevant to discuss customer relationship management (CRM) systems, which are being widely adopted by firms. CRM systems are sophisticated software packages that enable firms to essentially collect information about individual customers from all points of contact with a customer (called "touch points"), analyze this knowledge base, and customize the creation of new services or offers to valued customers. Some of the major players in the CRM market are Siebel Systems, Broadvision, and E*piphany (Deighton 2001). One such provider, Convergys, reports that its CRM software helped reduce by half the churn rate for a leading wireless service provider by analyzing billing data in conjunction with other customer information to identify relevant service upgrades for potential switchers estimated to be of considerable lifetime value (www.convergys.com/crm_casestudies.html). Thus, the concept of CRM is consistent with the theme of real-time marketing in that not only are services customized, but also they are adapted to customer needs based on the cumulative knowledge acquired about a customer.

Real-Time Marketing Vis-à-Vis Service Outcomes

Further insight how real-time marketing applies vis-à-vis service outcomes can be gained by analyzing service outcomes using Lovelock's (1983) typology. Lovelock classifies service outcomes according to (a) whether the service outcome is tangible (e.g., a haircut) or intangible (e.g., news) and (b) whether the recipient of the service is the person of the customer (e.g., hairdressing, newspaper) or a possession belonging to the customer (e.g., car repair). We adopt this classification to discuss how real-time marketing works when applied to service outcomes involving intangible and tangible actions, regardless of whether these actions are performed on the person or the possession of the individual customer.

Real-Time Marketing of Intangible Actions

In Lovelock's framework, services such as education and broadcasting are intangible actions directed at people's minds, whereas services such as banking and stock trades are intangible actions directed at people's possessions. The earlier example of an electronic newspaper is an example of an intangible service product directed at the mind of the consumer. An excellent example of an intangible service action directed at a possession or object is the breakdown-prevention service provided on some Xerox machines. These machines maintain continuous online connections with a centralized database, which they provide with continuous performance feedback so that, when things go wrong, they are able to repair themselves automatically by receiving the appropriate online instructions.

It is easy to see that services that constitute intangible actions are most amenable to the practice of real-time e-Service. This is because such services have a high information content that can be stored, customized, and modified based on an analysis of the accumulated information collected about an individual. It is interesting to note that such services have already taken ready root on the Internet and Web (e.g., online banking, online trading, online classes, online newspapers, online counseling, online medical diagnosis, online tax consultancy). A recent product that employs real-time marketing in e-Service is the popular TiVo. This product, which digitally records consumer-specified cable TV shows, also records, on its own, new programs and shows that it believes a consumer may be interested in, given its analysis of the consumer's viewing choices.

Real-Time Marketing of Tangible Actions

With regard to the remaining two categories, namely, tangible actions directed at people or at their possessions, the application of real-time marketing becomes more challenging. This is because the service requires physical activity, often by a human service-provider outside of the cyberworld of e-Service (e.g., "haircut" in the case of tangible action on the body of a person; "lawn care" in the case of tangible action on possession).

By default, good human service-providers practice real-time marketing when they adapt their service to the changing needs (and moods) of customers within the boundaries set by the nature of the service provided. For example, good waiters and waitresses at restaurants are able to pick up on what their regular clientele need even before the need is articulated.

Conceivably, some services could be automated in the future, and this would open them up to Web-enabled e-Service. For example, it is not impossible that the haircuts of the future could be delivered by mechanical devices, akin to the dryers of today, that are connected to a central database that feeds information about the particular customer to the device, which then uses this information along with local information about the state of an individual's hair to make decisions as to the most optimal haircut. Note that this device has embedded intelligence that allows it to make decisions based on contextual information, possibly as a result of advancements in artificial intelligence and robotics.

Similarly, car repairs (tangible service on possessions) could be done much differently in real-time marketing given the technological advancements currently available. Each car could be equipped with communications chips that transmit information about the state of the car at regular intervals to a central computer via satellite, which a robot could download through an online connection when that particular car drives in for service. Interestingly enough, a similar device for monitoring the health of humans has been developed by a company called Applied Digital Solutions. Its Digital Angel product employs chips powered by body heat that use biometric technology to monitor a body's vital statistics, which are then beamed via wireless broadband or via Global Positioning System's network of satellites to a remote monitoring system. This unique product can be worn either as a wristband or patch or implant (Della Bitta 2000a).

Overview

Service performances are information-intensive and context-dependent, both of which are integral elements for an effective real-time marketing strategy. As we have seen, the information content in services is amenable to transmission, storage, and analysis over the Internet and Web. Contextual information can be gathered from local sensors (electronic chips in the case of physical goods or automated services) or via elicitation or from an analysis of past behavior. However, for real-time marketing to have truly taken place, the service must be able to reconfigure itself in real time to meet the changing preferences of customers. This ability is possible in the case of services with intangible outcomes, as the medium of delivery is often Web-related and the product digitized information (e.g., electronic newspaper). In the case of services involving tangible outcomes, "intelligent" mechanisms embedded in the automated robots that perform the service could be made to adapt to the changing needs of customers. In most instances, though, the support services that facilitate the delivery, installation, and use of a product or service can be made to respond to the differing and changing needs of individual customers since these services are information-intensive and can be delivered online.

Future Trends

When people think of the Web, the image most often conjured up is that of a bulky desktop connected to the Internet via modem or cable. However, we may soon have to disabuse ourselves of this notion as computers become smaller and sleeker and customers use wireless broadband to access the Internet ("Study Says . . ." 2001). The implication of these twin trends is the enhanced *mobility* of Internet-connected devices and the *constancy* in linkage with the Internet backbone. Thus, given the present trends, it would be possible for information to be collected (either locally or centrally) from more locations at greater frequency, dramatically increasing the scope of real-time marketing. For example, a consumer could be beeped about a special, customized offer at a nearby location about a product of potential interest when he/she is strolling through the malls. An early peek into this new world of possibilities is provided by Streetbeam, a New York–based company that enables kiosks and billboards to beam passers-by's Palm Pilots with relevant information about the product being advertised. This information could be in the form of "some content or call to action" such as "there's a store around the corner, go there now and get $30 off" (Della Bitta 2000b).

Besides the enhanced mobility and connectivity, the current advances and continued research in voice recognition technology and natural language interfaces (e.g., the ability to understand the "fuzzy" language of consumers) would make the access to the Internet more seamless and natural, further increasing the scope of e-Service and real-time marketing in future years.

Strategic Issues in Implementation of Real-Time Marketing in e-Services

Organizational Structure

Effective implementation of strategy requires an organization structure in harmony with that strategy (Jain 1983). It is clear that organizations that adopt a real-time marketing approach will need to process vast amounts of information. Real-time marketing companies will need to process information generated not only externally but also internally. In real-time marketing, firms will need to store and process elements of customer information such as preferences, purchase history, and customer feedback at an individual level. In addition to this externally generated information, coordinated implementation of real-time marketing would require intense communication both within and between the various departments of marketing, design, manufacturing, and distribution. Faced with this quantum jump in information, firms will need to organize themselves to process this information efficiently.

Achrol (1991) posits that in dynamic environments, either of two organizational structures—the marketing exchange company or the marketing coalition company—is possible. Briefly, the marketing exchange company is an organization that functions analogously to the modern-day stock exchange, matching customer needs with the supply from downstream companies. Marketing coalition companies, on the other hand, are comprised of a network of strategic alliances, each partner specializing in a particular functional area.

In each instance, however, the principle is the same. Subunits (separate organizations in the instance of marketing coalition companies, separate functional areas in the instance of marketing exchange organizations) specialize in a narrow range of operations whereas the marketing company—the company with the customer interface—coordinates activities. Such organizational forms—disaggregate in nature—combine flexibility with efficiency and give firms the leverage to compete efficiently in dynamic environments. Hence, firms will need to explore the applicability of such structures for the effective realization of real-time marketing strategies.

Should One Lead or Follow?

However, organizational change is not without risk, and the decision on whether a firm should lead or follow rests on a comparison of first-mover advantages with first-mover disadvantages (Porter 1985). If the first-mover advantages were to outweigh the first-mover disadvantages, then a pioneering strategy would be advocated. Some of the benefits of a first move are that firms get to define the industry standard, preempt competition in key markets, establish lock-ins with individual customers, gain insights into the market, stabilize operations before competitor entry, and enjoy early profits (Porter 1985). In contrast, some of the disadvantages are the cost of overcoming the structural inertia within the company, the cost of educating consumers, and the cost of gaining regulatory approvals from government bodies (Porter 1985).

Real-time marketing favors a pioneer strategy. A central point in most discussions on order of entry (e.g., Porter 1985, Glazer 1991) is whether the knowledge that a first mover acquires can be kept proprietary for future profits and be used to establish a better lock-in with existing customers. We argue that in real-time marketing, the most important resource that a company acquires is knowledge about customer preferences and that this information is proprietary by its very nature. Hence, firms that move first can gain *and sustain* their competitive advantage by being the first to establish a lock-in with customers. Furthermore, companies that internalize the philosophy of real-time marketing at an earlier stage can keep abreast of later competition by capitalizing on its proprietary learning curve to serve its customers better. The interested reader is directed to Leonard-Barton (1988) for an interesting discussion of implementation issues with respect to new technologies and to Ramasesh and Jayakumar (1992) for the economic justifications for adopting advanced technology.

Challenges to Real-Time Marketing in e-Services

Consumer Acceptance of Technology

With the increased use of Web-enabled, automated delivery of services, we envisage the service environment to change from a "high-touch, low-tech" environment to a "low-touch, high-tech" environment (cf. Bitner, Brown, and Meuter 2000). This would require consumers to be comfortable with technological interfaces, and since technology is constantly changing in terms of being improved upon, consumers would also need to be open to accepting newer versions and forms of technology.

While the upside of technologically enhanced interfaces are greater personalization and increased responsiveness, the downside is that in some instances, some consumers may miss the socialization experience that comes from interacting with live service providers (the assumption being that most interactions are friendly!). Hence, we anticipate that there will be segments of customers who would choose to opt out of technology-enhanced interfaces, much like the segments of individuals who prefer to interact with a teller rather than an ATM. It is encouraging to note that Bitner and her colleagues (e.g., Bitner, Brown, and Meuter 2000; Meuter et al. 2000) have begun researching the impact of technology-enhanced interfaces on service constructs in a programmatic fashion and are providing fresh impetus to earlier research along these lines by Dabholkar (1996) and A. Parasuraman (1996).

Privacy Issues

Real-time marketing is information-intensive in that it is dependent upon the availability of longitudinal information about the behavior and preferences of consumers, so that the differing and changing needs of customers can be served. However, polls show that consumers fear the collection of data about themselves, and some privacy advocates have sought to limit the information that can be collected about individual purchase and preference patterns (Borrus and Dwyer 2001). In Europe, there are strict rules about the collection and use of individually identifiable information since the information is believed to belong to the individual, whereas in the United States, the rules are less stringent, as the firm collecting the information is seen to have partial rights over the information (Jones and Meller 2001). Given the benefits of customization in real time on the one hand and the legitimate fear of consumers about the loss of security and privacy on the other, it would seem that firms that practice real-time marketing would need to reassure consumers about the legitimacy of the use of information collected, especially since some firms have reneged on their assurances to keep customer information private (Green 2001). Experts have suggested that firms advertise an explicit privacy policy on their Web site or in any form of online transactions and adopt the more rigorous default of giving customers the choice to "opt in" instead of requiring customers to "opt out" of an e-marketing program (Davidson 2001).

The debate on privacy rages on, and as yet, there is no clear consensus as to whether self-regulation or federal laws will govern how firms collect and use customer information. However, in the heat of the debate over privacy, it is easy to lose sight of the fact that access to certain private information is more problematic than others. From an informal analysis of the articles on privacy, it would appear that consumer groups are more vigorous in protecting information rights in the domain of medical and financial records (e.g., Hulme and Khirallah 2001). As real-time marketing seeks to collect information needs that relate to consumer preferences and behavioral patterns, it is possible that in medicine and banking and other such sensitive areas of service, marketers can expect to operate under federal regulations governing the use of private information. In other services, real-time marketing may just need to adhere to industry regulations. Further, given the recent high-profile instances of firms reneging on their privacy policies (e.g., eToys selling information about their customers when going under despite earlier pledges to keep information private), firms may explore authenticating their privacy policies by a nonprofit, third party like TRUSTe, which monitors adherence to privacy policies by member organizations and whose "trustmark" is supported by the Electronic Frontier Foundation (Greenstein and Feinman 2000).

Future Research

A rich agenda for future research presents itself within the paradigm of real-time marketing as it applies to e-Service. In this section, we present a few of the possible research ideas that could be advanced, the results of which would be welcome additions to the body of literature on real-time marketing in e-Services.

Given the importance of access to information for the practice of real-time marketing in e-Services, marketers would benefit from a more careful examination of the kind of information consumers would be willing to share with firms and the context in which they would choose to do so. More formally, marketers could explore economic models that treat information as a tradable commodity or economic good. This approach would enable firms to negotiate "information" rights from individuals in lieu of economic incentives and allow such information to be traded between firms, within prevailing rules and regulations. For instance, it is not inconceivable that an ethnic food store that has information about an individual's recent food purchases could seek to trade this information with an ethnic restaurant in the individual's area of residence, or vice versa. In this context, Rust, Kannan, and Peng (Forthcoming) is an early paper that employs a formal economic model to examine the value of customer information and the willingness of firms to pay for that information.

Similarly, models that explore how best to extract relevant information from customers, either directly or indirectly, in the least amount of time should be explored. In this context, the paper by Raghu et al. (2001) that focuses on developing easy-to-use methods for *dynamic* profiling of customers when offering customized products and services over the Internet is a welcome addition to the literature on real-time marketing in e-Services.

Concomitantly, researchers may consider studying the value of the information gleaned from consumers. From a product management perspective, it would be interesting to quantify the extent of customer information incorporated into product design, given that in real-time marketing the extent of person- and context-related information incorporated into product design is the driver of product value. In this context, concepts and results from information theory (e.g., Raisbeck 1964) could possibly prove helpful.

Lastly, from the point of view of implementing real-time marketing in e-Services, which is so dependent on timely information, it would be important to study how best to communicate across departments and organizations so that a fast, coordinated response can be made to the changing needs of a consumer. In this context, the work by Griffin and Hauser (1992) and Van den Bulte and Moenaert (1998), which examines the communication patterns among marketing, engineering, and manufacturing departments within an organization, provides some initial directions.

Note

The author thanks the editors, as well as Albert Della Bitta, Allan Graham, and Rohit Rampal for their helpful comments on an earlier version of the article.

References

Achrol, Ravi S. 1991. "Evolution of the Marketing Organization: New Forms for Turbulent Environments." *Journal of Marketing* 55: 77–93.

Bitner, Mary Jo; Stephen W. Brown; and Matthew L. Meuter. 2000. "Technology Infusion in Service Encounters." *Journal of the Academy of Marketing Science* 28(1): 138–149.

Borrus, Amy, and Paula Dwyer. 2001. "The Stage Seems Set for Net Privacy Rules This Year." *Business Week*, March 5, p. 51.

Dabholkar, Pratibha. 1996. "Consumer Evaluations of New Technology-based Self-Service Options: An Investigation of Alternative Models of Service Quality." *International Journal of Research in Marketing* 13(1): 29–51.

Davidson, Paul. 2001. "Marketing Gurus Clash on Internet Privacy Rules: Opt In or Opt Out." *USA Today*, April 27, p. B-1.

Deighton, John. 2001. "Branding Customers: Marketing in the Information Age." Presentation made at University of Rhode Island, May 4.

Della Bitta, Michael. 2000a. "Digital Angel: The New Eye in the Sky." *Foxnews.com*, October 16: www.foxnews.com.

———. 2000b. " New Street Ads Leave People Beaming." *Foxnews.com*, December 16, www.foxnews.com/scitech/121600/streetbeam.sml.

Glazer, Rashi. 1991. "Marketing in an Information-Intensive Environment: Strategic Implications of Knowledge as an Asset." *Journal of Marketing* 55: 1–19.

Green, Heather. 2001. "Your Right to Privacy: Going . . . Going . . . " *Business Week*, April 23, p. 48.

Greenstein, Marilyn, and Todd M. Feinman. 2000. *Electronic Commerce: Security, Risk Management, and Control*. New York: Irwin McGraw-Hill.

Griffin, Abbie, and John R. Hauser. 1992. "Patterns of Communication Among Marketing, Engineering, and Manufacturing—A Comparison Between Two New Product Teams." *Management Science* 38(3): 360–373.

Heim, Gregory R., and Kingshuk K. Sinha. 2001. "A Product-Process Matrix for Electronic B2C Operations." *Journal of Service Research* 3(4): 286–299.

Hoffman, Donna L., and Thomas P. Novak. 1996. "Marketing in Hyper Media Computer Mediated Environments: Conceptual Foundations." *Journal of Marketing* 60 (July): 5–68.

Hulme, George V., and Diane Rezendes Khirallah. 2001. "Protecting Privacy." *InformationWeek.Com*, April 16, pp. 22–23: www.informationweek.com

Jain, Subhash C. 1983. "The Evolution of Strategic Marketing." *Journal of Business Research* 11: 409–425.

Jones, Jennifer, and Paul Meller. 2001. "U.S., E.U. Divided on Standards." *Infoworld*, April 2, p. 12: www.infoworld.com.

Leonard-Barton, Dorothy. 1988. "Implementation as Mutual Adaptation of Technology and Organization." *Research Policy* 17: 251–261.

Lovelock, Christopher H. 1983. "Classifying Services to Gain Strategic Marketing Insight." *Journal of Marketing* 47 (summer): 9–20.

McKenna, Regis. 1995. "Real-Time Marketing." *Harvard Business Review* (July–August): 87–95.

Meuter, Matthew L.; Amy L. Ostrom; Robert I. Roundtree; and Mary Jo Bitner. 2000. "Self-Service Technologies: Understanding Customer Satisfaction with Technology-Based Service Encounters." *Journal of Marketing* 64 (July): 50–64.

Oliver, Richard L.; Roland T. Rust; and Sajeev Varki. 1998. "Real-Time Marketing." *Marketing Management* (fall/winter): 29–37.

Parasuraman, A. 1996. "Understanding and Leveraging the Role of Customer Service in External, Interactive, and Internal Marketing." Frontiers in Services Conference, Nashville, TN, October 5.

Porter, Michael. 1985. *Competitive Advantage: Creating and Sustaining Superior Performance*. New York: Free Press.

Raghu, T.S.; P.K. Kannan; H.R. Rao; and A.B. Whinston. 2001. "Dynamic Profiling of Consumers for Customized Offerings Over the Internet: A Model and Analysis." *Decision Support Systems* 32(2) (December): 117–134.

Raisbeck, Gordon. 1964. *Information Theory*. Cambridge: MIT Press.

Ramasesh, R.V., and M.D. Jayakumar. 1992. "Economic Justification of Advanced Manufacturing Technology." *OMEGA* 21(3): 289–306.

Rust, Roland T. 2001. "The Rise of E-Service." *Journal of Service Research* 3(4): 283.

Rust, Roland T., and Katherine N. Lemon. 2001. "E-Service and the Consumer." *International Journal of Electronic Commerce* 5(3) (spring): 85–103.

Rust, Roland T., and Sajeev Varki. 1996. "Rising from the Ashes of Advertising." *Journal of Business Research* 37(3): 173–181.

Rust, Roland T.; P.K. Kannan; and Na Peng. Forthcoming. "The Customer Economics of Internet Privacy." *Journal of Academy of Marketing Science*.

"Study Says Wireless Use Growing in U.S." 2001. *Computerworld*, March 12, p. 56.

Van den Bulte, Christophe, and Rudy K. Moenaert. 1998. "The Effect of R&D Team Co-location on Communication Patterns among R&D, Marketing, and Manufacturing." *Management Science* 44 (11, part 2): S1–S18.

Varki, Sajeev, and Roland T. Rust. 1998. "Technology and Optimal Segment Size." *Marketing Letters* 9(2): 147–167.

9

A Survey of Recommendation Systems in Electronic Commerce

Chih-Ping Wei, Michael J. Shaw, and Robert F. Easley

Introduction

Advances in information and networking technology not only have facilitated the creation, distribution, and access of online information, they have also fostered conducting business transactions on the Internet. The amount of data in this global information space is increasing far more rapidly than the ability of an individual information user or online customer to process it. As a result, information overload has become a critical challenge facing individuals, giving rise to an e-Service opportunity: developing recommendations that are typically personalized for individuals. In providing this service, merchandisers seek not only to increase sales, but also to better manage customer relationships that lead to higher loyalty and greater competitive barriers. Recommendation systems (also known as recommender systems) have emerged as a new class of e-Service product to address the challenge of information overload by suggesting information or products of greatest interest to users (from the information user or online customer perspective) and to facilitate the management of customer relationships or even to provide personalized services to customers (from the merchandiser or information provider perspective).

Recommendation systems typically suggest items (information, products, or services) that are of interest to users based on customer demographics, features of items, or user preferences (e.g., ratings or purchasing history). In the context of content-based sites, recommendation systems can be used to facilitate selective dissemination from a large stream of information to users or to support effective management of information on the part of individuals. For instance, GroupLens provides personalized recommendations of Usenet news items from a high-volume, high-turnover discussion list service on the Internet, based on the opinions of other users (Resnick et al. 1994; Konstan et al. 1997). Using the ratings of news articles evaluated by users, GroupLens identifies other users whose information needs or tastes are similar to those of a given user and recommends news articles that they have liked. Siteseer, developed by James Rucker and Marcos J. Polanco (1997), is a Web-page recommendation system that uses an individual's bookmarks and the organization of bookmarks within folders for predicting and recommending relevant pages. Essentially, Siteseer looks at each user's folders and bookmarks and measures the degree of overlap of each folder with other people's folders. Accordingly, Siteseer forms dynamically defined virtual communities of interest, particular to each user and specific to each of the user's categories of interest. Siteseer provides as recommendations those pages that have been bookmarked by the user's virtual neighbors, giving preference to pages drawn from folders with the highest overlap as well as those held within multiple folders in the neighborhood. The digital library of the Association for Computing Machinery (ACM) (www.acm.org/dl), on the other hand, suggests to a user new binders to be included in his/her personal bookshelf based on binders of other users who share similar professional memberships or subscriptions.

Recommendation systems have also seen considerable success on e-commerce sites to suggest products to their customers. An early entrant into the e-Service area—and one that capitalized on a new form of customer data, the navigation and browsing habits of customers across many different sites—is Double-click.com, which provides the service of pushing personalized advertisements into ad slots on Web sites. The data are acquired from cookie files, which track the movements of customers through many Web sites and can be used to deduce customers' product preferences. Recently, recommendation systems have been used—for example, by Bostondine to recommend restaurants in and around Boston; by Sepia Video Guide to make customized video recommendations; by Movie Critic, MovieFinder.com, and Morse to recommend movies; by CDNow.com to recommend albums related to the album located by a user; and by Amazon.com to recommend books (Schafer et al. 1999; Ansari et al. 2000). A well-known example of this practice is

Amazon.com's service of offering a personalized recommendation based on a customer's past purchases and interests, and on the preferences of similar customers. Such recommendations provide a customer service whose quality is commensurate with the customer's assessment of the value or appropriateness of the recommendation. If the quality of this service is high, the recommendations may lead to increased customer satisfaction and loyalty, as well as increased sales.

The difficulty and importance of making a quality recommendation underlie the development of a wide range of technical approaches to developing recommendations, a survey of which is the main focus of this chapter. The remainder of the chapter is organized as follows. In the next section, a framework for recommendation systems will be presented. The following section proposes a taxonomic classification for recommendation systems whose differences will be illustrated using the proposed framework. Various recommendation approaches will be detailed in the next four sections. Finally, a summary of the chapter and important practical considerations and research issues will be provided in the last section.

Framework for Recommendation Systems

Recommendation systems are used to determine a set of items (information, products, or services) that are of greatest interest to users. As shown in Figure 9.1, in a typical recommendation scenario, there is a set of n users $U = \{u_1, u_2, \ldots, u_n\}$ and a set of m items $I = \{i_1, i_2, \ldots, i_m\}$. Each user u_i may be associated with his/her demographic data and has a list of items I_{u_i} (where $I_{u_i} \subseteq I$ and I_{u_i} can be an empty set) on which the user has expressed his/her preferences. The preference of a user u_i on an item i_j (denoted as p_{ij}) can be a subjective rating explicitly stated by the user or an implicit measure inferred from purchase, browsing, and navigation data in user activity. On the other hand, a set of features may be used to describe each item $i_j \in I$. Thus, a recommendation system is often based on user demographics, features of items, or user preferences for deriving its recommendation decisions. Although other types of information may be adopted by some recommendation systems, we limit our discussions on these three information types commonly used for reaching recommendation decisions. Regarding the recommendation decision itself, it can be made for a specific user u_a (where $u_a \in U$), called an active user, on those items that have not explicitly been rated or chosen by this user. Alternatively, it may suggest a new item i_{new} (where $i_{new} \notin I$) to those users who might be interested. In the following subsections, potential information for and types of recommendation decisions will be discussed in detail.

Information for Recommendation Decisions

User demographics, meaning the characteristics of users that potentially affect their likes and dislikes, represent one type of information on which recommendation decisions can be made. User demographics typically include such attributes as age, gender, occupation, income level, education level, hobbies, and so on. For instance, based on the heuristics "teenage boys like basketball" and "medical doctors like golf," items related to basketball and golf can be suggested to customers with those demographic characteristics, respectively.

A second type of information that can be used for making recommendation decisions is the set of attributes of the items themselves. Items can be described by their features, extrinsic or intrinsic. Extrinsic features (e.g., color, brand, manufacturer, and subcategory/category of a product) refer to those that are difficult or impossible to derive by automatically analyzing the content of items and, if required, need to be supplied by other sources (e.g., domain experts). Conversely, intrinsic features are derivable by the analysis of the content of items, such as representative keywords extracted from news articles or Web pages. It is worth mentioning that information about category hierarchy of items, if needed, can also be captured in the feature set for describing the items.

The third type of information relevant to recommendation decisions is user preferences. The user preference score[1] on an item can be a binary measure (of preference or choice) or on a discrete numerical scale (representing degree of preference). User preferences can be explicit ratings provided by users or implicit measures inferred from available user activity data (Herlocker et al. 1999; Claypool et al. 2001). Explicit ratings are directly obtained from users by instructing them to evaluate and rate each item typically on a numerical scale. Even though explicit ratings are often observed in real-world practices, requiring users to provide explicit ratings may alter users' normal patterns of browsing in online settings. Unless users perceive potential benefits, they may not have any incentive to provide explicit ratings. As manifested by a study conducted by Badrul Sarwar et al. (1998), users are reading a lot more articles than they are rating. Thus, explicit ratings may not be as reliable as often presumed (Claypool et al. 2001). On the other hand, implicit ratings are derived from data sources such as purchase history, Web logs, or cookie data for user browsing and navigation patterns (e.g., time spent reading or the amount of scrolling on a Web page), thereby leveraging data already collected for other purposes (Breese et al. 1998; Herlocker et al. 1999; Claypool et al. 2001). Implicit ratings may be less accurate than explicit ones for measuring users' preferences. Nevertheless, there is evidence that the time spent on a page, the amount of scrolling on a page, and their combination may strongly correlate with explicit ratings (Claypool et al. 2001).

Any given recommendation system may use all or some part of the three types of information shown in Figure 9.1. In fact, the review of existing recommendation systems shows that each of them only uses a subset of information to arrive at recommendations. No system uses all the three types of information for recommendations.

Types of Recommendation Decisions

A recommendation decision may suggest a set of items from among those that have not explicitly been rated or chosen by an active user u_a. Alternatively, it may select a subset of users that may be interested in a newly available item i_{new}. Accordingly, three types of recommendation decisions can be:

- *Prediction:* Prediction expresses the predicted preference for item $i_j \notin I_{u_a}$ for an active user u_a. This predicted value is within the same scale as for the user preferences (Sarwar et al. 2001).
- *Top-N recommendation:* This is a list of N items, $I_r \subset I$, that the active user u_a will like the most. The recommended list must be on items not already rated or chosen by u_a, that is, $I_r \cap I_{u_a} = \emptyset$ (Sarwar et al. 2001).
- *Top-M users:* For a newly available item i_{new}, a recommendation system suggests a list of M users who will like i_{new} most. In some recommendation approaches, the recommendation on the top-M users for a new item can be viewed as a set of *prediction* decisions, each of which is made for a user. Subsequently, the top-M users who are predicted to like i_{target} most are recommended.

The first two types of recommendations (prediction and top-N recommendation) can be further categorized along a degree-of-personalization dimension. A recommendation decision can be personalized to specific users or nonpersonalized if it is independent of users. For instance, the average customer ratings displayed by Amazon.com and MovieFinder.com are nonpersonalized top-N recommendations, while Amazon.com's book recommendations that are based on a customer's past purchases and interests are personalized top-N recommendations.

Classification of Recommendation Systems

Many recommendation systems have been proposed in the literature. Based on the type of data and technique used to arrive at recommendation deci-

Figure 9.1 Framework for Recommendation Systems

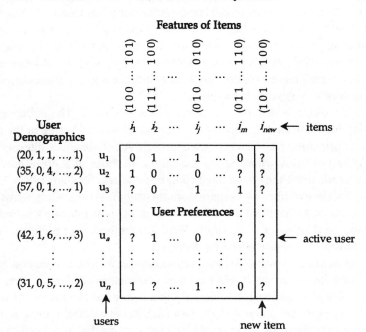

sions, recommendation systems can broadly be classified into the following approaches:

1. *Popularity-based recommendation approach:* In real-world practices, customers often want to know about the most popular items within a given community as a means of finding out what they should pay attention to. This approach has precedents in best-seller lists in physical store settings. Using user preferences as input, the popularity-based recommendation approach computes within-community popularity measures (e.g., percentage of customers who purchased an item) or summaries (e.g., number of customers who purchased an item, average ratings for an item, and so on) (Schafer et al. 2001). Thus, the most popular items are recommended to users. The popularity-based recommendation approach serves to clarify the sense in which personalization techniques form only a subset of recommendation systems, since this approach does provide recommendations without personalization. Although this approach can deliver only nonpersonalized recommendations, it is popular due to its simplicity and efficiency.

2. *Content-based recommendation approach:* The content-based recommendation approach rests on the notion that the features of items can be useful in recommending items. It conforms to content-based information fil-

tering that assumes that the degree of relevance (to a particular user) of an item can be determined by its content (represented by its features) (Alspector et al. 1998). The content-based recommendation approach tries to recommend items similar to those a given user has liked in the past (Balabanovic and Shoham 1997; Herlocker et al. 1999). Thus, the features of items and a user's own preferences are the only factors influencing recommendation decisions for the user with this approach.

3. *Collaborative filtering recommendation approach:* The collaborative filtering recommendation approach is also called social filtering or the user-to-user correlation recommendation approach. A collaborative filtering system identifies users whose tastes are similar to those of a given user and recommends items they have liked (Balabanovic and Shoham 1997). Users of a collaborative filtering system share their opinions regarding items that they consume so that other users of the system can better decide which items to consume (Herlocker et al. 1999). With this method, user preferences are the sole input to recommendation decisions.

4. *Association-based recommendation approach:* The association-based recommendation approach relies on user preferences to identify items frequently found in association with items that a user has chosen, or for which a user has expressed interest in the past (Schafer et al. 2001). Item-associations can take the form, for example, of a set of items that have been rated as similar to a particular item, or of cooccurrence of items that users often preferred or purchased in common. Such item-associations, once identified, can then be employed to recommend items to users. For instance, the prediction of the preference score of an active user on an item can be based on the active user's preference scores over similar items.

5. *Demographics-based recommendation approach:* This approach recommends items to a user based on the preferences of other users with similar demographics. Unlike other recommendation approaches in which recommendations are made at the item level, a demographics-based recommendation system typically generates recommendations at the more general category level. As such, this approach involves learning and reasoning with relationships between user demographics and expressed category preferences, where the expressed category preferences of a user are derived from individual user preferences stated previously and the category hierarchies of items.

6. *Reputation-based recommendation approach:* This approach focuses on identifying users that a user respects (directly or transitively) and then using the opinions of these selected individuals as a basis for recommendations. The reputation-based recommendation approach has its roots in social practices involving reviewers or opinion leaders (Lynch 2001). It captures a totally different aspect of socially based information discovery, where one

makes assessments about people in a more general way rather than directly comparing preferences.

Table 9.1 summarizes the characteristics of each recommendation approach. The popularity-based recommendation approach involves simple techniques for recommendations. On the other hand, the reputation-based recommendation approach is still in its conception stage. To the best of our knowledge, although few reputation mechanisms have been proposed for electronic marketplaces (Zacharia et al. 2000), no existing recommendation systems have incorporated a reputation mechanism for delivering reputation-based recommendations. Thus, in the following sections, we will only review representative techniques for the remaining recommendation approaches.

Each recommendation approach has its strengths and limitations. To complement one's limitations by another's strengths, several hybrid techniques have been proposed. For example, Fab, proposed by Balabanovic and Shoham (1997) is a hybrid content-based, collaborative filtering recommendation system for suggesting Web pages to users. Badrul M. Sarwar et al. (2000) propose a recommendation technique that integrates collaborative filtering and association-based approaches. Due to space limitation, hybrid techniques will not be discussed in further detail.

Content-Based Recommendation Approach

For a given user, content-based recommendation systems recommend items similar to those the user has liked in the past (Balabanovic and Shoham 1997; Herlocker et al. 1999). The content-based approach automatically learns and adaptively updates the profile of each user. Given a user profile, items are recommended for the user based on a comparison between item-feature weights and those of the user profile. If a user rates an item differently than a recommendation system suggested, the user profile can be updated accordingly. This process is also known as *relevance feedback*. The content-based recommendation approach has its roots in content-based information filtering and has proven to be effective in recommending textual documents. Examples of the content-based recommendation systems include Syskill & Webert for recommending Web pages (Pazzani et al. 1996), NewsWeeder for recommending news-group messages (Lang 1995), and InformationFinder for recommending textual documents (Krulwich and Burkey 1996).

Assume the set of items that a user has rated or chosen to be the training set with respect to the given user. As shown in Figure 9.2, the phases involved in a content-based recommendation system generally include:

Table 9.1

Characteristics of Different Recommendation Approaches

Recommendation approach	Information used	Types of recommendations	Degree of personalization
Popularity-based	User preferences	Top-N recommendation	Nonpersonalized
Content-based	Features of items and individual user preferences	Prediction, top-N recommendation, and top-M users	Personalized
Collaborative filtering	User preferences	Prediction and top-N recommendation	Personalized
Association-based	User preferences	Prediction and top-N recommendation	Personalized
Demographics-based	User demographics, individual user preferences, and features of items (specifically, category hierarchy of items)	Prediction, top-N recommendation, and top-M users	Personalized
Reputation-based	User preferences and reputation matrix	Top-N recommendation and, possibly, prediction	Personalized

Figure 9.2 **Process of Content-Based Recommendation Approach**

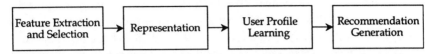

1. *Feature extraction and selection:* Extract and select relevant features for all items in the collection.
2. *Representation*: Represent each item with the feature set determined in the previous phase.
3. *User profile learning:* Automatically learn or adaptively update the user profile model for each user based on the training examples pertinent to the user.
4. *Recommendation generation:* Generate recommendations by performing reasoning on the corresponding user profile model.

Feature Extraction and Selection

The feature extraction and selection phase is undertaken to determine a set of features that will be used for representing individual items. If items involve extrinsic features, they need to be specified by domain experts. For example, Joshua Alspector et al. (1998) developed variants of content-based recommendation systems for movie selection based on such features as category (e.g., comedy, drama), MAPP rating, Maltin rating, Academy Award, length, origin, and director of movies. However, if intrinsic features are involved, extraction of features by analyzing the content of items is required. An automatic feature extraction mechanism is only available for limited domains. In the domain consisting of textual documents, the most effective domain of the content-based recommendation approach, the text portion of the documents is parsed to produce a list of features (typically consisting of nouns or noun phrases), none of which is a number or part of a proper name, or belongs to a predefined list of stop words.

After the feature specification (for extrinsic features) or extraction (for intrinsic features), feature selection is initiated to choose a small subset of features that ideally is necessary and sufficient to describe the target concept (Piramuthu 1998). The feature selection process not only improves learning efficiency but also has the potential to increase learning effectiveness (Dumais et al. 1998). Various feature selection methods have been proposed, using such techniques as statistical analysis, genetic algorithms, rough sets theory, and so on. For example, in statistical analysis, forward and backward stepwise multiple regression are widely used to select features. In the forward stepwise multiple regression, the analysis proceeds by adding features to a subset until the addition of a new feature no longer results in an improvement in the explained variance (R^2 value). The backward stepwise multiple regression starts with the full set of features and seeks to eliminate features with the smallest contribution to R^2 value (Kittler 1975). Wojciech Siedlecki and Jack Sklansky (1989) adopted genetic algorithms for feature selection by encoding the initial set of f features as f-element bit string with 1 and 0 representing the presence and absence, respectively, of features in the set, with classification accuracy employed as the fitness function. Maciej Modrzejewski (1993) proposed a rough set-based, feature-selection method to determine the degree of dependency of sets of attributes for selecting binary features. Features resulting in a minimal preset decision tree, with minimal length of all paths from root to leaves, are selected. For interested readers, a summary of and empirical comparisons on various feature selection methods can be found in Piramuthu (1998).

However, in the case of recommending textual documents, hundreds or thousands of features can be extracted, and the feature-selection methods described above may become computationally infeasible. Thus, most feature-selection methods developed for textual documents adopt an evaluation function that is applied to features independently. A feature-selection metric score is then assigned to each feature under consideration. The top k features with the highest feature-selection metric score are selected as features for representing documents, where k is a predefined number of features to select. Several evaluation functions for feature selection have been proposed, including TF (within-document term frequency), TF x IDF (within-document term frequency x inverse document frequency), correlation coefficient, mutual information, and an X^2 metric (Dumais et al. 1998; Lam and Ho 1998; Lewis and Ringuette 1994; Ng et al. 1997).

Representation

In the representation phase, each item is represented in terms of features selected in the previous phase. Each item in the training set is labeled to indicate its preference (dependent variable) by a particular user and assigned a value for each feature (independent variable) selected. The task of representing extrinsic features of an item is straightforward and is essentially achieved during the feature extraction and selection phase. Feature values of an item originally supplied by domain experts are used. On the other hand, for representing a textual document by a set of intrinsic features extracted and selected in the previous phase, a binary value (e.g., indicating whether or not the feature appears in the document) or a numerical value (e.g., frequency of occurrence in the document being processed) is assigned to each feature. Different document representation schemes have been proposed, including binary, TF, IDF, and TFIDF (Yang and Chute 1994).

User Profile Learning

For each user, the purpose of this phase is to construct a user profile model for establishing the relationship between preference scores (dependent variable) and feature values (independent variables) from the training examples pertinent to the user. The learning implementation can draw on statistical, inductive learning, and Bayesian probability methods. For example, Joshua Alspector et al. (1998) adopted the statistical method (specifically, a multiple linear regression model) and inductive learning algorithm (specifically, CART) for movie recommendations. Raymond J. Mooney and Loriene Roy (2000) used the Bayesian probability method for learning user profiles in order to obtain book recommendations.

A multiple linear regression model is based on the most natural assumption of a linear influence of each of the features involved on the preferences. Thus, it takes the form of:

$$p_{im} = \sum_{j=1}^{k} w_j f_{mj} + b$$

where p_{im} denotes the preference score of the user i on the item m,
w_j is the coefficient associated with the feature j,
f_{mj} is the value of the jth feature for the item m, and
b represents the bias.

Creation of such a user profile model for each user is essentially equivalent to a multiple linear regression on the set of features, and its solution can be obtained using the least-squares technique (Alspector et al. 1998).

To address the potential nonlinear dependencies between individual features, inductive-learning algorithms have been adopted for learning user profiles in the content-based recommendation approach. In this inductive-learning framework, preference scores on items in the training set can be treated as a continuous decision or a discrete class membership, while the features of the item are attributes potentially affecting the decision. Consequently, a decision tree induction algorithm (e.g., ID3 [Quinlan 1986]) or its descendant C4.5 (Quinlan 1993), CHAID (Kass 1980), or CART (Breiman et al. 1984), a decision rule induction algorithm (e.g., CN2 [Clark and Niblett 1989]), or a back-propagation neural network (Rumelhart et al.1986) can be employed to address the target learning task.

A decision tree induction algorithm is a supervised learning method that constructs a decision tree from a set of training examples. It typically adopts an *iterative* method to construct decision trees, preferring simple trees to complex ones, based on the theory that simple trees are more accurate classifiers for future instances. On the other hand, a decision rule induction algorithm induces from training examples a set of decision rules, each of which is represented by an "if <complex> then predict <class>" format, where <complex> is a conjunct attribute test and <class> represents a decision outcome. The rule construction proceeds in an iterative fashion, and each iteration searches for a better and significant complex for predicting a decision class via a general-to-specific or specific-to-general search strategy.

A back-propagation neural network is a multilayered, fully connected network (Rumelhart et al. 1986). The network has one input layer, one or more hidden layers, and one output layer. Typically, each layer contains multiple nodes, each of which is connected to every node in the next adjacent layer through a weighted link. In a back-propagation neural network, training is achieved by adjusting its weights each time it sees an input-output pair (i.e., a training example). Each iteration requires a forward pass and a backward pass. The forward pass involves presenting the training example to the network and letting activations flow until they reach the output layer. During the backward pass, the actual output of the network produced from the forward pass is compared with the target output of the training example, and error estimates are computed for the output nodes. The error estimates of the output nodes are then employed to derive error estimates for the hidden nodes. Accordingly, the weights connected to the output nodes can be adjusted in order to reduce those errors in output layer. Finally, errors are propagated back to the weights stemming from the input nodes. Through repeatedly presenting the set of training examples to the network, the weights between nodes are expected to converge. As a result, the user profile model is encoded in the weights within the selected network topology.

Recommendation Generation

Once user profile models are induced, recommendations can be generated. Since the features of items and a user's past preferences are the only factors influencing recommendation decisions, all of the three types of recommendations can be suggested. To estimate the predicted preference score on item $i_j \notin I_{u_a}$ for an active user u_a, the item is first represented with the features selected previously. Subsequently, the reasoning on the user profile model (e.g., a regression model, a decision tree, a set of decision rules, or a trained back-propagation neural network) corresponding to the active user is performed to predict the preference score of u_a on the item i_j. To produce the top-N recommendation for the active user u_a, the predicted preference score on each item that has not explicitly been rated or chosen by u_a is obtained as described previously. Afterward, the top-N items with the highest predicted preference score are included in the recommendation list. To recommend the top-M users for a new item i_{new}, a set of prediction decisions are made, one for each user, followed by the selection of the top-M users who are predicted to like i_{new} most.

Summary

The content-based recommendation approach recommends for a given user items similar to those the user has liked in the past. Since individualized user profiles are induced, personalized recommendations can be achieved. Due to the relevance feedback process, a content-based recommendation system can adaptively update the profile of each user. As mentioned, items are recommended based on features of items rather than on the preferences of other users. This allows for the possibility of providing explanations that list content features that caused an item to be recommended, potentially giving readers confidence in the system's recommendations and insight into their own preferences (Mooney and Roy 2000).

However, the content-based recommendation approach has several shortcomings. In many domains, the items are not amenable to any useful feature extraction methods (e.g., movies, music albums, and videos). For such domains, the efforts of domain experts to specify for extrinsic features and to assign feature values for each item are unavoidable, thus limiting the applicability of content-based recommendation approach. Furthermore, overspecialization is another problem associated with this approach. When the system can only recommend items scoring highly against a user's profile, the user is restricted to seeing items similar to those the user has liked in the past (Balabanovic and Shoham 1997).

Collaborative Filtering Recommendation Approach

The collaborative filtering recommendation approach is very different from the content-based one. Rather than recommending items because they are similar to items a user has liked in the past, the collaborative filtering approach recommends items based on the opinions of other users. Typically, by computing the similarity of users, a set of "nearest neighbor" users whose known preferences correlate significantly with a given user are found. Preferences for unseen items are predicted for the user based on a combination of the preferences known from the nearest neighbors. Thus, in this approach, users share their preferences regarding each item that they consume so that other users of the system can better decide which items to consume (Herlocker et al. 1999). The collaborative filtering approach is the most successful and widely adopted recommendation technique to date. Examples of collaborative filtering systems include GroupLens (Resnick et al. 1994; Konstan et al. 1997), the Bellcore video recommender (Hill et al. 1995), and Ringo (Shardanand and Maes 1995). Amazon.com also uses a form of collaborative filtering technology, though the specifics of their implementation are not published.

As mentioned, the collaborative filtering approach utilizes user preferences to generate recommendations. Several different techniques have been proposed for collaborative filtering recommendations, including neighborhood-based, Bayesian networks (Breese et al. 1998), singular value decomposition with neural net classification (Billsus and Pazzani 1998), and induction rule learning (Basu et al. 1998). Due to space limitation, we will only review the neighborhood-based collaborative filtering techniques since they are the most prevalent algorithms used in collaborative filtering for recommendation. As shown in Figure 9.3, the process of a typical neighborhood-based collaborative filtering system can be divided into three phases (Sarwar et al. 2000):

1. *Dimension reduction:* Transform the original user preference matrix into a lower dimensional space to address the sparsity and scalability problems.
2. *Neighborhood formation:* For an active user, compute the similarities between all other users and the active user to form a proximity-based neighborhood with a number of like-minded users for the active user.
3. *Recommendation generation:* Generate recommendations based on the preferences of the set of nearest neighbors of the active user.

Dimension Reduction

The dimension-reduction phase transforms the original user preference matrix into a lower dimensional space to address the sparsity and scalability problem often encountered in collaborative filtering recommendation scenarios. The original representation of the input data to a collaborative filtering system is an nm user preference matrix, where n is the number of users and m is the number of items. This representation may potentially pose sparsity and scalability problems for collaborative filtering systems (Sarwar et al. 2000). In practice, when a large set of items is available, users may have rated or chosen a very low percentage of items, resulting in a very sparse user preference matrix. As a consequence, a collaborative filtering recommendation system may be unable to make any recommendations for a particular user. On the other hand, a collaborative filtering recommendation

Figure 9.3 **Process of Collaborative Filtering Recommendation Approach**

system requires the user similarity computation that grows with n and m, and thus suffers a serious scalability problem.

To overcome the described problems associated with the original representation, the sparse matrix can be transformed into a lower dimensional representation using the Latent Semantic Indexing (LSI) method (Sarwar et al. 2000). Essentially, this approach uses a truncated singular value decomposition to obtain a rank-d approximation of the original nm user preference matrix. This reduced representation alleviates the sparsity problem as all the entries in the nd matrix are nonzero, which means that all n customers now have their preferences on the d meta-items. Moreover, the performance on computing user similarities and its scalability are improved dramatically as $d \ll m$ (Sarwar et al. 2000).

Neighborhood Formation

The goal of neighborhood formation is to find, for an active user u_a, an ordered list of l users $N = \{n_1, n_2, \ldots, n_l\}$ such that $u_a \notin N$ and $sim(u_a, n_i) \geq sim(u_a, n_j)$ for $i < j$. This phase is, in fact, the model-building process for the collaborative filtering recommendation approach. Several different similarity measures have been proposed (Shardanand and Maes 1995; Herlocker et al. 1999; Sarwar et al. 2000), including

• *Pearson correlation coefficient:* The Pearson correlation coefficient is the most commonly used similarity measure in collaborative filtering recommendation systems. It is derived from a linear regression model. The similarity between an active user u_a and another user u_b using the Pearson correlation coefficient is calculated as:

$$sim(u_a, u_b) = \frac{\sum_i^m (p_{ai} - \overline{p}_a)(p_{bi} - \overline{p}_b)}{\sqrt{\sum_i^m (p_{ai} - \overline{p}_a)^2} \sqrt{\sum_i^m (p_{bi} - \overline{p}_b)^2}}$$

where p_{ai} represents the preference score of the user u_a on item i,
           $\overline{p}_a$ is the average preference score of the user u_a, and
           m is the number of items or meta-items in the reduced representation.

• *Constrained Pearson correlation coefficient:* The constrained Pearson correlation coefficient takes the positivity and negativity of preferences into account (Shardanand and Maes 1995). A preference score below the midpoint of the scaling scheme (e.g., 4 in a 7-point rating scale) is considered as negative, while a preference score above the midpoint is positive. Accordingly, the constrained Pearson correlation coefficient is used so that only when both users have rated an item positively or both negatively, the correlation coefficient between them will increase. The similarity between an active user u_a and another user u_b using the constrained Pearson correlation coefficient is given as:

$$sim(u_a, u_b) = \frac{\sum_i^m (p_{ai} - mp)(p_{bi} - mp)}{\sqrt{\sum_i^m (p_{ai} - mp)^2} \sqrt{\sum_i^m (p_{bi} - mp)^2}}$$

where mp is the midpoint of the rating scale.

• *Spearman rank correlation coefficient:* The Spearman rank correlation coefficient, a nonparametric method, computes a measure of correlation between ranks instead of actual preference scores:

$$sim(u_a, u_b) = \frac{\sum_i^m (rank_{ai} - \overline{rank}_a)(rank_{bi} - \overline{rank}_b)}{\sqrt{\sum_i^m (rank_{ai} - \overline{rank}_a)^2} \sqrt{\sum_i^m (rank_{bi} - \overline{rank}_b)^2}}$$

• *Cosine similarity:* Two users u_a and u_b are considered as two vectors in the m dimensional item-space or in the d dimensional meta-item-space in the reduced representation. The similarity between them is measured by computing the cosine of the angle between the two vectors, which is given by:

$$sim(u_a, u_b) = cos(\vec{a}, \vec{b}) = \frac{\vec{a} \cdot \vec{b}}{\|\vec{a}\|_2 \|\vec{b}\|_2} = \frac{\sum_i^m p_{ai} \cdot p_{bi}}{\sqrt{\sum_i^m p_{ai}^2} \sqrt{\sum_i^m p_{bi}^2}}$$

• *Mean-squared difference:* The mean-squared difference, introduced in Ringo (Shardanand and Maes 1995), measures the dissimilarity between an active user u_a and another user u_b as:

$$dissim(u_a, u_b) = \overline{\sum_i^m (p_{ai} - p_{bi})^2}$$

According to an empirical evaluation study conducted by Jonathan L. Herlocker et al. (1999), the Pearson correlation coefficient, whose performance was similar to that of the Spearman correlation coefficient, outperformed the cosine similarity and the mean-squared difference. Upendra Shardanand and Pattie Maes (1995) empirically evaluated different similarity measures (including Pearson correlation coefficient, constrained Pearson correlation coefficient, and mean-squared difference) and suggest that the constrained Pearson correlation coefficient achieved the best performance in terms of the tradeoff between the prediction accuracy and the number of target values that can be predicted. On the other hand, the mean-squared difference outperformed its counterparts in prediction accuracy, but it produced fewer predictions than others did.

After the $n \times n$ similarity matrix is computed for n users using a desired similarity measure, the next task is to actually form the neighborhood for the active user. There are several schemes for neighborhood selection (Herlocker et al. 1999; Sarwar et al. 2000), including:

• *Weight thresholding:* This scheme, used by Shardanand and Maes (1995), is to set an absolute correlation threshold, where all neighbors of the active user with absolute correlations greater than the given threshold are selected.

• *Center-based best-k neighbors:* It forms a neighborhood of a prespecified size k, for the active user, by simply selecting the k nearest users.

• *Aggregate-based best-k neighbors:* The aggregate-based best-k neighbors scheme, proposed by Sarwar et al. (2000), forms a neighborhood of size k for the active user u_a by first selecting the closest neighbor to u_a. The rest $k-1$ neighbors are selected as follows. Let us say at a certain point there are j neighbors in the neighborhood N, where $j < k$. The centroid of the current neighborhood is then determined as $\vec{C} = \frac{1}{j}\sum_{\vec{V} \in N} \vec{V}$. A user w, such that $w \notin N$ is selected as the $j+1$-st neighbor only if w is closest to the centroid $\vec{C}$. Subsequently, the centroid is recomputed for $j+1$ neighbors, and the process continues until $|N| = k$. Essentially, this scheme allows the nearest neighbors to affect the formation of the neighborhood and can be beneficial for very sparse data sets (Sarwar et al. 2000).

Recommendation Generation

After the nearest neighbors of the active user are identified, subsequent recommendations can be generated. Since the collaborative filtering process is initiated for a particular user, the collaborative filtering recommendation approach is typically for prediction and top-N recommendation decisions. The collaborative filtering recommendation approach is not applicable to produce the top-M users for a newly available item since no user preference is available for this item.

To estimate the predicted preference score on the item $i_j \notin I_{u_a}$ for an active user u_a, the following methods can be employed:

1. *Weighted average:* To combine all the neighbors' preference scores on the item i_j into a prediction, the weighted average method is to compute a weighted average of the preference scores, using the correlations as the weights. This basic weighted average method, as used in Ringo (Shardanand and Maes 1995), makes an assumption that all users rate on approximately the same distribution.

2. *Deviation from mean:* The method, taken by GroupLens (Resnick et al. 1994; Konstan et al. 1997), is based on the assumption that a user's preference score distribution may center on different points. To account for the differences in means, the average deviation of a neighbor's preference score from that neighbor's mean preference score is first computed, where the mean preference score is taken over all items that the neighbor has rated. The average deviation from the mean computed across all neighbors is then converted into the active user's preference score distribution by adding it to the active user's mean preference score. Using the deviation-from-mean method, the predicted preference score of the active user u_a on the item i is calculated as:

$$p_{ai} = \overline{p}_a + \frac{\sum_{u=1}^{k}(p_{ui} - \overline{p}_u) \cdot sim(u_a, u_u)}{\sum_{u=1}^{k} sim(u_a, u_u)}$$

3. *Z-score average:* To take into account the situation where the spread of users' preference score distributions may be different, the z-score average method was proposed by Herlocker et al. (1999) by extending the deviation-from-mean method. In this method, neighbors' preference scores on the item i are converted to z-scores and a weighted average of the z-scores is derived as the predicted preference score of the active user u_a on the item i:

$$p_{ai} = \overline{p}_a + \frac{\sum_{u=1}^{k} \dfrac{(p_{ui} - \overline{p}_u)}{\sigma_u} sim(u_a, u_u)}{\sum_{u=1}^{k} sim(u_a, u_u)}$$

An empirical evaluation study conducted by Herlocker et al. (1999) showed that the deviation-from-mean method performed significantly better than the weighted average method. However, the z-score average method did not perform significantly better than the deviation-from-mean method, suggesting that differences in spread between users' preference score distributions might have no effect on prediction accuracy.

To produce the top-N recommendation for the active user u_a, the predicted preference score on each item that has not explicitly been rated or chosen by u_a is derived first. Afterward, the top-N items with the highest predicted preference score are included in the recommendation list.

Summary

The collaborative filtering approach delivers personalized recommendations based on the opinions of other users and provides several advantages that are not provided by the content-based recommendation approach (Balabanovic and Shoham 1997; Herlocker et al. 1999). By using other users' opinions rather than features of items, the collaborative filtering approach can be employed to recommend items whose content is not easily analyzed by automated feature extraction techniques. Furthermore, this approach is capable of recommending items on the basis of quality and taste. Finally, since other users' opinions influence what is recommended, the approach is able to provide serendipitous recommendations to a user (i.e., recommend items that are dissimilar to those the user has liked before), thus avoiding the overspecialization problem associated with the content-based recommendation approach.

However, in addition to the sparsity and scalability problems, the collaborative filtering approach incurs other problems of its own. Items that have not been rated or chosen by a sufficient number of users cannot be effectively recommended. Thus, the collaborative filtering approach potentially tends to recommend popular items (Mooney and Roy 2000). On the other hand, although newly available items are frequently of particular interest to users, it is impossible for the collaborative filtering approach to recommend those items that no one has yet rated or chosen (Balabanovic and Shoham 1997; Condliff et al. 1999; Mooney and Roy 2000). Furthermore, for a user whose tastes are unusual compared to the rest of the population, there will not be any other users who are particularly similar, leading to poor recommendations (Condliff et al. 1999). Finally, different items may be highly similar in their features. The collaborative filtering approach cannot find this latent association and treats these items differently (i.e., the synonymy problem). Thus, the lack of access to the content of the items prevents similar users from being matched unless they have rated the exact same items (Sarwar et al. 2000).

Association-Based Recommendation Approach

The association-based recommendation approach relies on user preferences to identify items frequently associated with those items that a user has expressed interest in or chosen in the past (Schafer et al. 2001). Depending on the technique used for such association discovery, item associations can be classified into two types: item correlations and association rules. For a target item, an item-correlation technique searches for items that have been rated as similar to the target item. Once the set of similar items is identified, the predicted preference score of an active user on the target item is then based on the active user's preference scores for these similar items (Schafer et al. 2001). Apparently, item-correlation techniques are best applicable to the multipoint scaling scheme used for describing user preferences.

Alternatively, the association rule discovery technique (Agrawal et al. 1993; Agrawal and Srikant 1994) can be adopted to find interesting co-occurrences of items in a set of transactions, where each transaction in this recommendation context corresponds to a distinct user and consists of a list of items that the user liked or purchased. Since the association rule discovery technique is concerned mainly with the cooccurrence of items, the user preferences need to be transformed into the described representation of transactions. An association rule is an implication of the form X Y, which represents the notion that if the set of items X occurs, another set of items Y will often occur. To recommend items to an active user, if his/her transaction supports the left-hand side (X in the previous example) but not the right-hand side (Y in the previous example) of an association rule, the set of items Y will be recommended. In the following subsections, the item-correlation and association rule techniques for recommendations are detailed.

Item-Correlation Techniques for Recommendations

Taking user preferences as input, an item-correlation technique searches for a set of items that have been rated as similar to a target item. Assume the set of k most similar items to be $\{i_1, i_2, \ldots, i_k\}$ and their corresponding similarities to be $\{s_{i1}, s_{i2}, \ldots, s_{ik}\}$. Once the set of similar items is identified, the prediction of the preference score of an active user on the target item is then computed by taking a weighted average of the active user's preference scores on these similar items (Schafer et al. 2001). Based on this process, an item-correlation technique for recommendations consists of two main phases: similarity computation and recommendation generation.

To determine the similarity between two items i and j, the users who have rated both of these items (called corated users) are first selected, and a similarity method is then applied to determine the similarity measure between items i and j. Different similarity measures have been proposed, using such methods as cosine similarity, Pearson correlation similarity, and adjusted-cosine similarity (Sarwar et al. 2001). In the cosine similarity method, two items are thought of as two vectors in the p dimensional user-space (where p is the number of corated users). As with the cosine similarity measure discussed in the previous section, the similarity between two items is measured by computing the cosine of the angle between these two vectors. Similarly, the Pearson correlation coefficient measures the similarity between two items i and j based on the set of co-rated users U, as follows:

$$sim(i, j) = \frac{\sum_{u \in U} (p_{ui} - \overline{p}_i)(p_{uj} - \overline{p}_j)}{\sqrt{\sum_{u \in U} (p_{ui} - \overline{p}_i)^2} \sqrt{\sum_{u \in U} (p_{uj} - \overline{p}_j)^2}}$$

where $\overline{p}_{ui}$ denotes the preference score of the user u on the item i, and $\overline{p}_i$ is the average preference score of the i-th item over the set of corated users U.

The cosine similarity does not take into account the differences in rating scale between different users. Accordingly, the adjusted cosine similarity standardizes a user's preference score by his/her average and measures the similarity between items i and j as:

$$sim(i, j) = \frac{\sum_{u \in U} (p_{ui} - \overline{p}_u)(p_{uj} - \overline{p}_u)}{\sqrt{\sum_{u \in U} (p_{ui} - \overline{p}_u)^2} \sqrt{\sum_{u \in U} (p_{uj} - \overline{p}_u)^2}}$$

where $\overline{p}_u$ is the average of the u-th user's preference scores.

Once the set of similar items is identified for a target item using a similarity measure, the next phase is to combine preference scores of the active user on the set of similar items to arrive at a predicted preference score on the target item. The weighted average method is typically employed for deriving the prediction. In a manner similar to that discussed in the previous section, the weighted average method tries to capture how the active user rates similar items. It computes the prediction on the target item for the active user by taking the weighted average of the preference scores given by the active user on the items similar to the target item, using the item similarities as the weights (Sarwar et al. 2001).

To produce the top-N recommendation for the active user by an item-correlation technique, the predicted preference score on each item for which a preference score has not been given by the active user is derived as discussed previously. Subsequently, the top-N items with the highest predicted preference score are included in the recommendation list. However, as with the collaborative filtering approach, item-correlation techniques are not able to recommend the top-M users for a newly available item since no user preference is available for this item.

Association Rule Techniques for Recommendations

The association rule discovery technique represents another alternative to the association-based recommendation approach (Sarwar et al. 2000). It finds interesting cooccurrences of items in a set of transactions. Formally, the association-rule mining problem is defined as follows (Agrawal et al. 1993; Agrawal and Srikant 1994). Let $I\{i_1, i_2, \ldots, i_m\}$ be a set of items. Let D be a set of transactions, where each transaction T is a set of items such that $T \subseteq I$. In the recommendation context, each transaction corresponds to a user and contains a set of items that the user liked or purchased. An association rule is an implication of the form $X \Rightarrow Y$, where $X \subset I$, $Y \subset I$, and $X \cap Y = \emptyset$. The association rule $X \Rightarrow Y$ holds in D with confidence c if c percent of transactions in D that contain X also contain Y. The rule $X \Rightarrow Y$ has a support s in D if s percent of transactions in D contains $X \cup Y$. Given a set of transactions D, the problem of mining association rules is to generate all association rules that have support and confidence greater than the user-specified minimum *support* and minimum *confidence*. To efficiently find all association rules satisfying the user-specified minimum support and minimum confidence, the Apriori algorithm proposed by Agrawal and Srikant (1994) is often employed.

As mentioned, the association rule discovery technique concerns mainly the co-occurrence of items in a set of transactions. Thus, the user preferences need to be transformed into the described representation of transactions. If the user preference on an item is a binary measure, the transformation can be straightforward. An item i will be included in the transaction of a user a only if p_{ai} is 1. However, if the user preference is on a numerical scale, the decision of whether an item will be included in a user's transaction can be based on a prespecified threshold, a mean-based method, or other methods. For example, given a threshold α, an item i will be included in the transaction of a user a if $p_{ai} \geq \alpha$; otherwise, it will not be shown in the transaction. Likewise, in a mean-based method, an item i will be included in the transaction of a user a if $p_{ai} \geq \bar{p}_a$, where $\bar{p}_a$ is the average preference score of the user a. Other transformation methods can be developed to reflect the nature of user preferences and the target recommendation problem.

To recommend the top-N items to an active user based on the set of association rules discovered, we first find the association rules that are supported by the active user (i.e., association rules whose left-hand-side items appear entirely in the transaction of the active user). Let I_p be the set of unique items that are suggested by the right-hand side of the association rules selected and are not shown in the transaction of the active user. Afterward, those items in I_p are sorted based on the confidence of the selected association rules. If a particular item is recommended by multiple association rules, the highest confidence is used. Finally, the top-N items are chosen as the recommended set for the active user. Since association rules are discovered from a set of transactions, each of which contains what a user has liked or purchased previously, the association rule discovery technique is not suitable to recommend the top-M users for a newly available item because it will not be shown in any association rules found.

Summary

The association-based recommendation approach recommends items to users based on the correlations or associations between items. Since it takes the user preferences as its source input information, personalized recommendations can be achieved. Similar to the collaborative filtering recommendation approach, the association-based recommendation approach is capable of recommending items on quality and taste. Finally, because the correlations or associations between items are relatively static, item similarity or association rules can be precomputed to improve the online scalability of an association-based recommendation technique (Sarwar et al. 2001).

On the other hand, the association-based recommendation approach encounters problems similar to the collaborative filtering recommendation approach. When a large set of items is available, users may have rated or chosen a very low percentage of items, resulting in the sparsity problem. As a result, items rated or chosen by a limited number of users cannot be effectively recommended. Furthermore, as mentioned previously, the association-based recommendation approach is incapable of recommending the top-M users for a new item or including

Figure 9.4 **Process of Demographics-Based Recommendation Approach**

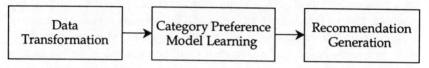

the new item in the top-N recommendation for a user. Finally, the synonymy problem (i.e., different items may be highly similar in their features) cannot be addressed in the association-based recommendation approach.

Demographics-Based Recommendation Approach

The demographics-based recommendation approach recommends items to a user based on the preferences of other users whose demographics are similar to those of the user. Unlike other approaches in which recommendations are made at the item level, a demographics-based recommendation system typically generates recommendations at the category level in order to deliver more generalized recommendations and to address sparsity and synonymy problems. Hence, this approach involves learning and reasoning with relationships between user demographics and expressed category preferences, where the expressed category preferences of a user are derived from individual user preferences stated previously and the category hierarchies of items. The demographics-based recommendation approach has been applied to deliver personalized advertisements on Internet storefronts (Kim et al. 2001).

Process of Demographics-Based Recommendation Approach

As shown in Figure 9.4, the process of a demographics-based recommendation system typically can be decomposed into the following phases:

1. *Data transformation:* Generate a set of training examples each of whose input attributes are the demographics of a user and decisions outcomes are category preferences of the user.
2. *Category preference model learning:* Automatically induce the preference model for each category based on the training examples pertaining to the category.
3. *Recommendation generation:* Given the demographic data of a user, generate recommendations by performing reasoning on the category preference models induced previously.

As mentioned, the data transformation phase generates a set of training examples for subsequent learning of the category preference model and generation of recommendations. Input attributes of a training example are the demographic descriptions of a user that potentially affect his/her category preferences. Given the demographic data of a user, the generation of input attribute values for a user is quite straightforward. However, if individual user preferences were expressed at the item level, the generation of a user's category preferences requires a transformation based on the category hierarchies of items. Several transformation methods have been proposed for deriving category preferences of users (Kim et al. 2001). We first assume that the user preferences are binary measures (e.g., like/dislike, purchased or not) where favorable preferences (e.g., like and purchased) are denoted as 1 while unfavorable preferences are denoted as 0. The described transformation methods can easily be modified for numerically scaled user preferences.

1. *Counting-based (frequency threshold) method:* This method uses the frequency of favorite preferences of a user on all items in a category to decide whether the user prefers the category or not. Let p_{ai} be the binary preference score of the user a on the item i, C_j be the category j, cp_{ai} be the derived binary preference score of the user a on the category j, and w be the prespecified frequency threshold. The counting-based method is as follows:

$$cp_{aj} = \begin{cases} 1 & \text{if } \sum_{i \in C_j} p_{ai} \geq w \\ 0 & \text{otherwise} \end{cases}$$

2. *Expected-value-based method:* This method takes into account the number of items in each category and determines whether a user prefers a category based on the expected value, as follows:

$$cp_{aj} = \begin{cases} 1 & \text{if } \sum_{i \in C_j} p_{ai} \geq \alpha \left(\sum_j \sum_{i \in C_j} p_{ai} \times \frac{N_j}{\sum_j N_j} \right) \\ 0 & \text{otherwise} \end{cases}$$

where α is a multiplier for the expected value and N_j is the number of items in the category j.

3. *Statistics-based method:* This method sets a threshold based on such statistical values as mean and median. For example,

$$cp_{aj} = \begin{cases} 1 & \text{if } \sum_{i \in C_j} p_{ai} \geq \alpha \left(\dfrac{\sum_j \sum_{i \in C_j} p_{ai}}{C} \right) \\ 0 & \text{otherwise} \end{cases}$$

where C is the number of categories.

For a main category, the category preference of a user can be derived from his/her preferences on its subcategories. For example, a user is considered to prefer a main category j if he/she prefers any subcategory of j or a certain percentage of the subcategories of j.

After the data transformation, each user corresponds to a training example with a binary preference decision on each category. Subsequently, the category preference model learning phase is initiated to induce a preference model for each category based on all the training examples pertaining to the category. As with the user profile learning phase in the content-based recommendation approach, a decision tree induction algorithm, a decision rule induction algorithm, or a back-propagation neural network can be employed for the target learning task. Accordingly, for each category in the category hierarchy, a classification model is constructed to capture the relationships between user demographics and preferences of the category. Once a set of category preference models is induced, recommendations can be generated for an active user. In this approach, all of the three types of recommendations are plausible since recommendations are generated using user demographics, the category to which a target item belongs, and the category preference models relevant to the target item. Given the demographic data of an active user and the category to which a target item belongs, the prediction on whether the active user will prefer the target item can be made by reasoning on the category preference models relevant to the target item. To produce the top-N recommendation for the active user, the preference prediction on each category is first obtained. Since inductive learning algorithms described above are capable of estimating prediction accuracy, the top-N items with the highest prediction accuracy are then included in the recommendation list. Finally, to recommend the top-M users for a new item, a set of prediction decisions can be made, one for each user, based on the category preference models associated with the target item's category and its supercategories. Subsequently, the top-M users who are predicted to like the new item most are selected.

Summary

The demographics-based recommendation approach recommends items to a user based on the preferences of other users whose demographics are similar to that of the user. Since it relies on individual user preferences and user demographics to arrive at recommendation decisions, personalized recommendations can be achieved. The demographics-based approach typically produces recommendations at the category level. Thus, the effect of the sparsity and synonymy problems on recommendation accuracy can be reduced. Finally, online scalability is improved with the demographics-based approach because the category preference models can be constructed offline and the resulting models are small in size and efficient in reasoning.

The demographics-based approach may encounter the following limitations. Although coarser granularity in recommendations has the advantage in addressing the sparsity and synonymy problems, a user may not like all the items within a category suggested by this approach. Conversely, a disrecommendation of a category does not necessarily mean that the user does not like all the items in the category. In other words, though the demographics-based approach may be able to achieve high-quality recommendations at the category level, its recommendation accuracy may suffer at the item level. Moreover, potential applications of the demographics-based approach may represent another source of limitation. User demographics cannot be assumed to be available, complete, and reliable. In many application domains, the acquisition and update of user demographics raises serious privacy issues and can be extremely difficult, if not impossible.

Conclusions

In an electronic commerce environment, recommendation systems have emerged not only to address the challenge of information overload for consumers of information or products, but also to facilitate the delivery of e-Services to customers. This chapter surveyed the major recommendation approaches and the techniques associated with their implementation. However, the techniques covered in this chapter are by no means exhaustive. For example, collaborative filtering recommendation systems using Bayesian networks, neural networks, and inductive learning algorithms were not covered. Various hybrid recommendation techniques that seek to seamlessly integrate different recommendation approaches are not reviewed in detail. As users demand higher-quality recommendations and as e-commerce expands its coverage into a wireless environment (the so-called mobile commerce or m-commerce), recommendation approaches will continue to evolve and new techniques will be devised, incorporating an ever richer set of data sources, such as precise real-time geographic location.

As with decision support tools, recommendation systems should be integrated with existing Web-based electronic commerce systems in which information users or online customers consume information or search-and-purchase products. In addition, a recommendation system may have strong implications for redesigning and personalizing e-commerce Web sites. As recommendation systems continue to evolve, frequent modifications of existing electronic commerce systems can be anticipated. Thus, component-based software development may represent a promising approach in achieving increased interoperability and reusability of electronic commerce systems.

A closer examination of successful e-commerce businesses suggests the appropriateness and importance of adopting multiple recommendation systems to support recommendation services to their customers. No single recommendation system can satisfy customers differing in their recommendation requirements, quality- or coverage-wise. From a practical viewpoint, it is desirable to investigate the effect of customer characteristics on the effectiveness of recommendation approaches. Furthermore, recommendation approaches may demonstrate varying degrees of effectiveness in supporting diverse commercial activities, such as advertising, marketing, or price discovery (e.g., through auctions). Empirical evaluations along this line of investigation represent an essential and interesting research direction with great practical implications.

Notes

The authors are grateful for the support from National Science Council, Taiwan, R.O.C., Beckman Institute for Advanced Science and Technology, Center for International Education and Research in Accounting at the University of Illinois at Urbana-Champaign, and Mendoza College of Business at the University of Notre Dame.

1. In many studies, preference scores are often referred to as ratings. However, in this chapter, we prefer preference scores to ratings since the former covers both explicit ratings and implicit ratings, while the latter typically implies subjective ratings (i.e., explicit ratings).

References

Agrawal, R.; T. Imielinski; and A. Swami. 1993. "Mining Association Rules Between Sets of Items in Large Databases." *Proceedings of the ACM SIGMOD International Conference on Management of Data*, Washington, DC, 207–216.

Agrawal, R., and R. Srikant. 1994. "Fast Algorithms for Mining Association Rules." *Proceedings of the Twentieth International Conference on Very Large Data Bases*, Santiago, Chile, 487–499.

Alspector, J.; A. Kolcz; and N. Karunanithi. 1998. "Comparing Feature-Based and

Clique-Based User Models for Movie Selection." *Proceedings of the Third ACM Conference on Digital Libraries*, Pittsburgh, PA, 11–18.

Ansari, A.; S. Essegaier; and R. Kohli. 2000. "Internet Recommendation Systems." *Journal of Marketing Research* 37 (August): 363–375.

Balabanovic, M., and Y. Shoham. 1997. "Fab: Content-Based, Collaborative Recommendation." *Communications of the ACM* 40(3): 66–72.

Basu, C.; H. Hirsh; and W. Cohen. 1998. "Recommendation as Classification: Using Social and Content-Based Information in Recommendation." *Proceedings of the Workshop on Recommender Systems*, AAAI Press, 11–15.

Billsus, D., and M.J. Pazzani. 1998. "Learning Collaborative Information Filters." *Proceedings of the Workshop on Recommender Systems*, AAAI Press.

Breese, J.S.; D. Heckerman; and C. Kadie. 1998. "Empirical Analysis of Predictive Algorithms for Collaborative Filtering." *Proceedings of the Fourteenth Conference on Uncertainty in Artificial Intelligence (UAI-98)*, San Francisco, CA, 43–52.

Breiman, L.; J. Friedman; R. Olshen; and C. Stone. 1984. *Classification and Regression Trees*. Pacific Grove, CA: Wadsworth.

Clark, P., and T. Niblett. 1989. "The CN2 Induction Algorithm." *Machine Learning* 3(4): 261–283.

Claypool, M.; P. Le; M. Wased; and D. Brown. 2001. "Implicit Interest Indicators." *Proceedings of the International Conference on Intelligent User Interfaces*, Santa Fe, NM, 33–40.

Condliff, M.K.; D.D. Lewis; D. Madigan; and C. Posse. 1999. "Bayesian Mixed-Effects Models for Recommender Systems." *Proceedings of Workshop on Recommender Systems: Algorithms and Evaluation*, Berkeley, CA.

Dumais, S.; J. Platt; D. Heckerman; and M. Sahami. 1998. "Inductive Learning Algorithms and Representations for Text Categorization." *Proceedings of the ACM Seventh International Conference on Information and Knowledge Management (CIKM '98)*, Washington, DC, 148–155.

Herlocker, J.L.; J.A. Konstan; A. Borchers; and J. Riedl. 1999. "An Algorithmic Framework for Performing Collaborative Filtering." *Proceedings of the Twenty-Second Annual International ACM SIGIR Conference on Research and Development in Information Retrieval*, Berkeley, CA, 230–237.

Hill, W.; L. Stead; M. Rosenstein; and G. Furnas. 1995. "Recommending and Evaluating Choices in a Virtual Community of Use." *Proceedings of the Conference on Human Factors in Computing Systems*, 194–201.

Kass, G.V. 1980. "An Exploratory Technique for Investigating Large Quantities of Categorical Data." *Applied Statistics* 29: 119–127.

Kim, J.W.; B.H. Lee; M.J. Shaw; H.L. Chang; and M. Nelson. 2001. "Application of Decision-Tree Induction Techniques to Personalized Advertisements on Internet Storefronts." *International Journal of Electronic Commerce* 5(3): 45–62.

Kittler, J. 1975. "Mathematical Methods of Feature Selection in Pattern Recognition." *International Journal of Man-Machine Studies* 7: 609–637.

Konstan, J.A.; B.N. Miller; D. Maltz; J.L. Herlocker; L.R. Gordon; and J. Riedl. 1997. "GroupLens: Applying Collaborative Filtering to Usenet News." *Communications of the ACM* 40(3): 77–87.

Krulwich, B., and C. Burkey. 1996. "Learning User Information Interests through Extraction of Semantically Significant Phrases." *Proceedings of the AAAI Spring Symposium on Machine Learning in Information Access*, Stanford, CA.

Lam, W., and C.Y. Ho. 1998. "Using a Generalized Instance Set for Automatic Text Categorization." *Proceedings of the Twenty-First Annual International ACM SIGIR Conference on Research and Development in Information Retrieval*, Melbourne, Australia, 81–89.

Lang, K. 1995. "NewsWeeder: Learning to Filter Netnews." *Proceedings of the Twelfth International Conference on Machine Learning*, San Francisco, CA, 331–339.

Lewis, D., and M. Ringuette. 1994. "A Comparison of Two Learning Algorithms for Text Categorization." *Proceedings of Symposium on Document Analysis and Information Retrieval.*

Lynch, C. 2001. "Personalization and Recommender Systems in the Larger Context: New Directions and Research Questions." *Proceedings of the Second DELOS Network of Excellence Workshop on Personalization and Recommender Systems in Digital Libraries*, Dublin, Ireland.

Modrzejewski, M. 1993. "Feature Selection Using Rough Sets Theory." *Proceedings of European Conference on Machine Learning*, 213–226.

Mooney, R.J., and L. Roy. 2000. "Content-Based Book Recommending Using Learning for Text Categorization." *Proceedings of the Fifth ACM Conference on Digital Libraries*, San Antonio, TX, 195–204.

Ng, H.T.; W.B. Goh; and K.L. Low. 1997. "Feature Selection, Perceptron Learning, and a Usability Case Study for Text Categorization." *Proceedings of Annual International ACM SIGIR Conference on Research and Development in Information Retrieval (SIGIR '97)*, Philadelphia, PA, 67–73.

Pazzani, M.; J. Muramatsu; and D. Billsus. 1996. "Syskill & Webert: Identifying Interesting Web Sites." *Proceedings of the Thirteenth National Conference on Artificial Intelligence*, Portland, OR, 54–61.

Piramuthu, S. 1998. "Evaluating Feature Selection Methods for Learning in Data Mining Applications." *Proceedings of the Thirty-First Annual Hawaii International Conference on System Sciences*, Kohala Coast, HI.

Quinlan, J.R. 1986. "Induction of Decision Trees." *Machine Learning* 1(1): 81–106.

———. 1993. *C4.5: Programs for Machine Learning*. San Mateo, CA: Morgan Kaufmann.

Resnick, P.; N. Iacovou; M. Suchak; P. Bergstrom; and J. Riedl. 1994. "GroupLens: An Open Architecture for Collaborative Filtering of Netnews." *Proceedings of the Conference on Computer Supported Cooperative Work (CSCW)*, Chapel Hill, NC, 175–186.

Rucker, J., and M.J. Polanco. 1997. "Siteseer: Personalized Navigation for the Web." *Communications of the ACM* 40(3): 73–76.

Rumelhart, D.E.; G.E. Hinton; and R.J. Williams. 1986. "Learning Internal Representations by Error Propagation." In *Parallel Distributed Processing: Explorations in the Microstructures of Cognition*, vol. 1, ed. D.E. Rumelhart and J.L. McClelland. Cambridge: MIT Press, 318–362.

Sarwar, B.M.; G. Karypis; J.A. Konstan; and J. Riedl. 2000. "Analysis of Recommendation Algorithms for E-Commerce." *Proceedings of Second ACM Conference on Electronic Commerce*, Minneapolis, MN, 158–167.

Sarwar, B.; G. Karypis; J. Konstan; and J. Riedl. 2001. "Item-Based Collaborative Filtering Recommendation Algorithms." *Proceedings of the Tenth International Conference on World Wide Web*, Hong Kong, 285–295.

Sarwar, B.; J. Konstan; A. Borchers; J. Herlocker; B. Miller; and J. Riedl. 1998. "Using Filtering Agents to Improve Prediction Quality in the GroupLens Research

Collaborative Filtering System." *Proceedings of the ACM Conference on Computer Supported Cooperative Work (CSCW)*, Seattle, WA, 345–355.

Schafer, J.B.; J.A. Konstan; and J. Riedl. 1999. "Recommender Systems in E-Commerce." *Proceedings of the First ACM Conference on Electronic Commerce*, Denver, CO, 158–166.

———. 2001. "E-Commerce Recommendation Applications." *Data Mining and Knowledge Discovery* 5(1): 115–153.

Siedlecki, W., and J. Sklansky. 1989. "A Note on Genetic Algorithms for Large-Scale Feature Selection." *Pattern Recognition Letters* 10(5): 335–347.

Shardanand, U., and P. Maes. 1995. "Social Information Filtering: Algorithms for Automating 'Word of Mouth,' " *Proceedings of Conference on Human Factors in Computing Systems*, 210–217.

Yang, Y., and C.G. Chute. 1994. "An Example-Based Mapping Method for Text Categorization and Retrieval." *ACM Transactions on Information Systems* 12(3): 252–277.

Zacharia, G.; A. Moukas; and P. Maes. 2000. "Collaborative Reputation Mechanisms for Electronic Marketplaces." *Decision Support Systems* 29(4): 371–388.

10

The Wireless Rules for e-Service

Critical Issues for Managers and Researchers

Katherine N. Lemon, Frederick B. Newell, and Loren J. Lemon

The Wireless Rules for e-Service: Critical Issues for Managers and Researchers

• Andy Gordon's Blackberry RIM device alerts him to a new e-mail from Kelli Christiansen, the project manager at his largest client. The server's gone down again. How soon can it be fixed?

• Christine Kahn uses her HP Jornada PocketPC to check in with her office one last time before the plane takes off for vacation. She finds that a key presentation document failed to arrive at the client's office as promised. With a few clicks of the stylus or keyboard, she has corrected the error.

• Barak Libai has just arrived in the United States for a week-long conference. Unfortunately, his luggage is lost somewhere between Tel Aviv and New York. Using his Palm VII device, he finds the closest clothing retailer, picks out a suit and a business casual assortment, and arranges for them to arrive at his hotel when he does.

What do these examples have to do with e-Service? Why is it important to understand the mobile customer and the mobile workforce as we seek to understand and manage e-Service? Consider the changing nature of work and communications. Over 30 percent of the U.S. workforce (or 35.7 million people) are out of the office traveling at any given time. By 2003, that number will increase to 39.5 percent. (*doubleclick.net* 2001). These numbers suggest that soon the number of workers with significant mobility in their jobs will outnumber those who sit at a desk. How real is this possibility? Accenture Norway, a management consulting firm, has transformed 80 percent of its employees into mobile workers (people working from anywhere with a laptop and a mobile phone). The move has allowed the company to drastically cut spending on computers, fixed telephone lines, and other office equipment. If workers need to go to the office, they book a space. All workers get a laptop and have their mobile phone bill paid by the company. This arrangement allows the mobile workers to set up an office virtually anywhere. Even the offices use mobile phones. Executives say the money they save on desk places can be spent on new IT equipment and training for their consultants (Johnsen 2000).

Combine the shift to mobile employment with the explosion of wireless devices on the planet. Experts estimate that there are over half a billion wireless devices in use by customers throughout the world. In the United States alone, over 200 million wireless devices will be in use by the end of 2001. By 2003, 219 million people in Europe, one-third of the population, will be surfing the Internet from their cell phones and an amazing array of wireless devices. By that year more than 60 percent of the populations of Britain, France, Germany, Italy, and Sweden will have cell phones. The number of cell phones in Britain alone nearly doubled to 24 million in 1999, and 66 percent of the population had gone wireless by the end of 2000 ("Phone Market" 2001). It is expected that by 2006 there will be more wireless data users in Japan than people because pets and cars will have subscriptions as well (Lightman 2000).

How widespread is this phenomenon? By 2010, experts expect that 40 percent of adults and 75 percent of teenagers in the developed world will have "always on" wearable wireless devices (Flisi 2000). The world's largest cell phone maker, Nokia Corp., estimates a billion users by 2002. According to International Data Corp., this number will reach 1.6 billion subscribers by 2005. The Boston-based Yankee Group estimates Web-enabled mobile devices generating as much as 63 percent of transactions on the Internet by 2003. Wireless Internet subscribers—users of Web-enabled cell phones, personal digital assistants (PDAs), and other devices—are expected to outnumber the wired by the end of 2002.

What does this mean for e-Service? Customers both business to business (B2B) and business to consumer (B2C), will expect firms to be able to interact with them and to provide service for and to them anywhere, anytime, and on any device. In this chapter, we will explore the effects of these major changes on e-Service. In particular, we will (1) help you understand the true value of wireless customer dialog and how it relates to e-Service, (2) highlight critical issues in wireless e-Service and the customer–firm relationship, and (3) uncover the critical challenges of wireless e-Service.

What Is Wireless e-Service and Why Do Firms Need to Worry About It?

As we will discuss below, these changes are affecting customer expectations and, therefore, the service solutions that firms must provide to survive and to retain critical customers. Specifically, in our research for our recent book on the effects of wireless on marketing and customer relationship management (Newell and Lemon 2001), we determined that firms will need to provide technological, marketing, and service solutions that:

- always recognize customers and serve customers the way they want to be served;
- enable customers to conduct transactions and interact with the firm anytime, anywhere—securely;
- maximize convenience and value in every interaction, across every channel;
- offer proactive relationship management ("your payment is due" or "you're close to your credit limit" or "your favorite wine just arrived");
- are always "on";
- encourage real dialog—a virtual "face-to-face" relationship.

To understand the breadth of opportunity and possibility that wireless technologies provide, let us take a look at a few pioneers.

To be sure they are serving customers the way the customers want to be served, Finland's largest bank, MeritaNordbanken, makes it possible for its e-banking customers to access their accounts via: automatic teller machines (ATMs), telephone, global system for mobile communication (GSM), personal computer (PC), Internet TV, and soon, wireless application protocol (WAP) phones, making its access mix one of the richest in the world. It offers basic banking, stock trading, investment fund transactions, purchase and sale of bonds, account opening, credit card ordering, credit card transactions viewing, general bill balances via GSM mobile, and loan authorization guaranteed within one hour—without any paperwork being signed. It has established open pages geared to building up life-event combinations to avoid offering straight deposits, loans, and payment products. It approaches CRM from a person's life events: going abroad, retirement, or the need to move. Merita has 600,000 Finnish e-banking customers—500,000 of which use the service on a monthly basis (representing 42 percent of its retail customer base in Finland). The take-up rate is about 15,000 customers per month;

current monthly log-on is 2 million per month (4 log-ons per active customer); 26 percent of all bill payment (1.5 million per month) takes place via the Internet (Engen 2000).

Chase Manhattan Bank announced that in early 2001 it would be able to offer its wholesale and retail customers the ability to conduct financial transactions anytime, anywhere, quickly and securely over a wireless device. Chase customers will be able to transfer data to and from any Web-enabled cellular phone or laptop computer or PDA using any wireless carrier. Using Tantau Software Inc.'s Wireless Internet Platform, Chase will be able to maintain a direct link with its customers versus an environment in which all transactions must go through a service provider's proprietary portal. This "ownership" of the transaction provides Chase with many additional benefits, including an uninterrupted relationship with its customers, a secure transaction environment, the ability to develop personalized user services, and ultimately the establishment of a stronger foundation for customer loyalty. In announcing the development, Dennis O'Leary, head of Chase.com, said, "Our customers deserve the best banking services available, and in today's mobile world, that includes the ability to bank from anywhere you happen to be" ("Tantau Bags" 2000).

With wireless, customers' communications options are fundamentally changing, and businesses that fail to capture this new moment will fail in the marketplace. We must all find new ways to move from the traditional company-centric tell-and-sell efforts to customer-centric listen-and-learn techniques in the have-it-right-now, have-it-right-here culture of wireless communication. As we begin to examine the critical issues in wireless e-Service, it is important to add a dose of reality to our discussion. Consider the sage advice of Kevin Clark, program director of brand management and strategy for IBM Mobile Computing:

> So what is the current role of wireless technology in marketing strategy? Unless you are part of the wireless industry, not much. In a few short years, however, wireless marketing practices will be entwined in the fabric of every part of the customer experience—from awareness, consideration, purchase, ownership, upgrade, service and support. Privacy and security will also be part of the conversation going forward because these practices will give customers the confidence to participate and use these new practices. (Clark 2001)

As firms make the shift from "not much" to "entwined in the fabric of the customer experience," they need to be able to answer the following questions:

- How can we initiate active discussion and innovation to prepare our firm for these challenges?

- How can we gain an understanding of how and why wireless changes the basic relationship between our company and our customers?
- How will the flow of products, service, and information have to change in our company?
- How can we build and leverage networks in the wireless world?
- How will m-commerce affect our offline and wired online service strategies?
- What will we have to be good at tomorrow, or next year, in order to stay relevant to wireless customers in ways that will affect our profit?

Finding and delivering on the answers to these questions will require significant changes and adaptations to traditional models of service. In the next section, we will examine the specific value that wireless technologies bring to the customer experience, and the role of e-Service in maximizing this value.

Understanding the Value of Wireless Solutions: A Framework

As we have studied the mobile revolution, we have come to understand that there are three primary avenues through which wireless or mobile devices add value to the customer–firm relationship. Mobile devices strengthen the customers (and the firm's) abilities in three areas: (1) accessibility, (2) alerting and averting, and (3) updating. Each of these can be thought of as an ability or competency that the firm and customer cocreate, thereby adding value to the customer experience and customer–firm relationship (see Figure 10.1). Let us examine each of these critical abilities in more depth.

Accessibility

Accessibility is defined as the *ability to reach the person (or information) you need, when you need it.* It is important to understand that accessibility is a two-way ability: to the extent that the firm enables the customer to reach the person or information the customer needs when the customer needs it, the firm can add value to the relationship. Similarly, the extent to which the firm is enabled (by technology and by the customer) to reach the customer (or the customer's information) when the firm needs it to provide maximum value to the customer, the firm can grow the value of the relationship (Rust et al. 2000; Zeithaml 1988, 2000).

New forms of access from the firm to the customer, from the customer to the firm, have begun to turn traditional notions of marketing and service on their heads. Customers now choose where and when to contact the firm;

Figure 10.1 **Understanding the Value of Wireless**

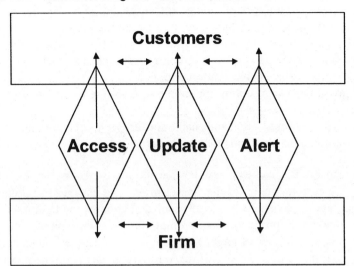

where, when, and how to do business with the firm; which channels to use—
it is almost as though the customer is now determining the marketing tactics
of the firm (Bowman and Narayandas 2001). And access—through wireless,
through the Web, through traditional call-centers and face-to-face interactions—is the key to this upside-down value-chain revolution. Through advances in accessibility—the two-way wireless interactions between the
consumer and the firm—customers can now:

- signal their interest in a product or service (in other words, that they are
  "open for bids");
- engage in self-service activities that give them a greater level of perceived control over the exchange than ever before—to track purchases,
  return, check status, FedEx, UPS, Amazon.com (Bettencourt 1997;
  Meuter et al. 2000; Moon and Frei 2000);
- engage in exchange transactions that require no human interaction throughout the entire decision-making process (as discussed in Moon 1999, 2000);
- search and find new possible solutions to any problem they face;
- renew (or end) subscriptions or service relationships;
- engage in new online communities to find a market for stuff or services
  the customer wants to market himself or herself (McWilliam 2000);
- offer or receive opinions or advice on potential purchases;
- get questions answered (by real live people, agents, or "bots") about
  purchasing, servicing, recalls, and so on (Hauble and Trifts 2000);

- save time buying, finding, returning, fixing, reordering;
- engage in new types of dialog with firms that provide unprecedented knowledge of the customer by the firm and unprecedented input into the firm's business practices by the customer (Oliver et al. 1998);
- gain new benefits without sacrificing traditional approaches;
- set price (or reveal reservation price);
- choose desired reception (distribution, from the firm's point of view) channel;
- initiate communication and enable specific forms of communication to/ from/with the firm and other customers.

These capabilities lead to a new look at the old marketing world—one in which the customer chooses the "target firms" and engages in "situational, psychographic, or benefits segmentation" and chooses the traditional "four Ps" of marketing (product, price, promotion, and place). Intelligent agents reduce the possibilities of target firms under the consumer's consideration. Regarding the traditional "Cs" of marketing (customer, company, competitors, and collaborators), the customer knows his or her needs, wants, preferences, and interests—the company's role is to solve the customer's problem, competition is now from the customer's point of view, and the collaborators serve to fit the company's solution to the customers' situational set of "what they want, how they want it, and when they want it."

Let us take a look at some specific examples of how wireless devices enable customer access in new ways. Rovenet now offers a free bathroom finder on Palm Inc.'s Palm.net wireless portal and the YadaYada.com wireless portal service. Where2Go 1.0 provides bathroom information in San Francisco and eleven other cities, including New York, Philadelphia, Miami, and Washington, DC. Rovenet's service provides locations for four-star commodes as well as one-star stalls ("Rovenet Unveils" 2000).

In business-to-business markets, consider the access available to Memorex Telex staff around the world. Memorex Telex salespeople are the first employees worldwide using WAP technology to access and update their customer management system. Using Digifone online services, the folks at Memorex can access and update their customer database from wherever they happen to be. The benefits are tangible. According to Paschal Naylor, managing director of Memorex Telex, "sales teams are not only instantly available, but they can dial in for up-to-the-second customer histories, pricing, deal information—anything that they previously had to be in the office to access. We are looking forward to speeding the sales cycle as our team can concentrate on selling rather than on administrative duties" ("Memorex Telex" 2000). That is great for the Memorex Telex sales staff, but a giant responsibility for the folks who have to make it work. Understanding the IT challenges will be critical as we move forward with these technologies (Cooper and Zmud 1990; Kannan and Rao 2001).

Ericsson has partnered with ICA Ahold, the Swedish retail chain, to experiment with what the companies believe is the world's first retail Bluetooth-enabled mobile phone service. Using their WAP mobile phones, users can move around the store, checking their account balance, paying for goods, and be notified of the latest offers in the store. Jurgen Wennberg, ICA Ahold vice president says:

> You can have customers walking around the deli, who can be notified (on their WAP-equipped mobile phones) of the latest offers of the day and as customers move into another section of the store, the messages can be changed as required. We can also spot our gold card customers when they enter the store, or a section of the store, and send them quite specific messages, such as special offers for them. The possibilities are endless. ("Ericsson" 2000)

When customers are ready to make a purchase, they go to the check out with their products and tell the operator they want to pay with their store account using their mobile. The clerk hits a button and the transaction is carried out using the shopper's mobile phone. Details of the purchases are then relayed to the user's mobile using Bluetooth personal area network (PAN) technology and, if the shopper agrees, he or she inputs a PIN code to the mobile phone, and the transaction is complete. This has significant implications for loyalty and retention programs (e.g., Bolton et al. 2000; Dowling and Uncles 1997; Sharp and Sharp 1997).

Alerting and Averting

Alerting/averting is defined as the *ability to provide the right information or the right interaction at just the right time.* One of the great advantages of wireless technologies is that employees (or customers) can be alerted "just in time" either to avoid some negative outcome or to take advantage of some potential positive outcome. The extent to which a firm enables the ability to send alerts (or averts) to customers or mobile workforces, the greater the value the firm will be able to extract from wireless technologies.

Why are alerts or averts important? In today's overfilled world in which customers and employees are often starved for time, or, more importantly, starved for RAM (random-access memory), reminders and alerts can mean the difference between a great customer experience and an irrecoverable service failure. Inconsistency in service and poor service can have significant negative implications for the firm (Boulding et al. 1993; Boulding et al.1999; Elliott et al. 2000; Hansen and Danaher 1999). Firms can utilize the power of wireless to:

- allow a sales rep to avert a potential "blow-up" situation on a call he or she is about to make on a critical client;
- alert a customer that one of his or her favorite items is now in stock and available;
- alert a customer or employee that it is time to take a certain action (take a pill, get on the plane, visit a client).

Consider the following examples. Customers can delegate simple reminders to their mobile phones or PDAs. With a process called short messaging service (SMS)—often shortened to "messaging" or referred to as "wireless alerts"—customers can set up their wireless devices to remind them to call mother at dinner time or send a message every four hours that says, "Take your pill now." Or, consider the following put forth by Daren Tsui, CEO at SkyGo, a leader in wireless interactive marketing:

> Say you're a collector of fine wines, and you could be notified that the private reserve cabernet you've been lusting after has just been released, and only 10 bottles will be available for sale to the general public. Would you pick up all 10 bottles if you just had to click on the "buy" button on your cell phone? Probably. ("Ericsson" 2000)

Several online booking services, such as Galileo.com, TheTrip.com, and Travelocity.com, and some airlines are now using messaging to notify travelers of their flight status, gate assignment information, upgrade confirmations, and even weather conditions in the destination city. The nice thing about this is that these can be discreet messages that will not interrupt your business meeting with a voice phone call.

Soon wireless alerts will be fully location sensitive. If you want the local weather every day at 8:00 A.M., the service will know if you are in San Diego or Boston and send the appropriate forecast. Even more valuable to some customers is a specific allergy-alert service in California. By sending alerts to their customers' pagers and cell phones, these companies help people avoid pollen and smog. Several companies now forward air-quality information for Los Angeles, Orange, Riverside, and San Bernardino counties to wireless subscribers. "This is much easier than having to go search the Web or check the newspapers every day for this information," said one subscriber.

"Even though this is important to me, I don't always have time to do that. This makes my life simpler" (Drouin 2000). Subscribers get five calls a day from the server, four in the morning, one in the afternoon, and a special beep is added if the air-quality index goes over 100 and a smog alert is issued. Morning messages include an air pollution forecast for the next day, one weather report, one pollution advisory, and an ultraviolet notice. A second weather forecast is issued each afternoon.

Updating

Updating is defined as the *ability to create and maintain up-to-date, real-time information sources*. Many back-end systems (SAP, CRM, ERP, and so on) require the field force to update information from customers and from customer–firm interactions on an ongoing basis and in a timely manner. Similarly, in many B2B environments and B2C e-environments, customers are asked to update information or requirements over time as well. Firms that find innovative ways to utilize wireless technologies to ease the burden of the updating process will add significant value to the firm and to the customer–firm relationship.

Wireless solutions (and their anytime, anywhere communication capabilities) may solve another longstanding sales force automation and service problem. One of the main reasons some service initiatives fail is that the users of the applications—in the B2B case, the field sales force—do not input the relevant customer data they acquire. As a result, the call center and other in-house service functions never get access to some of the most important customer knowledge needed to manage the customer relationship in anything resembling real time. Now, this information can enter the system wirelessly for immediate enterprisewide access at the point of customer contact. These new approaches can enable the firm to overcome adoption resistance to these new innovations (Ram 1989; Ram and Sheth 1989; Sheth 1981).

Direct Line Group, the leading insurer in the United Kingdom and a wholly owned subsidiary of the Royal Bank of Scotland, has a reputation for strong client relationships, offering various insurance policies and financial services like mortgages and personal loans. Their stated goal is to give customers fast, flexible service, letting customers buy products the way they want—via Internet, telephone, on-site. In the future the system will include access by interactive TV and Web-enabled phone. The important thing about Direct Line's CRM process is that it has made it possible for every agent to know all of a customer's transactions regardless of how the client does the transaction. In August 2000, Direct Line introduced RealTime Loans, personal loans approved immediately. By 2003, one loan every minute will be awarded through the Internet. By giving the agents full knowledge of each customer's interaction with the bank, the agents are able to make the most effective use of relevant data. When a client applies for a mortgage online, the application form contains all the necessary information for Direct Line's credit cards. This enables the agent to say, "You've also given me all the information needed to offer you our credit card. Since you have already qualified, may I send it to you?"

Ian Gray, director of systems and operations at Direct Line Financial Services, says:

> We are moving into our next phase of customer relationship management and as a direct to the consumer company, we want to offer all direct channels as they become viable options for customers. Our strategy is to initially offer more transactional services over the Web. The human touch is vital to our customers. Ultimately we will be able to deliver the full range of sales and customer service channels including interactive TV and WAP enabled mobile devices. ("Leading Insurer" 2000)

Health care is also jumping onto the wireless bandwagon with both feet. A great new service from epocrates.com offers a downloadable version of the Physician's Desk Reference, right onto your PDA. Think about what this means for the physician-patient relationship. The doctor can check, in real time anywhere, for possible drug interactions, or new pharmacological treatments that have recently been approved, while he or she is sitting with the patient in the hospital or exam room—up-to-the-minute medical technologies, now available at the point of patient-physician contact.

Wireless applications are transforming the world of real estate as well. You will not see real estate agents carrying that big, bulky (and probably outdated) Multiple Listing Service (MLS) book around in the backseat of their cars anymore. Nope. The MLS is now downloadable to a PalmVx PDA. Just place the Palm in its cradle, HotSync it, and the latest listings are automatically available, right in the "palm" of your hand. Think about it. With a wireless interface, an agent could "beam" a listing from her PDA to her customers' PDA or cell phone, where the customers could then easily make additional notes about a house they liked.

But the transformation of real estate does not stop there. Lockbox technologies have gone wireless too. Each day, the agent downloads the special electronic "key code" for each house the agent wants to show. At the end of the day, when the Palm "synchs," the codes for the houses that were visited are transmitted to the listing agent. Now the listing agent has a record of how often the house was shown—and to whom! Understanding who is looking at what listings provides valuable insight into marketing these high-ticket, high-involvement "products," not to mention a much needed element of security and control as well.

Prioritizing the Opportunities in Wireless

As noted above, the three abilities—accessibility, updating, and alerting/averting—are at least bidirectional. For example: firm => customer and customer => firm. In addition (as can be seen in Table 10.1), it may also be that the critical value of wireless may also accrue from intrafirm (firm => firm) or intracustomer (customer => customer or peer-to-peer) interactions. Research suggests that the early successes in implementing wireless solutions (and reaping significant value from such solutions) will be primarily in the intrafirm accessibility, updating, and alerting/averting quadrants. Why? First of all, these aspects of the customer–firm relationship tend to be transparent to the customer so that when systems fail (and they will), the failure is not readily noticable by the customer and may not be attributed to the firm (Folkes 1984). Second of all, the firm can exercise greater control of device integrity and can minimize device multiplicity, thereby increasing the effectiveness of the devices while at the same time reducing the overall costs to implement and maintain. Finally, it is in these critical communication areas within the firm that there is still a significant amount of inefficiency or "slack," and we believe that a firm can easily achieve a significant return on investment from minimizing communication inefficiencies.

In addition to the more transparent, firm-to-firm wireless solutions, successful firm-to-consumer solutions are also beginning to emerge. Specifically, we are seeing firms succeed in providing new forms of access to customers that actually result in increased revenue (and profit) for the firm. Consider the way Fidelity Investments has transformed the customer's experience. In 1998, Fidelity asked its brokerage customers (who were making five or more stock trades a year) the following question: "Was there a situation over the past year where if you had access to stock market information, you would have reacted with a trade?" (Courtmanche 2000). According to Fidelity spokesperson Jim Griffin, 40 percent responded affirmatively. Fidelity responded quickly, first with pager technology and soon with wireless interactive trading capability on a variety of platforms. Now, the firm offers wireless connections via: RIM Interactive 950 pagers (and Bell South), Palm VII PDAs (with the Fidelity software actually manufactured into the ROM of the Palm), Palm V (with OmniSky), and Verizon and Sprint mobile phones. Almost 30 percent of Fidelity's InstantBroker service are new Fidelity customers. (Courtmanche 2000) Fidelity investments created new avenues of

Table 10.1

Opportunities for Creating Value with Wireless Strategies

Factor	Customer-to firm	Firm-to customer	Intra firm	Customer-to customer
Accessibility	High potential		High potential	
Updating			High potential	
Alert/Avert			High potential	

accessibility for its customers in such a way that it both increased revenues from its existing customers and acquired new customers.

New technologies are on the way that will make the Fidelity example seem simplistic and ordinary. In the 2000 holiday season, the first electronic shopping street was created in the small town of Luleå, Norbotten, in Sweden. Called eStreet, it is a real-life laboratory that allows customers and firms to experiment with mobile technologies in an urban, retail setting. "With eStreet, we're stepping right from the lab onto the street. This gives us a unique test bed for mobile Internet and mobile services," said eStreet project manager Bo-Göran Stenman ("World-Unique" 2000). Residents of Luleå can volunteer to participate in the test pilot laboratory, and as of the end of December, 1,400 of Luleå's 75,000 residents have opted in ("Electronic Shopping" 2000). These customers will receive personalized information from up to a dozen firms participating in the project, based upon information they have asked to receive. For example, "the local pharmacy can send a message to inform a customer that a prescription is ready. Clothing shops can send out sale offers. The cinema can notify movie-goers of the number of seats available for the next showing. Commuters can find out when the next bus is leaving, etc." ("Christmas Shoppers" 2000).

The most exciting element of eStreet is the research laboratory approach. One of the project's key objectives is to serve as a test environment that can be used by companies and research organizations from all over the world to determine how to maximize the benefits of mobile applications—how to maximize the value of accessibility, alerting and averting, and updating. This real-life laboratory suggests the exciting opportunities for marketing research that wireless brings to firms. One can easily imagine using wireless to set up omnibus panels, and Harris Online Research is currently working on this application.

The advent of Global Positioning System and other location-based technologies will bring even more interesting possibilities for marketers and for e-Service. These technologies will make it possible to send location-based advertising to consumers on their wireless devices. Although we believe that consumer-based location marketing will arrive eventually, we believe that it will be adopted more slowly than many other wireless applications. However, it will be imperative to understand the extent to which consumers will accept such intrusions on their wireless devices.

Critical Issues and Challenges in Wireless e-Service and the Customer–Firm Relationship

Wireless e-Service is more than a function. It is an approach that must pervade the entire organization's relationships with customers. In Figure 10.3, we have outlined the overall framework for thinking about wireless e-Service and the customer–firm relationship. As you think about the firm's relationship with the customer over time (the long arrow), you can think of specific stages within that relationship: the customer acquisition process, the customer permission process, customer interactions over time (following acquisition), and the customer retention process (if it becomes necessary). The firm's customer information system (in blue) cuts across all these customer relationship stages. Similarly, the traditional customer service function covers all these stages (with less emphasis prior to customer acquisition) and relies heavily on the customer information system (see Figure 10.2). Let us take a look at each of these elements in turn.

Wireless e-Service and the Customer Relationship over Time

As the firm seeks to actively manage its relationships with customers, from acquisition through permissions, interactions, and, ultimately, retention efforts, it is important to understand the role of wireless e-Service. In the customer acquisition phase, access will be most critical. Customers must be able to locate the firm and be able to access the information they need to determine if the firm is a potential fit with their needs. In the permission phase of the relationship, firms must find ways to encourage the customer to "opt in"—to believe that there is significant value to be gained by allowing the firm access to the customer. This opens the door for the firm to begin engaging in alerting and averting behavior with the customer (Lemon 2002; Gilbert and Teinowitz 2000). It is in the customer interaction and retention phases of the relationship that the updating ability becomes most critical. Customers who have build ongoing relationships with the firm will expect the firm to have up-to-date and accurate information about the customer (with permission, of course). This approach is consistent with Melinda Nykamp's definition of customer relationship management (www.nykamp.com):

Figure 10.2 **e-Service and the Customer–Firm Relationship**

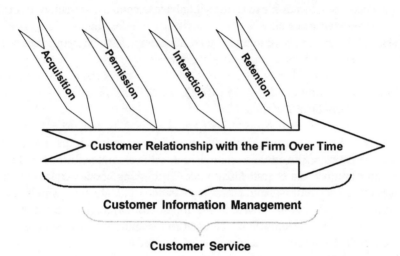

CRM is the optimization of all customer contacts through the distribution and application of customer information. It is your promise, that no matter how your customer interacts with you, you will always recognize who they are. And, in turn you will optimize the value of their experience, while also optimizing their value to you. (Nykamp and McEachern 2001)

Overall, we see wireless location technology as a great boon to marketers who, in all likelihood, will find numerous opportunities to upset customers with unwanted or untimely messages or alerts. But below are what we believe are the five key rules for wireless customer relationship management. If you follow these rules, you will build exciting, dynamic, and long-lasting relationships with customers who will truly believe that you have their best interests at heart. Ignore these rules at your own peril.

1. *Opt in.* Always get permission from customers before you ever send a location-based message. If you do not, they will really think Big Brother is watching them.
2. *Opt when and opt where.* When you get permission, find out when the customer is interested or willing to hear from you. Let the customer set the rules, but make sure you are clear on the windows of opportunity.
3. *Opt on.* Always wait for the customers to signal to you that they are willing to be in communication. Find ways to encourage customers to "turn their radar on" for your firm.
4. *Secure the customers' trust.* Beyond traditional privacy policies, the

opportunity for location-based interactive marketing requires that customers truly believe that we will only communicate with them if it is in their best interest.

5. *Never abuse the customers' trust.* No matter how tempting it may be, never, never, never engage in outbound location-based marketing without the customers' permission. Once you lose this trust, you will not be able to regain it.

When you have permission to call, your message is anticipated and your customer knows your message will be relevant. One way to gain this valuable permission is to ask something like this: "From time to time I will have information for you of immediate importance. I can send notes quickly and simply to your cell phone to catch you wherever you are and save you time. Please let me know the best time for me to reach you." Here, permission is everything. One unwanted invasion and you lose your access. If you lose your access, the best e-Service in the world will not save you.

Consistency, in the wireless e-Service world, means consistency across every contact on the selling floor, every sales contact in the field, every contact in the call center, every contact on the Web, and now every wireless contact (Bolton et al. 2002; Hansen and Danaher 1999). With your customers always "on," always reachable, always reaching out, always contactable, always contacting, always sending, always receiving—not just "opting in," but opting *on*, opting *when*, opting *where*, opting *how* and opting *now*, you *will* have to get them to give you permission to communicate in their terms, on their terms, and on their turf. That is the only way you can manage your customer relationships in the anytime, anywhere wireless world. That will be the only way to successful wireless e-Service, customer loyalty, and keeping your customers for life.

Customer Information Management

Delivering customer value starts with customer data integration—bringing all channels of customer information together in one record—and then demands the capability to link the customer knowledge with the integration of delivery mechanisms. In simplest terms, this means making all the elements of the customer experience accessible in real time for every customer-facing teammate at every customer-facing opportunity. Few companies are doing this well.

A recent research study sought to establish the attitude of financial services, telecoms, and utilities companies toward customer relationship management and whether they had strategies in place. In researching both IT and business respondents, the research was seeking to determine if there was a gap in the understanding of customer relationship management. While the respondents all recognized the benefits of customer relationship management, they had yet to fully understand the need for a seamless view of the customer.

> Customers require you to know their needs and be able to do business with them in one transaction. Therefore, this knowledge operation has to be seamless. Customers do not wish to call several times in order to carry out their business. It was therefore surprising that a large number of those companies researched, planned to operate the different channels and the information contained therein, independently.
>
> Perhaps these were the same companies who had yet to fully understand the strategic benefits of customer relationship management and had so far not seen that having a seamless view of the customer is a contributor to the success of that strategy. (Blue 2000)

In this real-time, wireless world you cannot operate just one part of a strategy. In order for customer relationship management to be truly effective, you have to practice all of it to fulfill the potential. Operating different channels of customer information differently and the information contained in them independently is no longer good enough.

Pulling all of the relevant customer information into one accessible form is not easy. Pulling information from legacy systems with different formats is difficult, and requires a strong team and a strong will to make it happen. The folks at Eddie Bauer give us a good example of the effort required and its worth. Troy Brown, director of Eddie Bauer's metrics and finance, and the man in charge of gathering and disseminating customer data at the big catalog retailer, says this of their effort:

> The task is daunting because it is so big and complicated. You need to look at every detail, which requires discipline and a commitment from people who know both the business and the technology. IT couldn't do it alone. A cross-functional team was the key. (McDonald 2000)

A team of fifty full-time people was committed to this initial CRM effort. Staff from both the technology and business functions worked side by side with outside systems integrators for ten months analyzing all lines of business and customer channels. Did it pay off? Michael Boyd, the company's director of customer relationship management, gives the answer:

> For the first time we could see the profitability of customers across multiple channels. Additional channels like the Web weren't cannibalizing our

retail or catalog businesses at all. Suddenly, we realized that our multichannel customers were our most valuable ones, and a cross-channel CRM solution was crucial to serving them well and adding value to their customer experience. (McDonald 2000)

Customer information management systems will be critical to maximizing the value from wireless solutions. More importantly, redundant systems will be critical for two reasons: (1) existing systems will not go away (at least for a long while); (2) your customers need a safety net. Let us look at each of these reasons in a bit more depth.

First, we do not think wireless communications will, for the foreseeable future, replace existing channels of communication with the customer. Rather, we believe they will augment existing systems. While wireless offers an exciting opportunity for your customers to reach you, this does not suggest that existing (nonwireless) systems will disappear. Get ready for the world of multifaceted, pervasive, multi-platform customer relationship management.

The recent dot.com boom-and-bust cycle provides some insight into this phenomenon. Companies that are using Web technologies successfully and, more importantly, profitably are those firms that have figured out how the Internet complements their existing business model. Consider the success of firms such as Land's End, JCPenney, Charles Schwab, and Fidelity. Each of these firms understood that the Web presented an opportunity to create an additional channel for their customers to reach them—the key word here is "additional." They did not seek out the Web as a means to get rid of brick and mortar stores, catalogs, phone communications, or office walk-ins. The Web was just another way for their customers to access and communicate with them. The brick and mortar doomsayers got it wrong.

Similarly, wireless solutions provide an additional new—and unique— opportunity for your customers to reach out and communicate with you. On the go, wherever they are, whatever they are doing, they now will have the opportunity to look you up, find your store, office or restaurant location, place an order, book a ticket, check on a flight arrival or departure—the list goes on and on. More control—more accessibility for the customer (cf. Hui and Bateson 1991). But that same customer will expect to be able to walk into your store (and get the same service he has come to expect), call your airline (and get the same attentive responses as she always does), or reach your tech support team via the multiple channels of phone, fax, e-mail, and Internet that have worked so well in the past. Again we say, mobile communications solutions will once again raise the bar, not just for wireless but also for the entire firm (no one will want to wait five minutes on a landline for customer service if they are used to immediate response via their WAP phone).

Do not lose sight of fulfilling customer expectations through traditional channels of communications (Oliver 1997; Oliver and Burke 1999).

Next, let us take a look at the need for the customer safety net. Many customers may come to rely on wireless systems as their primary (or even secondary) mode of communication with you. Therefore, you must have backup systems in place so your customers do not think they have fallen into the wireless equivalent of a black hole. Successful customer relationships are based on a fundamental trust built up between the firm and the customer (Dwyer et al. 1987; Hart and Johnson 1995; Shapiro 1987). When the customer believes that this trust has been violated (whether or not it is the "fault" of the firm), it is very difficult to regain trust and rebuild the relationship.

So, what should you do? We suggest starting with a very simple wireless strategy—one that allows you to control, insofar as it is possible, the downside risk when the systems break down. How simple? Consider Fidelity Investments' decision to embrace wireless trading. By developing its own software and imbedding the software in the Palm devices when shipped, it was able to reduce the likelihood of errors as customers seek to download their own applications to the device.

Or consider initial investments in wireless applications that build the customer relationship and yet are such that the customer will not come to rely on them (at least for a while). For example, if the customer opts in—and agrees to allow you to contact him or her when you have special offers of interest to the customer—you are less likely to be in a situation in which the customer is disappointed when the technology fails. If you fail to send the customer a customized, special-offer message on one occasion when the customer has "opted on," for example, the customer may just believe there was not a cool offer available ("They'll never know the server was down. . .").

Simple solutions are a great start, but backup systems will be critical. When customers come to believe that you are reachable anytime, from anywhere, you had better be. Have a backup server. Have customer service reps available 24/7. If your customers are expecting updates or reminders, and your automated system is not responding, be prepared to make these calls "by hand"—at least to customers you do not want to lose. You will need backup systems, so if the lights go out—or if there is no viable wireless portal—you (and your customers) can still function.

When you invest in the exciting world of wireless communications with the customer, be ready for a long ride. In addition to handling the always-on, always-available, from anywhere issues, the firm also has to address the any application, any device issue. You may offer a great solution for your customers to reach you via wireless—but your customers will be frustrated if, for example, it only works on a Nokia phone, or only if they are an AT&T

wireless services customer. How to avoid this dilemma? Some experts suggest that companies may want to partner with devices and create incentives for customers to migrate to a particular device or platform. But beware. Given the immature nature of the technology, you will want to be "nimble." An individual device will have a "life" of only six to eighteen months. Do not marry yourself to a single-device technology, because you can be out in the cold quickly.

Customer Service: The "Killer App"

Building long-term, profitable B2B relationships takes more than sales force automation and smart relationship development. Once the initial sale has been made, it also requires successful transition management, integration, and handoff to implementation and installation teams. Mobile transferability (within the firm) of customer intelligence—mobile access and utilization of the institutional knowledge about the customer—is critical. How does wireless help? From FAQs to customer data to dialog, mobile technologies are enabling the entire organization to serve the customer—without having to re-learn basic things about the customer at each turn.

Wheelhouse Corp., a Burlington, MA, B2B technology systems integrator, seems to understand this. Wheelhouse helps companies implement relational online analytical processing (ROLAP) databases—the next generation of relational databases for B2B CRM. As Frank Ingari, founder and chairman, puts it:

> Are you talking to a prospect, a first-time buyer or a repeat purchaser? Is that repeat purchaser satisfied or disgruntled? If your customer has just been on the Web for three hours researching a product before he phones his rep, that rep must know the guy was on the Web for three hours before he picks up the phone. (Libster 2000)

Gone are the days of customer willingness to wait seventy-two, forty-eight or even twenty-four hours to get a problem resolved—and to suffer the resulting downtime. Customers want problem-solving right now and right at the location of the problem. Enter the wireless solution. New technologies make it possible for customers to call your technical support center and complete entire, personalized, technical support transactions entirely by voice (without any humans on your end). Just so we are clear here—your customer uses only voice, hears only voice, but on your end it is all Web and computer. How does this work?

Conversay, a leader in speech technologies for mobile devices, and Integrated Information Systems, an Internet solutions firm, have developed a mobile-commerce application that allows users to conduct transactions entirely by voice, thereby providing a great solution for customers (cf. Moon 1999, 2000). According to Matt Scheuing, executive VP of marketing and sales at Conversay, "Users won't have to contend with difficult or frustrating input interfaces, such as tiny keypads, when trying to complete a transaction on their mobile device" ("Fall Comdex" 2000). The embedded speech technology is built around Conversay's proprietary small-footprint speech recognition and text-to-speech engine. It is purported to have a virtually unlimited vocabulary.

Companies such as Hewlett Packard have found ways to create organizational memory in their customer service (Glazer 1991). HP has created a system that remembers whom the customer speaks to during any customer service contact. When the customer calls again, he or she is given the option to be connected to the same contact from the previous call if desired. This enables the customer to avoid the frustration of tediously searching for the right contact in a muddled web of customer service personnel or an endless traditional menu or Interactive Voice Recognition (IVR) driven system. Whether the firm creates a sophisticated internal "memory" like Hewlett Packard, or a simple PDA-based system such as Fidelity Investments— through which its best customers can contact their Fidelity representatives wirelessly and simply with a few strokes of a stylus—the firm has created new and wirelessly enabled ways for the customer to interact *on his or her own terms* with the traditional customer-service function of the firm.

Overall, wireless transforms selling, sales management, and service processes (cf. Cannon and Perreault 1999). New wireless-enabled sales automation systems are offering simple solutions for managing the salesperson's often complex world of sales leads, contact information, forecasts, and customer information. Companies such as salesforce.com, upshot.com, and mynetsales.com provide wireless, easily "synchable" solutions for sales forces—the ultimate "on the go" application. For example, with sales force.com, salespeople can log on to the Web site from a PDA, check accounts, update a database, and get new information. Anytime. Anywhere. No additional software/middleware/hardware necessary. According to Tom Hughes, a customer of upshot.com and sales and marketing technology programmer at Hewlett Packard, "The payback was just phenomenal. This was about one-fifth of what the other stuff would cost" (Girard 2000). Sales automation and customer-relationship software is big business. The META group expects the market for such software to reach about $67 billion by 2004 (Girard 2000). Siebel Systems, the largest player by far in the CRM software and sales automation process, is developing offerings in the wireless space as well. Sales.com, a Siebel spin-off, is testing new mobile sales-automation and call-center CRM products that will be available soon. Start-up, first mover, or market leader, take your pick. But anytime, anywhere sales management and customer service is here. And moving fast.

Metrics for the New Wireless e-Service

If you seek to create, develop, build, and sustain successful relationships with customers—anytime and anywhere—it is important to examine tangible evidence from your customers to see if you are succeeding. How will you know? Your strategies are working if:

- Your customers have your phone number stored on their cell phone, your e-mail address on their PDA, and your Web address bookmarked on their WAP phone.
- Your customers have given you permission to engage and interact with them.
- Your customers ask you to contact them when you have something you think they would want to know.
- Your customers contact you regularly and know your names.
- Your customers buy from you on a regular (for them) basis, and plan to do so again.
- The long-term costs of maintaining relationships with your customers are less than the long-term revenue potential.

More generally, your strategies are working if you have achieved success in two key areas: share of customer purchases (current and future) and share of customer access (current and future). First, some basic definitions:

Share of customer purchases (current and future). What percent do you receive of customer purchases in the categories in which you have the opportunity to serve the customer? How likely is the customer to continue doing business with you? And do you expect the customer purchase stream to increase over time? Or decrease (cf. Blattberg et al. 2001; Rust et al. 2000)?

Share of customer access (current and future). When the customer engages with your product or service category, how much of that engagement—thinking, access, dialog, interaction—is devoted to your firm? Do you expect this category to grow more or less important to the customer over time? And do you expect your firm will become more or less important to the customer in this category?

It is critical to understand how well you are doing in these two areas. Current measures tell you how well your strategies are delivering results today. Future measures suggest opportunities or vulnerabilities present in your current strategies. Here is what you are after: You want a high share of customer purchases and a strong share of customer access—they buy from you (a lot and often), and they think of you (find you, talk to you) when they think of the category.

Measurement and Metrics

But how do you begin to get a handle on these success metrics? What do you need to measure? With the customer's permission, you need to understand the customer's perception of the relationship as it is manifested in five key areas: interaction, accessibility, opting, stickiness, and profitability (see Table 10.2). Let us look at each one in more depth—to understand what you would really like to know. Quick note: as you read through this list, do not panic. For some of the items on this list, the technologies may still be under development to adequately capture a solid measurement of customer activity in some areas. Remember—our goal in this book is to give you a glimpse of the wireless future—so do not worry if you cannot measure some of these right now. Do what you can.

Interaction

Dialog or monologue. Is there a real relationship? Is your customer interacting with you? Or merely reacting to you? The more you can get your customers to initiate contact with you, the stronger the bond between you and the customer. How can you tell? Here are some suggestions:

Inflow vs. outflow percentage. What percent of the communications between you and the customer are initiated by you? Firm-initiated communications would include outbound direct mail, e-mail, voice communications, or instant messages. What portion of communications is initiated by the customer? Customer-initiated communications would include incoming e-mail, voice communications (either via landline or wireless), instant messages (including responses to your outbound communications, although these are not as useful in building relationships).

Extent of interaction. To what extent does your customer engage in real-time interaction with your firm? Try to measure the length, intensity, and satisfaction of conversations and interactions between your customer and you.

Accessibility

How reachable does the customer perceive your firm to be? Here, we are trying to get a measure on how easy it is for the customer to interact with you

Table 10.2

Metrics for Wireless e-Service

Aspect of relationship	What to measure
Interaction	Inflow vs. outflow percentage Extent of interaction
Accessibility	Ease of access Ease of transaction
Opting	Extent of customer opting and permission Extent of self-disclosure
Stickiness	Megabyte share Learning relationships Word of mouth
Profitability	Revenue inflows from customers and customer relationships Cost outflows to manage customer relationship

and to do business with you. These measures are best captured via a customer survey.

Ease of access. How easy is it for your customer to contact you, her way, on her time? What difficulties has the customer experienced in the past three months trying to contact you or do business with you? What can you do better or differently to improve your accessibility in the eyes of the customer?

Ease of transaction. Once your customers reach you, how easy is it for them to successfully transact business? Get customer support? Get the information they need? What can you improve? Are there areas where you are overstaffed or understaffed? Are these systems that are not responding quickly enough to customer requests?

Opting

How successful have you been in getting the customer's permission—getting the customer to opt in, opt on, opt now? Here, we want to get a handle on how easily accessible your customers are to you—in effect, the extent to which your customers have opened up and given you "access" to their lives, so you can serve them better. How do you measure this?

Extent of opting and permission. As you develop your operational procedures for your customers to opt in and give you access to them, you should think of it (potentially) in terms of levels—low level permission would be equivalent to giving you their name and e-mail address. Midlevel permission might be equivalent to the customers' giving you permission to contact them via their mobile devices under specific circumstances. High-level permission would involve the customers' opting to have you contact them whenever you feel you have something important to tell them. By creating these levels of opting in, you can begin to understand the extent to which the customers have given you permission to be a part of their life.

Extent of self-disclosure. In addition to permission, you can gauge the strength of the customer relationship by examining how much the customers are willing to tell you about themselves. Do you know their names? E-mail address? Cell phone number? Home address? Home phone? Demographic and psychographic information? Preferences? When they shop? Develop a scale to understand how much your customers have been willing to reveal to you (always with permission, of course).

Stickiness

In addition to understanding the extent of interaction, accessibility, and opting, you also need to understand how committed your customers are to your firm. How likely are they to switch to a competitor? What is keeping them coming back to you? How can we measure customer stickiness in wireless?

Megabyte share. Where do you rate on their "radar screen"? Are you on your customers' list of "favorites"? Do they have your contact information in their wireless Rolodex? We highly recommend that you determine the answers to these questions through the use of a customer survey, rather than invasive cookie technology that may upset the customer. Understanding the extent to which your firm is integrated into their daily wireless lives is the key measurement here.

Learning relationships. To what extent do your customers take advantage of (and value) your customized offers and communications to them—based upon the knowledge you have gained about them over time? Try to get a sense of the value your customers place on customized communications— customized by place (where they are when you contact them), by content (what you offer them when you contact them), by context (how you make it easy for them to buy from you their way), and by time (when you contact them). The greater the value of these services to your customer, the greater the stickiness.

Word of mouth. Do your customers tell other people about you? And if so, do they say good things? Often, a customer's willingness to engage in positive word of mouth for a firm is a signal of the customer's commitment to the firm. Not everyone will tell the world how great you are. But you would like to know who does, and how much (Anderson 1998; Hogan et al. 2001). These folks tend to be hooked on your business.

Profitability

Building strong customer interaction, accessibility, opting, and stickiness will lead to successful (and profitable) long-term customer relationships. But it is critical to understand whether these initiatives are actually making money— on a customer-by-customer basis—to determine whether you are investing wisely in CRM. What should you measure?

Revenue inflows from customers and customer relationships. Where are the revenues coming from? How much do your customers spend? How often? (Recency, frequency, and monetary value are still relevant—it is just a bit more complicated in wireless). Are your customers generating revenues for you from new wireless partnerships? It is important to track the revenue streams from partnerships and alliances so you can determine if they will pay out in the long run. Examine the trend of customer inflows for each customer, if possible. Are the revenues growing over time? Decreasing? Measures of customer lifetime value are key, and they must take into account both the revenue side and the cost of serving the customer.

Cost outflows to manage customer relationships. If at all possible, try to allocate costs of serving customers at the customer level. In the short term, this may not be feasible, but it is a critical step in developing profitable customer relationship management strategies and systems in the long run. Certain customers may be too costly to retain, too costly to customize communications or offers for, too costly to develop m-CRM strategies for. You need to know which customers are worth the m-CRM efforts you are developing.

Customer Equity: A Strategic Tool

So, now you have a list of what you should be measuring. But once you have all that information, what can you do with it? You need to determine which aspects of your CRM strategy are working, which are paying off, and which are not. You need to figure out what things you are doing right (things you are doing that your customers think are important) and what you are merely wasting money and resources on. How can you begin to determine which investments are worthwhile? Your chief financial officer may have some ideas of his or her own, but here is an approach to get you started.

The customer equity framework (Rust et al. 2000) was designed to help firms determine the best way to invest marketing dollars. Throughout this chapter, we have suggested that you will need to invest in wireless technologies and develop wireless CRM solutions. The key question: Is the investment worth it? The customer equity framework provides a methodology to answer this question. Without going into great detail, the basic idea is as follows.[1]

You want to maximize your firm's overall customer equity—defined as the sum of the discounted lifetime values of all your current (and potential) customers (Blattberg and Deighton 1996; Blattberg et al. 2001). Therefore, you want to invest in those strategies that will grow the value of your overall customer base over time—thereby growing the total value of the firm. The strategies that build customer equity can be divided into three key areas: brand strategies, value strategies, and retention strategies. The model allows the firm to determine which of these is the key driver of customer equity for your industry, and for each customer. Once you know what the key drivers are for a customer, you invest in those strategies that will have the highest return on investment. The key element in the customer equity framework is that all marketing investments become financially accountable.

Why does this matter? In a recent survey, *Information Week* found that more than 80 percent of companies now require a return on investment (ROI) analysis before approving any information technology initiative. And Gartner Group has found that two-thirds of vendors are often asked to perform a total cost of ownership (TCO) analysis as part of a customer proposal for an IT investment (Hill 2000). In other words, you will have to justify any investment in wireless solutions. So you had better figure out a customer-based way to justify it.

The critical element as you consider the value of these investments: find a way to link your business decisions and actions to ROI, where "R" is measured in customer terms—the effect of an investment on growing the "customer asset."

One final note: As we move forward in our understanding of success in wireless environments, we foresee a real need for continued development of measures and metrics in this area. And we are not alone. The investment community is looking for new metrics as well. After being hard hit by the lack of diagnostic metrics for dot.coms over the past few years, we believe that the investment and financial community will be taking a new look at the key indicators of future success of m-commerce and m-CRM enterprises. We believe that the finance community will come around and will begin utilizing a new model—based upon the value of the customer asset—as key indicators of the health of mobile commerce enterprises. This is yet another reason to take steps to begin to measure interaction, opting, accessibility, stickiness—and, of course, profit.

Challenges for Researchers

As we move forward in our understanding and utilization of wireless technologies to enable the customer relationship, there is still much to be learned. Broadly, much research is needed to understand the following key issues:

Accessibility

Two-way dialog. How will the new, anytime, anywhere, two-way interaction possibilities that wireless and mobile devices give customers affect the "rules" of customer relationship management? Will customer decision-making processes change now that such two-way dialog is truly possible?

Self-service strategies. As new technologies make it possible for firms to encourage consumers to engage in self-service and consumers to choose to engage in self-service, how will this affect consumer expectations and behavior? How will these new approaches affect price and promotion strategies?

Business-to-business relationships. Does the increased accessibility of salespeople, service people, and customers change the rules for B2B marketing? Will definitions of trust, consistency, and dependability now depend on accessibility?

Alerting and Averting

Service-failure management. New mobile technologies may raise the bar for responses to service failures, both in B2B and B2C markets. How will these new technologies affect customer expectation formation and customer satisfaction (with respect to response to service failure) and, ultimately, retention?

Timeliness. As firms begin to develop these new capabilities, they will have opportunities to serve customers in new ways. How will the possibilities of alerting, reminding, and notification—especially when the technologies become location-sensitive—affect customer decision-making? Will these new possibilities change the rules of advertising and promotion?

Updating

Information technology management. The need for up-to-date, real-time information will create substantial challenges for IT. Research is needed to determine both the real value of this up-to-date information to the firm's field force and customer base and the most efficient methodologies to create and maintain the necessary real-time information.

Resistance to innovation. Customers and firms will be adopting new technologies in the wireless space at an incredibly rapid pace over the next several years. It will be critical for firms to understand how to reduce resistance to adoption of these new technologies, and to determine what strategies will be most successful in encouraging new adopter learning.

Permission

We now have technologies that allow us to invade our customers' lives like never before. Therefore, it will be critical to understand when such "invasion" is appropriate, warranted, and acceptable, and the conditions under which customers feel most comfortable granting permission for firms to interact with them in these very personal ways.

Metrics

Much research is needed in the area of customer metrics. Specifically, future research may want to investigate new metrics for measuring customer-firm interaction (e.g., inflow vs. outflow percentage, extent of interaction). In addition, new measures are needed to allow the firm to understand how accessible customers perceive the firm to be (both for communicating and transacting). Third, measures of strength or extent of permission granted to the firm by the consumer will be critical as we move forward. Finally, measures of the strength of the customer relationship and better measures of profitability (both the revenue and cost aspects of the wireless customer relationship) are sorely needed.

Challenges for CEOs: Are You Ready?

In closing, it is important to understand where the customer is heading, and what the customer will expect in the next few years. As a diagnostic starting point, consider the following questions:

- *Instant access*: Can customers find you all the time, everywhere, on any wireless device?
- *Consistent excellence*: Do you deliver excellence—all the time and everywhere: intelligent service, in person, m-service, internal agents, all the time, every time?
- *Anywhere, anytime ordering*: Can your customers buy on their terms, their way, all the time, anywhere?
- *Anywhere, anytime, delivery*: Can your customers get the goods they want, the way they want, on their schedule?

- *Alerting and averting*: Can your customer service or call center alert a member of your field force to unforeseen events prior to the field employee visiting the client?
- *Updating*: Do your systems enable every employee to easily update customer information (when necessary) from anywhere, anytime, and from any device?

Clearly, that is an overwhelming agenda for any firm. But we must recognize that customers' expectations are changing, and that in the not-too-distant future, customers will come to expect such service. It used to be that firms could make the decisions and figure out how to market to the customer—on the firm's terms. Now, customers carry with them, in their pockets, on their belts, in their purses, devices that enable them to interact with the firm whenever they see fit. Without realizing it, we have put the customer in control of the firm–customer relationship like never before.

Wireless has the potential to transform e-Service. Our advice: try not to be roadkill on the wireless communication superhighway. But remember: you must have a wireless strategy, even if it is "wait and see." Believe us. You will be dead in the water (or roadkill on the highway) if you do not.

Note

1. For more information, see Roland Rust, Valarie Zeithaml, and Katherine Lemon, *Driving Customer Equity: How Customer Lifetime Value Is Reshaping Corporate Strategy* (New York: Free Press, 2000).

References

Anderson, Eugene W. 1998. "Customer Satisfaction and Word of Mouth." *Journal of Service Research* 1(1) (August): 5–17.

Bettencourt, Lance A. 1997. "Customer Voluntary Performance: Customers as Partners in Service Delivery." *Journal of Retailing* 73(3): 383–406.

Blattberg, R., and J. Deighton. 1996. "Manage Marketing by the Customer Equity Test." *Harvard Business Review* 74 (July–August): 136–144.

Blattberg, Robert; Gary Getz; and Jacquelyn S. Thomas. 2001. *Customer Equity: Building and Managing Relationships as Valuable Assets*. Boston: Harvard Business School Press.

Blue, Hatton. 2000. "Customer Relationship Management: Hot Topic or Hot Air." www.crm-forum.com (January 22), pp. 3, 5.

Bolton, Ruth N.; P.K. Kannan; and Matthew D. Bramlett. 2000. "Implication of Loyalty Programs and Service Experiences for Customer Retention and Value." *Journal of the Academy of Marketing Science* 28(1): 95–108.

Bolton, Ruth N.; Katherine Lemon; and Matthew D. Bramlett. 2002. "Modeling Repeat Purchase Decisions: How Customers' Experiences over Time Influence

Their Renewal of Service Contracts." Working paper, Vanderbilt University, Nashville, TN.

Boulding, William; Ajay Kalra; and Richard Staelin. 1999. "The Quality Double Whammy." *Marketing Science* 18(4): 463–484.

Boulding, William; Ajay Kalra; Richard Staelin; and Valarie A. Zeithaml. 1993. "A Dynamic Model of Service Quality: From Expectations to Behavioral Intentions." *Journal of Marketing Research* 30 (February): 7–27.

Bowman, Douglas, and Das Narayandas. 2001. "Managing Customer-Initiated Contacts with Manufacturers: The Impact on Share of Category Requirements and Word-of-Mouth Behavior." *Journal of Marketing Research* 38 (August): 281–297.

Cannon, Joseph P., and William D. Perreault Jr. 1999. "Buyer-Seller Relationships in Business Markets." *Journal of Marketing Research* 36(4): 439–460.

"Christmas Shoppers Buy Gifts on the World's First Electronic Street, in Luleå, Sweden." 2000. Telia Press Release: www.estreet.lu/vin/pressinfo/pressinfo.html (November 21).

Clark, Kevin. 2001. "The Future of Marketing in a Wireless World." In *Wireless Rules: New Marketing Strategies for Customer Relationship Management Anytime, Anywhere.* New York: McGraw-Hill.

Cooper, R.B., and R.W. Zmud. 1990. "Information Technology Implementation Research: A Technological Diffusion Approach." *Management Science* 36(2): 123–139.

Courtmanche, John. 2000. "Trading Without Bounds." *1 to 1 Magazine* (September): 30.

Doubleclick.net. 2001. (November 5), p. 2.

Dowling, Graham W., and Mark Uncles. 1997. "Do Loyalty Programs Really Work?" *Sloan Management Review* 38(4): 71–82.

Drouin, Leon. 2000. "Latest Pollution Monitor: Cell Phone." *San Diego Union Tribune,* July 8, A3–5.

Dwyer, F. Robert; Paul H. Schurr; and Sejo Oh. 1987. "Developing Buyer-Seller Relationships." *Journal of Marketing* 51 (April): 11–27.

"Electronic Shopping Street Success Up North." 2000. www.ericsson.com/infocenter/news/eStreet.html (December 29).

Elliott, Kiersten; Julie Edell; and Katherine N. Lemon. 2000. "Who's to Blame? Consumers' Responses to Service Failure." Paper presented at Association of Consumer Research Conference, Salt Lake City, UT, October.

Engen, John R. 2000. "Banking on the Run." *Banking Strategies* (July/August): 16–25.

"Ericsson and ICA Ahold in World's First Trial of E-Payment Via Bluetooth." 2000. *Business Wire,* December 19, p. 21.

"Fall Comdex: Conversay, IIS Develop Voice-Enabled Mobile-Commerce App." 2000. www.wirelessnetnow.com, article 30088 (October).

Flisi, Claudia. 2000. "Mobile's New Floating World: As Voice and Data Move to the Mobile Phone, Will Commerce Be Far Behind?" *International Herald Tribune,* December 6, p. B-10.

Folkes, Valerie S. 1984. "Consumer Reactions to Product Failure: An Attributional Approach." *Journal of Consumer Research* 10 (March): 398–409.

Gilbert, Jennifer, and Ira Teinowitz. 2000. "FTC Raises Ante with Opt-In." *Advertising Age,* March 13, pp. 56–64.

Girard, Kim. 2000. "A Farewell to Software?" *Business 2.0,* September 26, pp. 41–43.

Glazer, Rashi. 1991. "Marketing in an Information Intensive Environment: Strategic Implications of Knowledge as an Asset." *Journal of Marketing* 55(3): 1–19.

Hansen, D., and P. Danaher. 1999. "Inconsistent Performance Within the Service Encounter: What's a Good Start Worth?" *Journal of Service Research* 1(3): 227–235.

Hart, Christopher W., and Michael D. Johnson. 1995. "Growing the Trust Relationship." *Marketing Management* (spring): 9–24.

Hauble, Gerald, and Valerie Trifts. 2000. "Consumer Decision Making in Online Shopping Environments: The Effects of Interactive Decision Aids." *Marketing Science* 19 (winter): 4–21.

Hill, Jeff. 2000. "Using ROI/TCO Tools in the ASP Sales Process: Do's and Don'ts." Silent Partner Software, Inc. Paper presented at DCI's Wireless Summit Conference, Orlando FL, September.

Hogan, John E.; Katherine N. Lemon; and Barak Libai. 2001. "Incorporating the Effect of Positive Word-of-Mouth into Customer Profitability Models." Working paper, Boston College.

Hui, M.K, and J.E.G. Bateson. 1991. "Perceived Control and the Effects of Crowding and Consumer Choice on the Service Experience." *Journal of Consumer Research* 18 (September): 174–184.

Johnsen, Aina. 2000. "Workers Go Wireless." *wap.com* (November 1), p. 1.

Kannan, P.K., and H. Raghav Rao. 2001. "Introduction to the Special Issue: Decision Support Issues in Customer Relationship Management and Interactive Marketing for E-Commerce." *Decision Support Systems* 32 (December): 83–84.

Lemon, Katherine N. 2002. "Gaining Customer Permission: The Role of Opt-in and Opt-out Strategies in Customer Relationship Management." Working paper, Carroll School of Management, Boston College, Chestnut Hill, MA.

"Leading Insurer in UK, Direct Line, Selects Chordiant E-Business Software to Support the Web and Call Centers." 2000. *M2 Communications Ltd.,* October 24, p. 1

Libster, Bernie. 2000. "Can B2B Marketers Personalize?" *1 to 1 Personalization: The Guide to Insights, Issues and Trends:* www.1to1.com/personalization/article2.html (November 15).

Lightman, Alex. 2000. "Wireless Standards Shootout." *destinationCRM*: www.destinationcrm.com/ff/dcrm_ff_article.asp?id=226 (November).

McDonald, Bruce. 2000. "Finding the Right Fit." *1 to 1 Magazine* (September): 22.

McWilliam, Gil. 2000. "Building Stronger Brands Through Online Communities." *Sloan Management Review* 41(3): 43–54.

"Memorex Telex Staff Enjoy World-Wide First in WAP Access of Customer Database." 2000. www.wapforum.org (July 15).

Meuter, Matthew L.; Amy L. Ostrom; Robert I. Roundtree; and Mary Jo Bitner. 2000. "Self-Service Technologies: Understanding Customer Satisfaction with Technology-Based Service Encounters." *Journal of Marketing* 64(3): 50–64.

Moon, Youngme. 2000. "Intimate Exchanges: Using Computers to Elicit Self-disclosure from Consumers." *Journal of Consumer Research* 26 (March): 323–339.

———. 1999. "When the Computer Is the Sales Agent: Consumer Responses to Computer Personalities in Interactive Marketing Situations." Working paper #99–041, Harvard Business School, Boston, MA.

Moon, Youngme, and Francis X. Frei. 2000. "Exploding the Self-Service Myth." *Harvard Business Review* 78 (May/June): 26–27.

Morgan, Robert, and Shelby D. Hunt. 1994. "The Commitment-Trust Theory of Relationship Marketing." *Journal of Marketing* 58 (July): 20–38.

Newell, Frederick, and Katherine Newell Lemon. 2001. *Wireless Rules: New Marketing Strategies for Customer Relationship Management Anytime, Anywhere.* New York: McGraw-Hill.

Nykamp, Melinda, and Carla McEachern. 2001. "Total Customer Relationship Management: Myth or Reality?" www.nykamp.com/crm_news/articles/totcust.html.

Oliver, Richard L. 1997. *Satisfaction.* New York: McGraw-Hill.

Oliver, Richard, and Raymond R. Burke. 1999. "Expectation Processes in Satisfaction Formation: A Field Study." *Journal of Service Research* 1(3): 196–214.

Oliver, Richard W.; Roland T. Rust; and Sajeev Varki. 1998. "Real-Time Marketing." *Marketing Management* 7 (fall): 28–37.

"Phone Market Saturated in Europe." 2001. *WirelessNetNow,* January 9, p. 11.

Ram, Sundaresan. 1989. "Successful Innovation Using Strategies to Reduce Consumer Resistance: An Empirical Test." *Journal of Product Innovation Management* 6(1): 20–34.

Ram, Sundaresan, and Jagdish N. Sheth. 1989. "Consumer Resistance to Innovations: The Marketing Problem and Its Solutions." *Journal of Consumer Marketing* 6(2): 5–14.

"Rovenet Unveils Wireless Toilet-Finder." 2000. *Wireless Net Now,* December 1, p. 2.

Rust, Roland; Valarie Zeithaml; and Katherine Lemon. 2000. *Driving Customer Equity: How Customer Lifetime Value Is Reshaping Corporate Strategy.* New York: Free Press.

Shapiro, Susan P. 1987. "The Social Control of Impersonal Trust." *American Journal of Sociology* 93 (November): 623–658.

Sharp, Byron, and Anne Sharp. 1997. "Loyalty Programs and Their Impact on Repeat-Purchase Loyalty Patterns." *International Journal of Research in Marketing* 14: 473–486.

Sheth, Jagdish N. 1981. "Psychology of Innovation Resistance." *Research in Marketing* 4: 273–282.

Srivastava, R.J.; T.A. Shervani; L. Fahey. 1998. "Market-Based Assets and Shareholder Value." *Journal of Marketing* 62(1): 2–18.

"Tantau Bags Wireless Deal With Chase Bank." 2000. *Wireless Net Now,* November 6, p. 1.

"World-Unique Mobile Test In Luleå—EStreet Is a Great Leap Forward for Mobile-Telephony Research." 2000. Telia Press Release: www.estreet.lu/vin/pressinfo/pressinfo.html (November 11).

Zeithaml, Valarie A. 1988. "Consumer Perceptions of Price, Quality, and Value: A Means-End Model and Synthesis of Evidence." *Journal of Marketing* 52(3): 2–22.

———. 2000. "Service Quality, Profitability, and the Economic Worth of Customers." *Journal of the Academy of Marketing Science* 28(1): 67–85.

Part III

Public-Sector Opportunities

11

e-Learning

Fifth-Generation Learning and Its Impact on Management Education

Richard W. Oliver

*"The illiterate of the 21st century will not be those who
cannot read and write, but those who cannot learn,
unlearn, and relearn."*

—Alvin Toffler, author of *Future Shock*

"Education is the killer application for the Internet."

—John Chambers, CEO, Cisco Systems

Introduction

The Internet and other digital information technologies are dramatically
changing many industries by transforming the most fundamental function of
a business: the nature of their interactions with consumers. Education (the
ultimate in bricks and mortar orientation), as a "business," is not immune to
the transformational power of the information technologies, most acutely
with its interaction with its "customer," the student. Digital communications
technologies have the power to touch and change nearly every segment of
education and virtually all the functions and processes of an educational
institution, from admissions to teaching to graduation and alumna affairs.

The process of teaching/learning, however, appears to be the area most
open to fundamental change (generally, collateral administrative functions

will simply be speeded up or made more efficient by information technologies) not only because it is at the heart of what education does, but also because it is the most interactive, personal, time- and space-sensitive, and information-rich function within the broad array of things that educational institutions do.

Further, the segment most likely to be on the cutting edge of this transformation is management education, and more specifically that segment of management education that aims to continuing educate a business manager well into a career. Generally, this area is known as "executive education," and for the purposes of this article can be thought of as including executive master's of business administration and shorter, nondegree courses and credentialing. It is important to note that this also includes the training of "managers" for K–12 education, health care organizations, the military, non-profit organizations and the like. For simplicity, this article refers to business or management education, but assumes inclusion of any manager anywhere whose skills and competencies are being enhanced.

While they will be explored more fully later in this chapter, it is worthwhile to note here that four important economic reasons will cause management education to lead the transformation of education service to an e-Service approach: currency of content; consistency of practice across the barriers of time and space; the need for cost-effective solutions; and private capital investment flows into this area. The chapter will also explore the efficacy of the results of this transformation to e-learning in management education, which may be even greater than currently estimated because of the transformational power of e-Services in general and e-learning in particular, namely: interactivity, personalization, and real-time content updates.

Living Is Learning

All living creatures are capable of learning. The distinguishing characteristic (other than their chemical composition) between organic and inorganic matter is that only the organic has the ability to learn from its environment.

It might be argued that the only skill necessary for life is learning. In the case of very low-level primitive organisms, such as primal ooze or plant species, learning is the genetic change that takes place over the course of generations. For higher-level mammals, learning may be rote, such as cows learning where the farmer will leave the hay, rats learning a maze, or Pavlov's dogs learning to sit when instructed or offered a treat.

For humans, learning is the essence of being. Learning begins at birth (crying brings mother's attention and food) and only ends with death. Not all learning is formal; much is the routine learning of small things that permit smooth functioning in society. More structured learning, called education, has over the past several thousand years become essential for those in developed societies. While an unfortunate few, for reasons of geography, tradition, culture, or economics, slip through the education "net," most people in the world receive at least a few years of formal education. The more fortunate receive twenty-three years (K–Ph.D.) or more.

It is impossible to measure precisely how much one "knows," and what portion of that knowledge is acquired in formal settings. Several popular culture icons suggest that the ratio is tilted in favor of learning outside formal settings: a popular book by Robert Fulghum suggests *All I Really Need to Know I Learned in Kindergarten* (1988); a business book promising business success by Mark H. McCormack is titled *What They Don't Teach You at the Harvard Business School* (1986); and a popular routine by Father Guido Sarducci of *Saturday Night Live* fame argues for the "Five-Minute University," where one learns in a matter of seconds everything they need to know about a particular subject (e.g., economics: supply and demand!).

While such popular perceptions have some basis in fact, the business of formal education is large and growing, not only in the West but around the world. In fact, as will be shown later, education is the second largest industry in the United States (health care being number one). The education industry has become an entrenched part of Western society and, despite its many detractors, operates relatively unfettered by outside influences.

Criticism of U.S. education in particular is relatively new and has been largely sparked by economics. In the 1980s, other countries appeared to best U.S. business, forcing a debate on "national competitiveness," which inevitably led to concerns about education efficacy. And while U.S. global competitiveness is no longer in question, education still is. Interestingly, such concerns come at a time when education is about to enter what I call the "fifth generation of learning."

Learning Versus Education

It is important at this early point to distinguish between learning and education.

All education is learning (or at least should be), but not all learning is education. In the popular vernacular, we use the term "learning" to mean all the activities that lead to greater understanding of life, while we use the term "education" to refer to that part of learning that is presented in a formal process, typically in an institution devoted to the process. A broad understanding of the process might be that learning is what we gain on our own *and* in formal settings, while education is only that portion of learning that is "provided" to us from other parties (i.e., at a distance). So, at least for the purpose of this chapter, learning can be thought of as what we as consumers direct ourselves, while education is that which is directed at us.

It is curious that the generally accepted term for this new form of education is "e-learning," and not "e-education." It may be a result of the fact that overtly or covertly (depending on your perspective), the "control" of the process has shifted from third-party educators to us as individual consumers. This chapter is focused on formal educational content and initiatives' being developed digitally and distributed across time and space as "e-learning." Implicit in this thesis is that this is the fifth generation of learning, and, as will be shown later, is evolutionary rather than revolutionary. However, this latest evolution brings learning back full circle to its early beginnings (more learning, less education), and represents a seismic shift of power to the user: the tyranny of education gives way to the democracy of learning (Figure 11.1). We are quick to add, however, that this is not a pejorative statement about education. Quite the reverse. Education in its purest sense has become and will continue to be the most powerful force for good—individually and collectively—on the planet.

The Value of Education

A wide variety of educational processes and institutions exists in the United States. It begins with prekindergarten, continuing with what is popularly referred to as K–12 (as well as the rapidly growing "home schooling" phenomenon) and culminating in various higher-education options. These include some 4,000 universities, 2,000 community and technical colleges, and a large number of technical and training institutions (where one can learn to drive a diesel truck or speak a foreign language, for example), both public and private (such as some 2,000 corporate "universities"). Globally, there are many times more institutions of all kinds, and they are growing daily in number and variety. The global education business expends some $2 trillion annually.

Studies have long demonstrated that an individual's years of formal education are highly positively correlated to income. More recently, a Harvard University study on longevity has indicated that length of education (among other factors) is positively correlated to length of life. One might suggest that the more one learns, the more one earns and lives to enjoy it. Unfortunately, with few exceptions, the formal system of education that has developed over the past several thousand years is highly structured to dump one into society at prescribed points with little more than lip service to the notion of "lifelong learning."

While this paper uses the term "learning" for the general process and

Figure 11.1   **Five Generations of Learning**

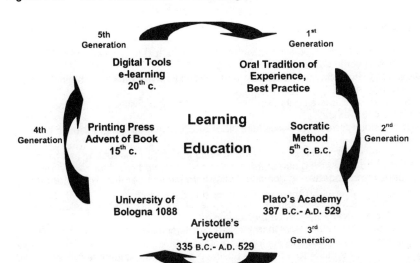

"e-learning" for the process of education via digital media, the focus is generally on the more formal process of education. However, the authors do not dispute the importance and growing power of nontraditional institutions and alternate forms of learning. Further, while other types of education will be affected, this chapter is focused primarily on higher education for managers, since management education has been the first and, to this point, at least, the biggest adopter of e-learning and distance technologies.

The field of e-learning is in its infancy. While there are many forms of e-learning being developed, we define e-learning simply as "the conversion of traditional (face-to-face) education into a digital form for use at a distance." Such learning can be synchronous (all students and instructors moving at roughly the same pace and schedule, often on line at the same time) or asynchronous (students completing course material at their own pace, on their own schedule). The many different variants of this basic structure are suggested by the definitions in Table 11.1.

The Fifth Generation of Learning: e-Learning

A Brief (and Biased) History of "Distance-Learning"

Many in the educational establishment are now leveling sharp and sustained criticism at the concept of distance learning or e-learning. A major contention of this chapter is that "learning at a distance" has been the dominant

Table 11.1

Definitions

Computer mediated: Process involving computers for text manipulation and electronic communication

Distributed: Students not necessarily in same geographic location as the lecturer or with each other

Synchronous: All participants experience all organized activities together, as in classroom learning

Asynchronous: Student activities take place at different times, after initiation by lecturer

Computer-mediated distributed asynchronous instruction: Instruction involving distributed class using computers with student-initiated times for receiving lectures and undertaking communication with the lecturer and with other students

Broadband: High-speed computer communication such as cable, DSL telephone lines, or two-way satellite communication

Face-to-face: As in classroom learning, the instructor seeing and being seen by students, not just students seeing each other

Socratic method: Instructor begins by posing a question for student response(s); he/she follows up with the same or other students to develop a theme, conclusion, or position. Instructor may "play the class like an instrument." Requires student discipline with respect to preparation for successful case treatment by this method.

Distance learning: Instruction in which instructor is geographically separate from at least some of the students

One-way communication: Instruction with one source and no discussion or feedback, except, perhaps, from student assignments or tests

Two-way communication: Instruction with the addition of feedback directly from student to instructor/lecturer, but not necessarily among students

Multiway communication: In addition to two-way communication, there is also communication among students, some *directed,* as required by the instructor, and some *undirected,* as takes place in open discussion in class

Directed communication: Communication required by instructor, for example, by calling on students in class or by requiring responses in electronic communication

Undirected communication: Communication incidental to the presence of receivers, for example, students listening to a class discussion or receivers of electronic communication directed only at an entire class.

Networked communication: Communication in which participants are geographically separated but can communicate via an electronic network, requiring use of a computer or similar device

Linear sequencing: Run-through of a lecture, text, or other presentation, explicitly or implicitly, without unplanned backtracking or jumps

Nonlinear sequencing: Sequencing of material as chosen by receiver, that is, the student, perhaps depending on hyperlinks embedded in computer-based media

Self-directed: Situation in which the decision to devote any particular time interval to an activity is made by each student, usually within an instructor-prescribed time frame

Groupware: Software to facilitate communication between individuals, specified groups, and other preselected patterns of communication

Threaded discussion: An integral part of a Knowledge Management System, threaded discussions are a workgroup communication tool. Discussion groups enable the immediate and far-reaching exchange of ideas and information over a network, helping a physically separated group to function as efficiently as if members shared the same room. Any user with network access can view and post messages via a Web browser. Following the thread of a discussion, a reader can immediately get up to speed on the history and flow of a conversation topic.

Source: Weingartner. 2000.

trend in education since humans first attempted to pass on what they had learned to others. The current effort to extend learning across time and space via electronics and networking represents not a revolution in education but the latest attempt to harvest the fruits of technology to provide learning to the greatest number of people. The author refers to this latest phase of "distance education" as the fifth generation of learning.

An overview of the main dimensions of the five generations of education is presented in Table 11.2.

Prior to writing, books, and schools, learning was essentially experiential (the first generation of learning). The individual essentially learned by doing. However, the substantive, albeit limited, "education at a distance" was the cave paintings and hieroglyphics of the ancients, meant, we assume, to instruct future generations about what had been "learned" by their painters and authors.

The first and most famous early "formal educational" process was developed in the fifth century B.C. in Athens with the advent of the Socratic method. Until that time, when this second generation of learning began, learning was very much a process of everyday experience (hieroglyphics notwithstanding). In effect, the idea of "learning" in an abstract setting (rather than from experience) also constitutes the first "learning at a distance," and the first formal education process that eventually gave rise to today's educational bureaucracy. The learning process tilted even more toward formal education in the third generation, with the academies founded by Aristotle and Plato, which continued as the dominant formal educational paradigm through the sixth century A.D. Much of Western education traces its roots to the Greek academy, however informal. In fact, as some critics of a more diverse educational system argue even today, "There's a Greek at every door of the academy!"

Importantly though, the early Socratic-Aristotelian academy for many years relied on the oral tradition of the "professor" reciting long passages of prose and poetry from memory, while students (without either language systems or writing technologies) memorized the recitation. Faculty and students then engaged in a dialogue to discover the truth. This oral dialogue between faculty and student pioneered by Socrates is still favored today by some educators.

Table 11.2

Five Generations of Learning

	1st Generation: Symbolic	2nd Generation: Didactic	3rd Generation: Institutional	4th Generation: Visual	5th Generation: Digital
Delivery	Hieroglyphics	Face-to-face	Face-to-face	Face-to-face/book	Distributed/networked
Perception	Visual	Auditory	Auditory	Visual	Multisensory
Communication	Limited	Limited	One-way	One-way	Interactive
Control	None	None	Faculty	Institutional	Student
Pedagogy	None	Socratic	Aristotelian	Passive	Active
Interaction	None	Dialogue	One-way	Limited	Extensive
Reach	Extremely limited	Highly selective	Selective	Broad	Ubiquitous

It should be noted at this point that this chapter is largely oriented to Western educational thought and history. The author acknowledges that Eastern and Asian cultures also have a rich and varied educational tradition, with the *sensei* (or teacher) being at the top or near the top of the social hierarchy of many cultures. Eastern tradition also has many anti-educational factions, such as some forms of Islam, that seem to prohibit education for all but religious scholars. While these are all important areas for consideration, for the purposes of simplicity this chapter traces the main sweep of Greco-Roman education history.

The Third Generation of Learning and the Advent of the University

The first known formal institution of higher learning was the University of Bologna, a private, for-profit organization that received a license to operate from the pope. It bore little resemblance to today's institutes of higher learning, however, since it predated the printing press by several hundred years. The origination of symbol systems by the Egyptians and Greeks led eventually to the formal writing of much of the world's codified knowledge in a document that became known as a book. The first books were extremely rare, and many writers, such as Plato, were severely criticized for introducing the book to the education system. In this early period, books were the exclusive domain of faculty. Instead of reciting lectures from memory, faculty read to students from handcrafted manuscripts. For reasons of economics and philosophy, students didn't have access to such books. The invention of the printing press erased the economic argument against students' having access to books and threw the philosophical arguments open for debate. As the book became the next technology of "distance learning," one can well imagine the faculty debate about whether or not knowledge and learning could take place away from the pontifications of the faculty "sage." The wide availability of books, however, eventually ushered in the fourth generation of learning, which has persisted until this time.

The University of Bologna spawned several other institutions around Europe, such as the University of Paris as well as Oxford and Cambridge, arguably the world's most famous universities. These Old World schools begat such North American counterparts as Harvard. An American innovation was the government-funded land-grant university, such as Cornell University, which added to the profusion of U.S. programs of higher learning. For many hundreds of years, the European and later American models of higher education have been widely emulated around the world. The advent of the book and the printing press added a major level of productivity enhancement that has resulted in over 90 percent of the developed world being literate. The latest U.S. census data show one in four Americans has earned a college degree. Roughly 60 percent of the developing world's population is now estimated to be literate, ranging from 18 percent (Burkina Faso) to 99 percent (Hungary). A study of developing countries by UNESCO found that at least one in twenty-five employed persons in developing countries worked in the education system. As we begin a new century and millennium, e-learning will lead us into the fifth generation of learning.

The Fifth Generation: e-Learning

For many individuals and companies, e-learning is like manna from heaven. It promises not only to provide a positive paradigm shift for students in traditional educational programs and to provide a new source of education to those geographically disadvantaged, but it may also provide a new, inexpensive source of education for the world's undereducated poor.

Anecdotal examples fill the pages of educational journals and, more frequently these days, the mainstream press as well. There is no shortage of stories: the family farm owner who takes agriculture courses from a college in the big city several hundred miles away, the working mom who is able to complete her degree in the wee hours, or the Brazilian business executive who is able to earn his M.B.A. from an American university without leaving Brazil. The explosion of e-learning options has been a boon to those with limited time, limited mobility, or long physical distances separating them from their goals.

In the postsecondary market, the proliferation of online courses is exploding. The two leading e-learning platform companies, Web CT and Blackboard, claim to have doubled their customer base in the 1999–2000 period, with more than 2,500 institutions actively using their software. Hundreds of other colleges and universities are using competing or homegrown platforms. The number of courses on offer is increasing exponentially, though many of these courses are merely supplements to the classroom experience rather than exclusive distance education programs.

In the corporate world, e-learning is becoming the standard rather than the exception in many companies, especially among those in the tech sector. Corporate America spent an estimated $62.5 billion on training its workforce in 1999. Less than 20 percent of that amount involved online training, but the huge advantages in both cost and effectiveness are causing many companies to shift to an electronic model for at least part of their training needs.

The total education market in the United States is $772 billion, which counts for 7 percent of the gross domestic product (GDP) (W.R. Hambrecht & Company). The e-learning market is expected to grab $46 billion of this market by 2005 (National Institute of Standards and Technology). Currently there are some 500 online learning providers worldwide, of which more than 300 are in the United States (*Fortune* magazine). The e-learning market is very fragmented: no company holds more than a 6 percent e-learning market share. Many firms are new and privately held (International Data Corporation). E-learning content providers are the largest segment with 66 percent market share, growing at an annual rate of 74 percent.

Figure 11.2 offers a general idea of the market segments involved in the e-learning space. For the balance of this chapter, we concentrate on content providers.

The most numerous among the first movers in the e-learning market are new, for-profit companies that do not have strong brand names in the traditional education market. E- learning companies have not yet fully positioned themselves in the market. Most of the companies have been focused on customized management training. A smaller number of the content providers— for-profit, traditional universities and new public-private partnerships—are offering degrees online.

The author expects competition in the e-learning space to resemble that in the traditional market in terms of brand positioning. However, the number of competitors will likely be greater, including most—if not all—of the traditional U.S. education institutions, a number of foreign institutions, and for-profit entities. A short description of a few of the current content segments follows:

Traditional Universities

While a few traditional universities are offering full degree programs online, most are constrained by administrative hurdles, faculty resistance, or fear of cannibalization of the on-campus student pool. As of this writing, only three of the top twenty-five business schools offer e-learning degrees (Prince Market Research 2000). Established universities are, however, taking a more active role in the online education market. Some of them have established their own for-profit subsidiaries for online learning (i.e., eCornell, NYUonline, Duke Inc., and Wharton Direct) or they have allied with for-profit companies. Some top twenty-five U.S. business schools have developed their executive M.B.A. (EMBA) programs for online delivery in part (such as University of North Carolina and Indiana University).

Business Week's fifth-ranked Fuqua School at Duke University has two programs, the Cross Continent M.B.A. program and a global EMBA

Figure 11.2   e-Learning Company Divisions

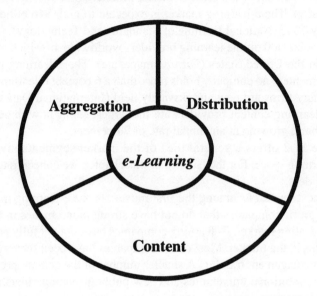

(GEMBA) program, which are partially or largely online. The Cross Continent program comprises eight terms, including a one-week residency and seven weeks of online education. The programs are designed for those who want to enhance their career path within their existing company.

For-Profit Universities

In the graduate program area, for-profit universities have quickly stepped in to fill the existing gaps, by either going it alone or by serving as the distance education arm of an established university.

Unext.com—Cardean University has an academic consortium with Carnegie Mellon, Columbia Business School, University of Chicago, Stanford University, and London Business School of Economics and Political Science. Currently, Unext.com focuses on management training, and its courses are open only to employees from partnering companies. In the future, Unext.com will have broader enrollment, and its students will be able to earn an M.B.A. degree from Cardean University. Unext.com will target people around the world who cannot attend a top business school and people with degrees who want lifelong learning.

Jones International University and *University of Phoenix Online* are both aggregated online universities. They offer online M.B.A. programs (among others) targeted to working adults. University of Phoenix Online is the biggest online university in the United States with more than 12,000 students and growing quickly.

Multifocus Content Complementors

Some new firms offer interactive management courses and create tailored knowledge communities for current content providers and directly for companies. Others focus on management training, instructional design, production, and technology in partnership with several business schools. At least one has developed a customized, partly online M.B.A. program together with a traditional university. Students for the program are generally based around the world and work for global companies.

Business schools are generally a U.S. phenomenon, but many international programs have been started in the last twenty-five years. Among the most active international business schools is INSEAD (France). Its primary focus is executive education. INSEAD opened a Singapore campus (100 students) and has plans to open a U.S. campus by 2003. As INSEAD's dean, Gabriel Hawawini, says: "Our goal is to create a global business school with a worldwide campus." INSEAD is typical of international business schools with a focus on U.S.-style management education.

There is no question that many traditional educational institutions own powerful brands that could potentially create real value in the executive education market. However, such schools frequently have institutional rigidities that inhibit their flexibility and speed in the fast-evolving e-learning market, particularly with degree programs.

Is e-Learning the Fifth Generation of Learning?

The previous section suggested that e-learning would revolutionize education by ceding power from the educator to the student/user. But will it really happen? The authors believe strongly that it will for three compelling reasons: user control; market forces that value the development of human capital; and increased productivity over traditional forms.

User Control

As in other markets, when the consumer takes control, or senses the ability to do so, there is no turning back. Consumers demand control and are reluctant to give it up once wrested from producers. While the "student" will have some measure of control, the real need for control in management education is with the "payer," the company for whom student-managers work. Costs and the need for more highly tuned training are driving companies to control their destinies through management training and education.

Market Forces

A 2000 study conducted by the American Society for Training and Development (ASTD) examined the average annual training expenditures of more than 500 U.S.-based publicly traded firms. The study concluded that firms in the top half of the group (i.e., firms that spent the most on training) had a total stockholder return 86 percent higher than firms in the bottom half and 46 percent higher than the market average.

As capital markets increasingly reward companies for their management of human equity at a rate far greater than for their stock of plant and equipment, growing a globally competitive workforce has leapt to the top of the CEO agenda.

Investing in human capital is a proven way to boost a firm's market cap. However, human capital is not something that is harvested from the earth, discovered on a shelf, or constructed from wood and steel. It is an asset that is derived solely from the individual and collective minds, creativity, energy, and collaborative culture of a firm's employees around the globe—particularly *high potential* managers.

Business owners know they need to offer high-quality management education in order to recruit and keep the best talent. At the same time, those with a widely dispersed workforce are challenged. Bringing executives to the United States for two years is expensive and disruptive, yet local universities do not meet the standards or consistency of what is offered in the United States.

Despite the layoff headlines currently making the news, there is a worldwide shortage of executive talent. A recent study commissioned by IBM and American Express noted that the shortage of qualified entrants into the workforce in the United States would become acute in the next several years. New entrants into the workforce, a critical resource for businesses, will decrease in absolute numbers by some 4.1 million people between 1996 and 2010. Companies are finding that skills needed by employees are changing rapidly and are constantly increasing in complexity. Companies are therefore turning to training of current employees to retain and upgrade their workforce in the United States and abroad (Oliver 2000).

Many of today's most successful companies are finding solutions through e-learning initiatives. With Web-based training, students around the world participate in a consistent program, using the same tools, language, and terminology. Time zones and geography become irrelevant and students can study when it is convenient for them, rather than when it is convenient for an institution. In addition, these courses offer the opportunity for global collaboration, allowing cross-continent discussions and perspectives that would not exist in a local classroom.

In addition, e-learning programs allow companies to monitor their students' progress and aptitude. In traditional classrooms, the instructor's perception is often the only gauge of whether the students are "getting it" or not. In an e-learning course, students are continually evaluated and challenged, with the results logged and tabulated. This process leads to a better understanding of the company's "return on learning."

Companies spend more than half their training budgets on travel and housing just to get instructors and students in the same room. Then there is time off the job. In this fast-paced economy, enterprises are reluctant to give up an employee for a two- or three-week course. "It's time, not money, that is the precious commodity in business these days," says Jeff Oberlin, vice president for course development and sourcing at Motorola University.

Motorola is widely cited for its belief that it receives $30 for every $1 invested in employee education and training. The message is spreading. A' 2000 study of corporate intentions to use e-learning suggests that nearly eight out of ten organizations will be using e-learning within three years.

Companies must ensure, however, that such programs do not merely replace the classroom experience with something cheaper and faster. Poorly developed e-learning courses will remove the classroom interaction that students enjoy and replace it with a flat, uninspiring course that offers little interactivity. In order to succeed, companies must be willing to invest the money in courses that replace the classroom with a richer, more effective learning experience that will produce true knowledge and skills development. The best courses will engage the learner with continual evaluation, interactive experiences, and simulations that prepare them for real-world environments.

Increased Learning Productivity

E-learning has the potential to dramatically improve the productivity of learning, converting it from an Industrial Age "hardware" manufacturing model (each time a professor goes into a classroom, it costs a little more than the last time) to an Information Age "software" model (creating the original version is very expensive, but there is virtually no incremental cost to the next copy). This potential is shown in Figure 11.3. This productivity enhancement occurs for both the teacher, who does not need to constantly restate course content material, and the student. The student-learning productivity

Figure 11.3   **e-Learning Costs**

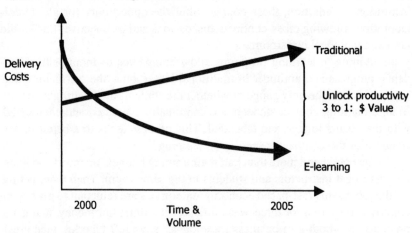

increases dramatically because students are no longer slowed by the pace of questions and other interruptions by their classmates. Further, enhanced interactivity can (at least hypothetically) occur because that student can seek out specific questions individually and quickly, given the one-on-one interactivity of the Internet.

Return on eLearning (ROeL)

ROI Versus ROL

The concept of return on investment (ROI) is a critical element of business decision-making that can be applied to any activity expected to yield a stream of future benefits. In the corporate environment, it is most frequently used in the context of physical investment, but, when properly used, it can provide valuable information about the payoff to investment in human capital via training and executive education—what this chapter refers to as "return on learning" (ROL). The chapter also extends this measurement to the fifth generation of learning by examining the return on e-learning (ROeL).

Application of ROI analysis to corporate training and education is in its infancy, largely because of difficulties in accurately quantifying its benefits. However, results of studies that take a variety of methodological approaches indicate that corporate investment in training provides an estimated ROI generally ranging between 10 and 200 percent (depending on the type of training analyzed, country studied, and methodological approach used).

While these figures provide a rough indication of how much net corporate performance improvement $1 of training expenditure will buy, a more specific question is what the ROI is for migrating corporate training programs from classroom or other non-computer-based format to computer-based training. In these cases, additional return can be generated from cost savings due to the migration. ROeL for these migrations varies widely—some case studies have reported figures in excess of 500 percent. Much of these savings stems from vastly reduced travel costs, as well as the ability to spread instruction costs over a larger number of students. Table 11.3 summarizes the results of six oft-cited studies published in the last ten years that use a large-sample econometric approach (studying large sample sizes using equations based on a standard economic growth model).

Table 11.4 summarizes the results of several studies undertaken by academics and corporations in the last ten years that use the case study approach (analyzing the costs and benefits of specific training programs at a single company or small number of companies). It provides an interesting window on ROL for different kinds of training. The most objective research (conducted by outside analysts) clearly shows that higher-level corporate education yields a much higher payoff than low-level remedial training. Three companies report ROL in excess of 100 percent, net of training costs.

Estimating ROeL

It is fairly clear that there is a substantial payoff to firms for engaging in employee training. An additional potentially large source of ROL is moving traditional training systems (including classroom settings and text-oriented computer-based training) to digitally based multimedia settings. The transition from classroom to computer-based training is happening throughout large corporations, and, with technology and bandwidth capacity growing, they are focusing on multimedia. As Table 11.5 shows, large U.S. companies have already embraced technology-mediated presentation and delivery techniques and plan to accelerate this shift in the next several years.

Numerous studies demonstrate that learning outcomes from distance education are not significantly different from classroom settings, but there is very little literature on how outcomes are affected by the move to distance education *and* computer-based learning. Also, as H. Martin Weingartner explains in "Quality of e-Learning" (2000), it is nearly impossible for research studies to accurately measure a learning method that is developing so quickly and evolving at the same speed as its underlying technology. For example, most research published thus far is based on studies done prior to the widespread availability of broadband Internet connections.

Table 11.3

Econometric Analyses of the Link Between Corporate Training and Performance

Author	Data	Type of training	Performance measure	Findings and comments
Bishop (1991)	Employment Opportunity Pilot Projects (2,594 employers)	New-hire training	Productivity index (scale of 0 to 100)	ROeL ranged from 11 percent to 38 percent, depending on empirical specification.
Bartel (1994)	Columbia Business School HR survey (155 manufacturing businesses)	All types	Value-added per worker	Implementation of formal training raised productivity by 19 percent over three years. Absence of training-cost data precludes true ROI estimate.
Huselid (1995)	Self-conducted HR practices survey (968 firms)	"High-performance work practices"	Tobin's Q statistic and rate of return on capital	Significant positive effect in cross-sectional model. Much smaller (even insignificant effect) in panel analysis. Nonmonetary expression of training precludes ROI calculation.
Lam and White (2000)	Self-conducted HR survey (235 manufacturing firms)	Compre-hensive HR develop-ment index	Return on assets, sales growth, and stock price appreciation	HR orientation is strongly and positively associated with growth in all three performance metrics. Model structure precludes ROI estimate.

Tan and Batra (1995)	World Bank survey of five non-OECD countries	All types	Value-added	Existence of formal company training programs raised productivity as follows:
				    Taiwan (2.8 percent)
				    Colombia (26.6 percent)
				    Malaysia (28.2 percent)
				    Mexico (44.1 percent)
				    Indonesia (71.1 percent)

Black and Lynch (1996)	EQW National Employers Survey (617 manufacturing establishments)	All types of off-the-job training	Net sales	Number of workers trained in prior years had no effect. In cross-sectional analysis, higher proportion of off-the-job training associated with higher sales. Results lose robustness in panel analysis. Absence of cost data precludes true ROI estimate.

Source: Based on information from Bartel (2000), and Lam and White (2000).

Table 11.4

Case Study Analyses of the Return on Investment in Corporate Training

Author and/or company	Employee group studied	Type of training	Performance measure	Findings and comments
Bartel (1995), large manufacturer	Professional employees	Management, communication, and technical skills	Wage growth and performance ratings	Estimated ROI of 49.7 percent. Controls for selection bias and employee-specific fixed effects.
Krueger and Rouse (1998), one manufacturing and one service company	Lower-skill employees	Remedial (reading, writing, and math improvement)	Wage growth and performance awards	ROI ranged from 0 to 7 percent. Controls for employee-specific fixed effects.
Federal Express	Twenty truck and van drivers	Driver safety and related training	Ten criteria including accidents, injuries, and errors	ROI of 24 percent. Increase in ROI is relative to a control group that did not receive training.
Garrett Engine	Maintenance teams	Team building	Dollar value of reduced downtime	Estimated ROI of 125 percent. Performance only monitored for four weeks following training. Small sample limits generalizability.
International Oil	Dispatchers	Customer service	Reduction in pullout and customer complaint costs	Reported gross ROI of 501 percent (does not net out key cost components). Estimated net ROI of 200 percent with cost adjustment.
Motorola	All employees	All types	Cost cutting, sales, and profit increases	Claim $30 saved for every dollar of training investment. Sales per employee doubled in five years. Unclear how they separate performance improvement due to training from that due to other factors.

Source: Based on information from Bartel (2000), Phillips (1996), Henkoff (1993).

Table 11.5

Use of Selected Nonclassroom Learning Technologies for Employer Training at Large U.S. Corporations, 1998 and 2001 Projections

	Percent of companies		Percent of training courses	
	1998	2001	1998	2001
Presentation techniques				
Computer-based training of all kinds	53.3	81.2	5.9	14.2
Multimedia	65.1	91.2	14.4	23.9
Teleconferencing	30.0	63.2	1.7	6.4
Virtual reality	2.9	20.9	0.3	2.3
Distribution techniques				
Intranet	32.2	77.1	4.6	16.2
World Wide Web	19.8	54.4	2.2	8.7
CD-ROM	56.3	87.0	5.9	15.1
Cable or satellite TV	12.5	28.0	0.7	2.5
Local area network	40.2	59.1	9.3	13.5
E-mail	40.6	62.4	8.0	13.2

Source: Based on information from American Society for Training and Development (2000).

ROeL is a critical element of planning corporate training and educational priorities. Growing literature on the subject indicates that these returns are very large, whether measured with respect to sales, productivity, or other broad metrics. Yet larger benefits are obtainable by migrating corporate education and training programs to carefully planned Web-based or other computer-mediated environments.

Valuing Human Equity

Historically, one of the key financial measures of corporate success has been return on assets (ROA), a measure that helps corporate strategists and financial investors compare management's use of the total assets of the firm to industry averages and to competitors.

While still a valuable tool, ROA becomes problematic in an era such as today's economy when the definition of "assets" is outmoded. Today a firm's assets are increasingly less tangible. In fact, for many firms, if not all, their principal assets are intangible and hard to identify, compare, count, and value. Those assets are in the form of intellectual capital (e.g., knowledge assets, process know-how, brands, public trust) and human capital.

While much work is being done to value knowledge and other intellectual capital (in the form of brands, for instance) for balance-sheet purposes, relatively less information and guidance is available to strategists on human assets.

This state of affairs is particularly troublesome since it is no secret to any CEO or business owner that quality people, especially quality leaders, are the key to corporate success. All the grand strategies are useless if capable management is not in place to execute them. The companies that can hire and retain top-tier managers will lead; those that cannot will rarely catch up.

According to Brandon-Hall.com, a training-research organization that benchmarks the successes of e-learning users, e-learning has produced training budget savings of 40 to 60 percent for large organizations such as Ernst & Young, the U.S. Internal Revenue Service, KPMG, and Rockwell Collins. Oracle estimates that it saves $100 million per year by utilizing e-learning, while IBM and Cisco each estimate they have saved over $200 million per year.

Surveys continually support the argument that well-designed e-learning courses not only save money and travel time, but also meet or exceed the effectiveness of the classroom experience.

What e-Learning Can and Cannot Do

True learning is not memorizing, but understanding. In most traditional classrooms, students show up at a specified time to hear the professor speak, they take tests that illustrate how well they have memorized what the professor and textbooks have stated, and they are graded accordingly. In a truly effective course, however, students learn principles and ideas that they can apply to other situations, and they develop abilities that will enable them to find answers and solutions.

John D. Bransford et al., editors of *How People Learn*, point out that our current deluge of information has made the educational goal of "knowing things" a futile pursuit. What we must teach all students now is how to learn, how to ask meaningful questions, how to innovate, and how to effectively search for the information that they require in order to achieve their fullest potential in a rapidly changing world.

E-learning is much more suited to the challenge of not just memorizing but understanding, of finding ways to find future answers rather than just learning today's answers. Real learning takes time, effort, and practice. A student cannot learn the principles of microeconomics in eight hours, in any learning situation. A student must be engaged for long periods in an environment that is interesting, stimulating, and effective. The student must have ample opportunities for practice and multiple opportunities to apply what has been learned at each stage. Table 11.7 details what can be done in an e-learning situation.

Table 11.6

Case Studies of the Benefits of Migrating Training Programs from Classroom-Based to Computer-Based

Company	Computer-based media	Type of training	Cost savings relative to classroom	Comments
Bell Canada (1999)	Web-based asynchronous and synchronous	Technical	ROI ranged from 28.3 percent to 69.7 percent for synchronous and over 30 percent for asynchronous.	Synchronous course had no multimedia, hence development cost was much lower than for others.
High-tech company (1997)	CD-ROM	IT	47 percent less, implying an ROI of just over 100 percent.	Bulk of savings came from reduced costs of travel and being absent from office.
Oak Ridge National Lab (1997)	Intranet	Safety and health	ROI of 84.5 percent (reflects net benefit of $1.51 million net benefit and $0.178 million cost).	50 percent of saving is from reduced travel costs, remainder is reduced training time and fewer instructor hours. More realistic travel cost estimate yields ROI of 61.6 percent.

Source: Based on information from Whalen and Wright (1999), and Schriver and Giles (1999).

What e-Learning Cannot Do

However, some subjects do require human contact to promote authentic practice. The effectiveness of course on presentation skills, for example, might be limited without practice in front of an instructor or classmates.

Some students miss the socialization with classmates that a small college class can provide, so e-learning courses must be designed to facilitate student interaction as a matter of course.

Table 11.7

What Can Be Done in an Online Course

Evaluate students by wider criteria than just assignment and test grades.

Create a quizzing structure that continually gauges comprehension.

Post grades as a group, subgroup, or individually, in real time.

Create a discussion board where all questions and answers are archived.

Post announcements that students must read before entering the course.

Host discussions that can take place across different schedules and time zones.

Easily push real-time information to students and allow them to share discovered material among themselves.

Regularly feature audio and video course material.

Continually use real-time case studies from today's news.

Refer to Web pages for examples and provide links to more in-depth information.

Create a different resource center (a virtual library) for each course, available 24 x 7.

Ensure that students are exposed to material in a variety of media and contexts.

Monitor how long students spend on the course, and in which areas.

What Works—Best Practices

One of the key findings of modern learning research is that students perform best when they can take control of their own learning. This ability is rather limited in a typical instructor-centric college course, but can be explored to its fullest in the more flexible online course. In the former, the instructor is a feudal king; in the latter, he or she is a facilitator. This is a key distinction: in a classroom setting the student body has little control, but in a properly run online course, both the group and the individual are in control of discussions, pacing, and which material demands the most interest.

In a well-designed course, this student control can ensure "attention till mastery," a concept that is impractical in a physical classroom setting, where all students are tied to the same limited time frame. If particular learners are having trouble with a particular problem or concept, they can be directed to run through a series of exercises and explanations in different contexts until they are able to grasp what they were missing.

Effective online courses can go well beyond the classroom approach in encouraging self-assessment and frequently gauging comprehension. All students are required to participate and to communicate on a regular basis, allowing continual knowledge sharing and deeper understanding. With proper ground rules set up at the beginning, there are no dominant students asking the professor all the questions and there are no wallflowers that never speak up.

Many online courses fail because they simply transfer classroom notes to a computer program. The student is expected to passively absorb information from a monitor and spit it back out when tested at the end. A successful course takes work to design well and must present information in different contexts to engage those who learn best by auditory, visual, or kinesthetic means.

Nonbusiness Applications for e-Learning

K–12

E-learning has the potential for bringing the world's resources to each and every child, tying parents directly to teachers, replacing rote learning with exciting interactive study, and cutting administrative costs.

The U.S. Department of Education recently estimated that 96 percent of the K–12 schools were connected to the Internet at the end of 1999, meaning we are likely at or near 100 percent today.

Providing courses and electronic field trips are among the principal applications for distance learning in pre-K through grade 12 education. Distance learning is also used to support rural and inner-city classes with student enrichment, student courses, staff development, and in-service training for teachers and administrators.

E-learning has also played a part in the recent boom in home schooling. With nearly unlimited course materials and teaching guides at their fingertips, parents are now able to match or exceed what is offered in the classroom. Bigchalk.com, for example, organizes more than 2,500 multimedia resources, including article collections, historical clips, and lessons built around sound collections from the Smithsonian. Classroom teachers or teaching parents can use these resources to make a static lesson come alive or arrange a "virtual field trip" to the tropical rainforest or the Arctic Circle.

Not surprisingly, some commercial enterprises are providing some of the richest online material. The Discovery Channel's DiscoverySchool.com provides a wealth of material on animals, nature, science, and space exploration. Minicourses and quizzes are available with a click of the mouse. National Geographic World online focuses on subjects of interest to children, and the Learning Network's "Fact Monster" site will help students complete almost any homework assignment.

Lifelong Learning

Hundreds of millions worldwide turn to the Web each day to learn something or to gather information. An increasing number are turning that thirst for knowledge into a desire for structured courses, either for career enhancement or personal development.

E-learning started out as a platform for career-minded learners to hone their computer skills or to become certified on a specific software program. The explosion of technology in the workplace has accelerated this trend. As *Industry Standard* editor Bob Cohn put it, "It used to be that education was something you pursued before you took your first full-time job. But in the new economy, learning is a lifelong enterprise." Universities have played a large part in this movement, especially companies such as Jones International University and the University of Phoenix. Both have marketed continuing education to the masses. Regional and community colleges have also expanded their non-degree-seeking ranks by growing and marketing their e-learning initiatives.

One of the most interesting developments has been the growth of courses offered through commercial Web sites. Rather than being a line of business, these offerings are typically an attempt at building a loyal community of customers. BarnesandNoble.com offers free courses on everything from wine to astronomy to Shakespeare, and sells plenty of course books on the side. Financial advice site The Motley Fool offers reasonably priced courses for beginning investors, while Morningstar.com conducts dozens of free courses on everything from analyzing a mutual fund's performance to reading a cash flow statement. Similarly focused courses are showing up on other sites that cater to aspiring gardeners, decorators, or novel writers.

Conclusion

The overriding factors that are stimulating the growth of e-learning across the educational spectrum are the same as those propelling an entire range of e-Service applications in a wide spectrum of industries: interactivity, personalization, and real-time content availability. The use of e-learning in management education is leading the trend because of market forces, globalization, and the increasing financial commitment by organizations and investors to the development of "human capital." By eliminating the constraints of time and space, e-learning, as in all e-Services, puts the user in control, increases satisfaction, and ultimately increases the productivity of the transaction for both consumer and service provider.   •

Historically in education, the teacher/institution schedule was paramount. No learning took place that did not fit the academic calendar. In e-learning, the student is in charge and a teacher's schedule becomes irrelevant. The student is in control of both the amount of time dedicated to study and the pace of that study. Content that is not relevant to the student can be skipped.

Content requiring further study can be allotted more time. A course that was formerly confined to a rigid semester of time can instead be finished in two months or ten.

The elimination of distance means that a student's physical location is not an issue. A rural student three hours from the closest university can get the same quality of education as one on campus. A business student in Calcutta or Caracas can get a world-class M.B.A. from an institution anywhere in the world. Any student in the world can study Shakespeare in London, study Arabic in the Middle East, or study medicine in Baltimore—all from wherever he or she lives. Globalization is an unstoppable force that is transforming the practices of nearly every country on Earth. With e-learning, another promise of globalization is at the fingertips of anyone with a computer and a modem.

E-learning allows education to evolve beyond the fragmented, very local institution it has been for thousands of years. A small percentage of students have always studied abroad, including at least a half million that come to the United States each year, but economic and social factors limit the number of people who have this option. With education from any developed country available in the home, global education becomes a reality for the masses, and universities will face tremendous challenges in order to adapt and thrive.

References

American Society for Training and Development. 2000. *ASTD 2000 State of the Industry Report.* Alexandria, VA: American Society for Training and Development.

Bartel, Ann P. 1994. "Productivity Gains from the Implementation of Employee Training Programs." *Journal of Industrial Relations* 33(4) (November): 411–425.

———. 1995. "Training, Wage Growth, and Job Performance: Evidence from a Company Database." *Journal of Labor Economics* 13 (July): 401–425.

———. 2000. "Measuring the Employer's Return on Investments in Training: Evidence from the Literature." *Journal of Industrial Relations* 39(3) (July): 502–523.

Bishop, John H. 1991. "On-the-Job Training of New Hires." In *Market Failure in Training?*, ed. D. Stern and J.M.M. Ritzen. New York: Springer-Verlag, 61–98.

Black, Sandra, and Lisa Lynch. 1996. "Human Capital Investments and Productivity." *American Economic Review* 86 (May): 263–267.

Bransford, John D.; Ann L. Brown; and Rodney R. Cocking, eds. 2000, *How People Learn: Brain, Mind, Experience and School.* Washington, DC: National Academic Press.

Henkoff, Ronald. 1993. "Companies that Train Best." *Fortune,* March 22.

Huselid, Mark. 1995. "The Impact of Human Resource Management Practices on Turnover, Productivity, and Corporate Financial Performance." *Academy of Management Journal* 38 (June): 636–672.

Krueger, Alan, and Cecelia Rouse. 1998. "The Impact of Workplace Education on Earnings, Turnover, and Job Performance." *Journal of Labor Economics* 16 (January): 61–94.

Lam, Long W., and Louis P. White. 2000. "Human Resource Orientation and Corporate Performance." *Human Resource Development Quarterly* 9(4) (winter): 351–364.

Oliver, Richard W. 2000. "The Future of Small Business." w.smallbusiness2000.com.

Phillips, Jack J. 1996. "Was It the Training?" *Training and Development* (July). American Society for Training and Development.

Schriver, Rob, and Steve Giles. 1999. "Real ROI Numbers." *Training and Development* (August). American Society for Training and Development.

Tan, Hong W., and Geeta Batra. 1995. "Enterprise Training in Developing Countries: Incidence, Productivity Effects, and Policy Implications." Mimeo, World Bank.

Weingartner, H. Martin. 2000. Quality of e-Learning: Report on Computer-Mediated Distributed Asynchronous Instruction." White paper, American Graduate School of Management.

Whalen, Tammy, and David Wright. 1999. "Methodology for Cost-Benefit Analysis of Web-Based Tele-learning: Case Study of the Bell Online Institute." *American Journal of Distance Education* 13(1): 24–44.

12

The Customer-Centric Digital Department

e-Service in Government

Jeffrey O. Bollettino

Introduction

As the dot.com bubble expanded and grew to full size, there was a near avalanche of e-business books touting the meaning of "e-" as the quest to create and capture profits in "new ways." In hindsight, however, it is clear that the implicit connection between e-business and "new ways of profits" had more to do with Wall Street mania than reality. The irony is that it is the government arena, where the focus on profits is absent, that provides the most potent insights on the value and realities of e-Service. This is because in a government context, we can remove from our thinking the factors that were the main drivers for e-business during the dot.com boom—namely, and succinctly, fear and greed. Fear arose from the many predictions, and some actual observations, that traditional businesses were being "blown to bits" (Evans and Wurster 2000). It appeared that nearly all traditional businesses were in line to be toppled by Internet-savvy teenagers at work in their garages. For this reason, e-business jumped overnight to the top of nearly every CEO's agenda as pressure from stockholders, customers, and competitors rose to a peak. Running hand in hand with fear was greed, about which, as an ardent capitalist, I certainly make no negative value judgment, for, to paraphrase a classic movie line, "Greed is often good." Greed led to soaring stock values and the creation of new dot.com fortunes, although many would subsequently be lost. As hyped by the media, greed drove the message that e-business was the only path to profits in the "new economy."

During this same period of time there came to be quite a lot of interest in something called electronic government or e-government, although it was not clear initially what it meant. Was it e-business applied to government? Was it a call for governments to operate like a business? While a lot was not clear at the time, what was clear was e-business did not create a comparable level of fear and greed within government organizations as it did in the private sector. While every CEO had a strong "burning platform" to become an e-enterprise, and was moving out aggressively on e-business, managers and leaders in government were left wondering what it all really meant in a government context. When the author, working with government clients in the information technology (IT) realm, began to ponder this question in the late 1990s, a number of key questions were formulated to guide our initial thinking about e-Service for governments:

1. What is our goal with e-Service? Our goal in discussing "e-Service" is not to learn how to provide *any* level of service electronically, but rather to seek to *transform* our delivery of government services through an electronic medium. Transformation represents our desire for improvements that are nonincremental—to achieve service that is significantly better, or of greater value, than that provided through traditional channels. The intention to go beyond simply making today's processes electronic stems from a recognition that, for some time, government organizations have been making greater and greater use of information technology. For example, the U.S. government already spends more than $45 billion annually on IT. E-Service couldn't simply be a call to use more IT or engage the Internet more fully. It also had to be more than taking today's processes and making them electronic. Replacing a form mailed physically with an electronic version transmitted by e-mail, while a good improvement in its own right, would clearly be incremental improvement. Thus, while incremental improvement would be good and welcome, we were going to aim at *transformational change*—change that has a much greater impact than the simple automation of existing processes.

2. Is this something new, or a rehash of the old? Our answer in short form is both. We observed that, in the past, a number of schools of thought had offered the promise of transformation, but none of them alone had been successful on a wide scale. These "schools" were driven separately by the gurus of information technology, management innovations such as business process reengineering (BRP), and government reinvention (e.g., see Osborne and Plastrik [1998]). In the hands of skilled implementers, each of these schools offered the potential for transformational change, but looking back at successful projects showed that when transformational change occurred, all three were usually present. As illustrated in Figure 12.1, our approach to e-Service was then built around the intersection of IT, BPR, and reinvention, in that we would seek to:

- fully exploit the rich electronic connection to customers that was now available via the Internet and other networks;
- reengineer processes around the customer, rather than the organization;
- use the out-of-the-box methods and cross-organizational thinking exemplified by government reinvention approaches.

3. Do government organizations want transformation? A most vexing question to consider was whether government managers and staff really had a desire to make a transformational change in the level of service provided. Would government employees support transformation efforts, especially when such efforts could render significant change in the status quo? Government managers must often contend with the tension that exists between the view of a public institution as a "must fund" entity, where improvements in service are optional, and the view that budgets will only be appropriated to the extent that the institution adds value. Government organizations in general have no "burning platform" that drives its leaders to focus on electronic service as a top priority. However, there are situations where effective platforms for change arise:

- Congress, particularly when in concert with the mood of the public, can create the environment for massive change, as it did in the mid- to late 1990s in demanding a revamping of the Internal Revenue Service (IRS). This move enabled the implementation of a massive e-Service program that is still being rolled out as of mid-2002.
- Elected leaders, such as governors and mayors, have created effective platforms for change when it is a high priority in their administration and when senior leaders are given the authority and resources. An example was Mayor Steve Goldsmith of Indianapolis who, starting in 1992, drove a platform for change by requiring city workers to compete with the private sector for their jobs (Osborne and Plastrik 2000).
- Career and appointed government executives with exceptional leadership skills have been able to create platforms for change when they can define for their staff why change is needed, show how the organization will get there, and provide the resources to do so. This is a daunting task, as any manager in any organization, private or public sector, can attest. While a discussion of change management is beyond the scope

Figure 12.1   **e-Service Operates at the Intersection of Three Schools of Thought**

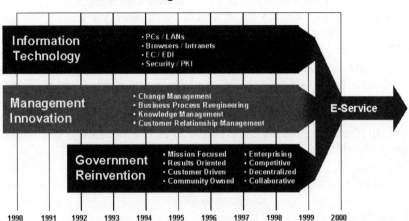

of this chapter, there are celebrated examples[1] available that demonstrate where government leaders have driven the level of change required for e-Service.

The situations above are not meant to be all-inclusive, as there are other situations and conditions that enable change. With these in mind, the conclusion reached was that some organizations, under the right conditions, *will* have an appetite for transformation, and those are the ones for whom an e-Service approach will be appealing. We also recognize that other organizations will initiate deliberately nontransformational efforts, and wrap them for convenience with the "glitter" of e-Service. While incremental gains from these projects do not represent our goal of transformation, they *do* represent progress, even if not at the desired level.

So with a goal of transformation, a recognition that our toolbox would include tricks from the IT, BPR, and reinvention worlds, and a belief that there would be leaders who would step up to the challenge, we considered what was at the core of e-Service—what is the essence of e-Service? A review of the "lessons learned" from the e-business world revealed that its thinking was so driven by the "fear and greed" factors that its use "as is" was impossible. So we posed the thought question: "If you start with e-business, and subtract the parts driven by fear and greed, what are you left with?" The answer we found is at the true core of what e-Service means, and that has everything to do with a new orientation to those being served.

In a government context, there is no universally accepted name for those being served. At times it may be appropriate to call them citizens, although sometimes they are not citizens (e.g., issues regarding immigration). In some cases, the entity served is a constituent or stakeholder. The author prefers to use the term "customer" at all times because it most closely evokes the attitude that is required of those serving to achieve the new orientation to those served. We'll use the term "customer" in this chapter to represent any individual, entity, or organization that uses the results of what you do. In this usage a customer could be a citizen, constituent, business, government employee, Congress, another government organization, or many other descriptors. In identifying the set of customers, it can be valuable to use the four categories defined by David Osborne and Peter Plastrik (1998):

Primary Customers	The individual or group your work is primarily designed to help.
Secondary Customers	Other individuals or groups your work is designed to benefit—but less directly than your primary customers.
Compliers	Those who must comply with laws and regulations, for example, taxpayers in relation to the Internal Revenue Service.[2]
Stakeholders	Individuals and groups that have an interest in the performance of a public system or organization, for example, teachers in the public schools.

A good example of a government organization that has worked to identify its primary customers is the Department of Housing and Urban Development (HUD). A snapshot of HUD's Web site is shown in Figure 12.2, and the upper-right corner provides a list of customer groups that HUD has identified. HUD has used events such as county fairs and other public gatherings to test and refine its list of customers. For each customer group, HUD provides content that is targeted to its special needs.

To understand why e-Service is so fundamentally oriented toward customers, we need to look at the underlying transformation occurring in our connection with those we serve and seek to understand the implications for how we provide service.

Foundations for e-Service

It is often, and mistakenly, believed that e-business is the foundational driver for many of the changes occurring today in business and technology. However, a more fundamental force is at play, which futurist author

Figure 12.2 **Customer Groups Identified on HUD's Web Site**

George Gilder describes as the *telecosm* (Gilder 2000). Gilder describes the telecosm as "the world enabled and defined by new communications technology" that will make human communications universal, instantaneous, unlimited in capacity and essentially free. The telecosm follows on the heels of the *microcosm*, the age driven by Moore's Law—the doubling of computing power, or the halving of its cost every eighteen months. Gilder argues that the age of the microcosm is ending, not because it has failed, but because it has succeeded so fully that it is omnipresent and no longer the force for change. His new force for change is the telecosm, where the world becomes so fully and richly connected, and bandwidth so abundant and inexpensive as to be wasteable. Bandwidth then replaces computer power as the driving force of technological advances. The telecosm has many fascinating implications but of central importance to e-Service is the recognition that we now have what we did not have just a few years ago—a high-speed[3] digital connection to virtually[4] every customer. These connections ride over not just the Internet, but through the many private and government networks covering local and wide area geographies. Previously we could not connect to customers, and, more importantly, customers could not connect to governments, through a remote mode that offers the:

- intimacy of an e-mail;
- permanent and self-documenting nature of written mail;
- interactivity of a phone call or face-to-face interaction;
- immediacy of radio;
- rich visual and dynamic display ranging between full-color magazines and television;
- competence of predesign, rather than the hit-or-miss results of typical face-to-face interactions.

These characteristics of intimacy, permanence, interactivity, immediacy, visual stimulation, and competence combine for a very powerful connection mechanism that is unlike any previous medium. The observation has been made by others that each new technology tends to be used initially in the same manner as its predecessor, until it is understood more fully. The first television shows were formatted much like their radio show predecessors, and so on. In the same ways, early e-Service initiatives have tended to format e-Service around thinking rooted in printed material—brochures, catalogs, and forms. To be successful in using the electronic mode to provide, at a minimum, competent and ultimately transformative levels of service requires an understanding of the new medium. Today's more limited understanding of these qualities has led to a proliferation of Web pages with little transformation. For example, as of mid-2001, the U.S. government manages 31 million Web pages of content, but has very little transformative change to show for it. The hard truth of e-Service, as shown in Figure 12.3, is that we have to change what is behind the Web site—the people, processes, culture, and organizations that make government work. The reasons are rooted in the key implications of the *telecosm*.

Telecosmic Implications

The telecosm encompasses a trillion-dollar infrastructure, already in place and ready to be used by anyone, at such little cost that it is essentially free. This has made information available far more cheaply and universally than at any previous time, and enables transaction costs to be reduced toward zero. Customers have ready access to so much information that they can easily observe the agility of an organization and the progress, or lack of it, being made. So the implication is *transparency*—organizations live in "glass houses." Transparency is the quality that eliminates the asymmetry of information that traditionally existed between customers, who were left guessing, and providers, who really knew what was happening. This has changed the balance of power from providers to customers. Now being more powerful,

Figure 12.3 **We Have to Change What Is Behind the Web Site**

the customer is able to demand and get greater levels of service that are customized to his/her specific needs. Therefore, *customer expectations have never been higher*, raising the demands on all public- and private-sector organizations.

The worldwide Internet infrastructure is a global, borderless platform for applications and communications. It enables customers to easily reach out to one another to talk about your organization, whether you facilitate it or not. Many organizations, particularly governments, cringe at the notion of facilitating public discussions among their customers. The fear is that the resulting image may not be uniformly positive, and they are probably correct. However, what is underappreciated is that customers can and do establish these discussions themselves, and the results can be far more negative. Consider, for example, the Web site www.untied.com, a customer forum created by passengers of United Airlines (UAL) as shown in Figure 12.4. Untied.com was created in 1996 following an unsatisfactory response to a passenger complaint letter. The site draws an average of 15,000 user sessions per month and has grown to document the complaints of contributors in categories that include rudeness, misinformation, incompetence, special needs, refund problems, and premier class. As the Web site declares, "We have, from the very early days, made it clear that these web pages exist not as an 'anti-UAL' site, but rather to raise attention to—and help address—the serious problems within the airline." Many other companies have seen similar sites (e.g., Starbucked.com) created by their customers, and several multicompany "gripe

Figure 12.4   **Customers Are Talking—Is Anyone Listening?**

sites" (e.g., PlanetFeedback.com, eComplaints.com, Vault.com, AskAn Owner.com) are also in operation. From a review of any of these sites, it is difficult to imagine that one facilitated by the company could be less flattering.

The message here is that in an age of e-mail, Web sites, instant messaging, and other means, customers can easily and inexpensively find ways to contact each other and discuss their experience and level of satisfaction with what you do. Their motivations in making these discussions public is generally not to be malicious, but instead to bring about positive change. To create this positive change in an e-Service context requires that we address the customer feedback from these channels at two levels. The first and more basic level is a simple complaint system, where we achieve incremental improvements by accepting the complaints in electronic form. A 1996 government study (www.govinfo.library.unt.edu) on customer service identified the following five best practices for resolving customer complaints:

1. *Make it easy for your customers to complain, and your customers will make it easy for you to improve.* Informed customers know how your services should work. If things are not working, customers are the first to know.

2. *Respond to complaints quickly and courteously with common sense, and you will improve customer loyalty.* A speedy response can add 25 percent to customer loyalty, which in government terms means increased confidence.
3. *Resolve complaints on the first contact and (1) save money by eliminating unnecessary additional contacts that escalate costs and (2) build customer confidence.* Research, and common sense, indicate that resolving a complaint on the first contact reduces the cost by at least 50 percent.
4. *Technology utilization is critical in complaint-handling systems.* Develop a database of complaints that can be used to spot trends, and use the database to present summaries of complaint data to everyone, especially management.
5. *Recruit and hire the best for customer service jobs.* Complaint resolution positions in leading customer service organizations tend to be highly sought-after positions, and since these employees get to know the organization so well, they are also able to get promoted into other roles.

The comprehensive implementation of these best practices can have a significant impact on customer service levels. To address customer feedback at a second level with the potential for transformation, we need to consider how wide a swath of the organization will gain the direct benefit of the message from customers. As illustrated in Figure 12.5, most customer communications are through a relatively "thin" channel between a small set of customers (e.g., those who are surveyed or happen to submit a complaint) and a small set of employees (e.g., customer service representatives or sales staff). Thus relatively few people in the organization have a true feel for what is happening on the "front lines." However, we can use the Internet to create online forums that make it easy for our customers to have a conversation with each other, and that is convenient for our employees to listen to. This has the added benefit, when compared with a complaint system, in that the customers are having a *dialogue with each other*, rather than submitting issues for the organization to respond to.

The important question is, how much better would your organization perform if a significant number of employees would tune in to the dialogue among customers? Too many organizations view the Internet as only a broadcast channel when in fact its unique power is as a listening tool. Customers are out there having a dialogue, and chances are they are willing to let you listen in. So the implication is *listening*—organizations must find ways to tune in to the customer dialogue. An early government example is found on the Web site of the U.S. Department of Housing and Urban Development (HUD). As shown in Figure 12.6, HUD's customers, who are often inhabitants of low-income housing, can reach out to one another to discuss problems of mutual interest. HUD

Figure 12.5   **Use the Internet to Tune in to the Customer Dialogue**

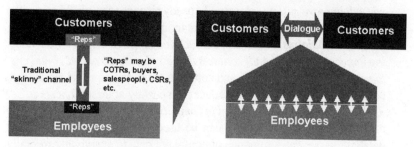

makes clear on the site that it does not monitor the discussions for the purpose of answering questions, which it need not do since the forums are a dialogue between customers. But the power of these forums is the potential for a broad base of HUD employees to "tune in" and develop a daily understanding of the issues and problems that confront its customers.

Listening to customers must be done smartly. The quote "People don't want quarter-inch drill bits—they want quarter-inch holes" illustrates what this means. Listening to customers is more about understanding the problems they face, the results they want, and the value we can add than it is about literally doing whatever they say. When we observe customers buying "quarter-inch drill bits," we need to be smart enough to understand that they really want quarter-inch holes. If we have a better way to create those holes, then we have an opportunity to add more value.

Now, if we combine *transparency* and *listening* we uncover another implication. Customers can now see past the packaged services of an organization's total value chain, and now have a clearer view of the *individual pieces* of the value chain. For example, a typical government may have a general services or administrative division that supplies contracts and procurement officials to help various agencies with their acquisitions. As shown in Figure 12.7, a simple view of their value chain would include contract officers (CO) and contract vehicles. However, other agencies also offer contract officers for hire, and can award their own contracts. Through transparency and customer dialogues, customers can rate the subpieces of the value chain, for example, rating the COs from one agency as an A+ and those from another as a B+. With similar ratings for the contracting ability, customers can pull together a custom value chain using the highest-rated pieces for their needs. Thus, customers can access the individual pieces of the organization's value chain, and to be successful, the subpieces must be competitive in their own right. The implication for all organizations, including governments, is to *understand your true competencies as well as your customers do*, and to consider partnering or outsourcing the pieces that are rated B+ and below.

Figure 12.6   HUD Creates Online Dialogues Between Customers

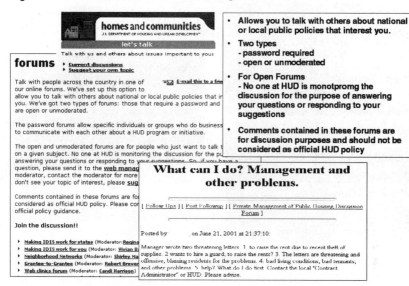

The Customer-Centric Mindset

Customer-centricity is a mindset that begins with the question "What are the customers' needs and what do they value?" This question is most likely to lead to transformation when the answer is developed without the stovepiped constraints of the services provided by any particular agency or department. This is perhaps the most difficult barrier to overcome, as focusing on what a particular agency does, being *agency-centric*, has been ingrained in the organizational culture for a long time. Figure 12.8 illustrates the problem by representing four government entities, labeled as Agencies A, B, C, and X. These may be four branches in the same agency, four departments in an overall government, or entirely different levels of government (i.e., federal, state, local). As shown by the dotted lines, these organizations typically provide their "stovepipe" of services. For customers one, two, three, and four, this is fine since, as represented in the figure, their needs fit within the services offered by the agencies A, B, C, and X. But customers five, six, and seven have needs that are not met alone by A, B, C, or X, and increasingly, this is how today's government customers exist. Meeting the needs of these customers requires *integrated service delivery*, by starting with their needs and working back to whichever agencies offer the necessary services. I emphasize the difficulty of doing this—it is not a natural act for any organization, particularly governments. It is counter to historical thinking and is often contradicted and made more difficult by the

Figure 12.7 **Customers Create Their Own A+ Value Chains**

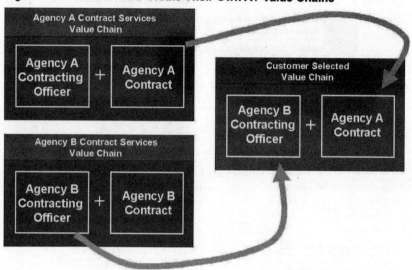

budget appropriation process.[5] Nonetheless, the integration of service delivery is fundamental to customer-centric transformation.

How do we learn enough about customer needs to become customer-centric? It is made difficult because, as described by Adrian Slywotzky and David Morrison (1998) "we don't see things as they are, we see things as *we* are." Seeing things as "they are," from the customer's perspective, requires a regular inflow of feedback. This is the reason for our previous emphasis on finding ways to tune into the dialogue that is happening between customers. A once-per-year customer conference or survey will not provide us with the richness of continual feedback needed to understand how customer needs are continually changing. Managers need to look at the customers' problems through the customers' eyes, which is difficult to impossible to accomplish if the input comes through a survey report. Part of being customer-centric is recognizing that we can only add value where the customer will let us, and therefore we need to be able to listen to their changing needs. Succeeding with e-Service means letting customers establish the agenda for what services you provide and how you provide them.

e-Service Qualities

A simple definition of a government e-Service organization (an e-government) is one that is focused on customers and uses technology to optimize the delivery of service. If we use the catchy phrase "digital department" to represent the idea of optimized service through technology,

Figure 12.8   **Customer-Centric Thinking Leads to Integrated
Service Delivery**

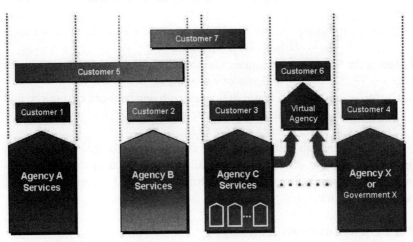

If your agency is "Agency A." who else serves the same
customer?

we can think of e-governments as customer-centric digital departments.
This definition is sufficient at a high level, but we offer greater detail in
the form of eight essential characteristics. The first three stem from the
simple observation of what happens with any electronic Web connection:

1. Open When Needed   Provides services 24 hours per day, 365 days per year.
2. Accessible   Provides easy access to its information, overcoming the barriers of time and distance.
3. Electronic   Minimizes the use of paper wherever possible.

The next two reflect the process goals for how we develop e-Service approaches:

4. Knowledge-Driven   Derives the maximum value from information and knowledge.
5. Collaborative   Develops solutions collaboratively with government, citizen, and industry partners.

So far, the characteristics represent good electronic practices but are not
transformational. Unfortunately, this is where many current electronic solu-

tions stop. However, when transformational uses of the Web are studied, there are three underappreciated qualities that drive the transformational difference:

6. Mass Customizing   Customizes services to the specific needs of each individual customer.
7. Seamless   Integrates services seamlessly with other agencies or levels of government.
8. Customer-Led[6]   Creates dialogues with and between customers, and aligns with customer groups.

These last three qualities reflect what is different about the electronic Web medium, and these differences make all the difference in the ability of a government organization to achieve transformation, and not just automation, through e-Service.

The Path to Customer-Centricity

As we embark toward customer-centric government, we need to recognize two sobering realities: (1) The path to creating customer-centric government organizations is not altogether clear, and (2) the only piece of it that *is* clear is that it will be hard.

We cannot offer a prescription here that will work automatically in any organization, nor can we provide a simple three-step process to follow, for every organization, situation, and leader is different. What we can share are four tools that can help leaders in driving change that increases the influence of and focus on customers.

Creating a Focal Point Team

My colleagues at Booz Allen Hamilton (Ahlquist et al. 2001) have studied how traditional organizations, which I will assert describes governments, have been successful in implementing e-Service. A key finding is that organizations need to create a "focal point" team to move out of the grassroots phase of e-initiatives and into a phase where lessons are learned and captured, efforts are coordinated, and one consistent strategy is implemented. The grassroots phase is valuable because it unleashes ideas and creativity, but it tends to constrain e-Service ideas to being about the organization's Web site. The focal point team is a central group with a visionary, results-oriented leader. Its initial role is to inventory all the existing e-Service opportunities and to prioritize the subset where the organization should concentrate its resources. The team can drive customer-centricity by prioritizing those opportunities of greatest value to customers, and by integrating those that serve the same customer groups. At the same time, the focal point team creates the climate for successful e-Service by coordinating with program managers, obtaining buy-in, developing organizationwide standards, and building a center of excellence for e-Service.

Organizing by Customer Group

Every decision on how to structure an organization places one priority over all the others. If we want customer service to be our top priority, it is enormously powerful to organize the agency by customer group or, at a minimum, to organize the front-line organization by customer group. The Internal Revenue Service (IRS) serves as an example of a large, complex organization in transition to a customer-centric culture. The effort began in 1996 when there was a growing concern in Congress and a broad public consensus that the IRS was off track, culminating in the passage of comprehensive restructuring legislation. The 1998 IRS Restructuring and Reform Act called for a transformation in the way IRS operates and relates to its *customers*. After bringing in new leadership, the IRS redefined its mission statement as being an agency that is customer-centric:

> Provide America's taxpayers top-quality service by helping them understand and meet their tax responsibilities and by applying the tax law with integrity and fairness to all.

The IRS annually processes 225 million tax returns, collects $2 trillion in taxes, refunds $200 billion and yet was able to recognize that it has only four main customer groups:

- Wage and investment customers
- Small business/self-employed
- Large and mid-size businesses
- Tax-exempt/government entities

The IRS restructured into four new operating divisions based on these four groups—all with renewed commitments to hear more clearly the voice of the customer and to provide enhanced, specialized services. Having each division focused on a different category of taxpayer means both that employees are better able to provide support to the customers they serve and that they are better prepared to detect and address any irregularities that appear on filers' returns.

To become an e-Service organization, the IRS has implemented other measures, including:

- *Establishing an award-winning Web site* (www.irs.gov) that offers information and forms twenty-four hours a day, seven days a week. The site offers forms, publications, and answers to tax questions, and continues to draw record numbers of taxpayers every year. The Web site had more than 1 billion hits in 1999 and 87 million tax form, publication, and other tax document downloads.
- *Expanding electronic filing*, including Telefile, E-file, and On-line Filing, which together accounted for more than 29 million returns in 1999.
- *Implementing increased taxpayer (customer) protections and rights*, including more inclusive protections on certain penalty and interest provisions, strengthening taxpayer rights in collection and audit situations.
- *Overcoming barriers of time and distance,* by including twenty-four-hour-a-day/seven-day-a-week telephone service, expanded walk-in service hours, translators for taxpayers who do not feel comfortable using English, and problem-solving days to help taxpayers with particularly difficult issues to find solutions.
- *Measuring what counts*, by implementing metrics that recognize employee satisfaction, customer satisfaction, and productivity all together.

The IRS is well on the way to being an organization that focuses on customers and uses technology to optimize the delivery of service. They have recognized that tax compliance and high-quality customer service can be pursued simultaneously.

Asking the Right Questions

Customer-centric thinking can be applied at any level of an organization, from the smallest branch or team, to the department or government as a whole. Whether our concern is an entire governmental department, or the office of procurement within that department, or the document printing team within the procurement shop, some questions that lead toward customer-centricity are:

1. *Who do we serve?* They are our customers.
2. *How do they group themselves?* As a starting point, what are the three to five customer groupings, as viewed by the customers themselves?
3. *Who else serves these same groups?* We are not the only ones who serve these groups. Are we each just serving a small piece of the customer's needs?
4. *How can we work together to serve the complete needs of the cus-*

tomer? We need to find ways to integrate our services with others who serve the same customer groups.

5. *How do we listen to what they need?* How do we know how well we are meeting the customer's needs? Do we have a means to get regular (daily, weekly) insights into what the needs are, how they are changing, and how successful we are being? Have we found a way to tune into the conversation that our customers are having about us?

6. *How can we customize to individual needs?* We know things about specific individuals that we can use, with their concurrence, to make the individual interaction with us better.

7. *Has anything improved for customers who continue to access us through traditional channels?* If our electronic initiatives have not had an impact on our traditional service channels, the chances are that we have not changed what is behind the Web site. Did we simply "pave the cowpath"?

Instituting Policies that Increase Customer Influence

A number of policies can be used to raise the influence customers have on the behavior of the organization.

• *Standards and compensation.* The use of performance standards is a well-known management tool. To apply these in a customer-centric manner, we need to ensure that the standards directly reflect what is valued by the customer. In a government setting, this is often measured in terms of time, such as time spent waiting in line or time for an application to be processed. Once the organization is committed and able to meet the standard, it should be published widely. Failure to meet the standard should result in some form of compensation back to the customer.

• *Decision-making participation.* Sharing decision-making power with a board of customers can be a dramatic step. The decisions that such arrangements could cover include the approval of new initiatives that are intended to benefit the customer, or allocation of resources across existing services, or the approval of key leaders. Ceding power to customers requires a partnership mindset, where we trust customers to be able to appropriately establish the priorities that best serve them.

• *Customer impact on capital planning.* Government organizations are making better and more rigorous use of capital planning for information technology. Focusing on measures such as return on investment, level of risk, mission impact, and so on is a strong management tool for funding the best initiatives. An additional criterion to help make IT initiatives more customer-centric is to require that the initiative identify the customer group served, identify the other systems that serve the same customer groups, and indicate how the new initiative improves service to the customer group as a whole. Systems built in isolation can result in customers facing a confusing array of partial solutions. With the right policies, system planners can be required to address the impact on customers of additional new systems.

• *Evaluations and complaints.* To "close the loop" on the performance of e-Services, organizations may institute a mechanism for independent evaluation of the service levels actually provided. The feedback provided through customer complaint systems should also be evaluated to identify the means to learn from complaints and raise performance levels.

As discussed at the beginning of this section, these approaches are only tools to be considered in the quest to drive customer-centric behavior throughout an organization. As with any change program, the necessary elements of leadership, communication, incentives, and other measures must be present for progress to be achieved.

From Customer-Centric to Mission-Centric

While customer-centricity has been the focus of this chapter, and is a worthy goal, we recognize that it is a means to an end, and not an end unto itself. For government organizations, the end must be the best possible achievement of the mission that taxpayers are funding the organization to accomplish. In general, we believe that customer-centric behavior will be fully consistent with better mission accomplishment, but there are a few special cases where some additional thinking is required.

Redefining the Customer to Serve

Within the massive U.S. Department of Defense is a tiny, thirty-staff-member organization that operates under the initials ESGR, for National Committee for Employer Support of the Guard and Reserve. ESGR was established in 1972 to promote cooperation and understanding between National Guard and armed forces reserve members and their civilian employers and to assist in conflicts arising from an employee's military commitment. When ESGR wanted to embrace the use of the Internet and e-enable the organization for greater effectiveness, a key issue to address was how to define their customer. Clearly, they had to have an impact on creating a more comfortable work climate for the Guard and reservists, and thus much of the thinking was that they were the customers. However, ESGR also has a network of fifty-four state committees, staffed by ex-military volunteers who work their influence at local levels. By considering that ESGR would be truly successful in achieving its mission only if the state committees were empowered and effective, ESGR's e-Service initiatives were built around serving the committees as ESGR's customers, and letting the ultimate Guard and reservists be the customers of the committees. The result has been a much more effective use of resources that greatly magnifies the impact of a tiny organization. The lesson here is that providers of government e-Service need to consider whether applying their resources to another entity will ultimately be more effective in accomplishing the mission.

The e-Regulator

How does customer-centricity apply to organizations whose mission is to regulate an industry or otherwise serve as a "watchdog" of some kind? In many of the e-government conferences I have attended, there is a reluctance to believe that regulators should think in terms of customers. However I believe that in such cases a customer-centric mindset still applies but needs a little shaping to make sense. I have placed this discussion under the mission-centric portion of this chapter, because a customer-centric regulator needs to be viewed in terms of best mission accomplishment. Take, for example, an organization that monitors environmental compliance. Such an organization clearly wants to catch and punish those who illegally damage the environment, but at a level more important to the mission, they want to prevent the environmental damage from happening in the first place. As shown in Table 12.1, the e-regulator works to achieve compliance by working to show the regulatees *how* to comply with environmental law. This changes the orientation from one of policing to one of serving customers. The emphasis is on making it easier to comply, educating about how to comply, and sharing best practices, rather than thinking only in terms of detection and stronger punishment. As with all customer-centric organizations, the e-regulator needs to find ways to tune into the customer dialogue to understand the ways in which it is difficult to comply and attempt to provide solutions.

Government to Mission (G2M)

Put yourself in the mindset of being the newly appointed leader of a brand new government agency being created sometime between 1920 and 1950. As a hypothetical example, let's say that this agency is the Department of Boater Safety in a state government. You assemble your team and decide that the best way to improve the safety of the boating community is to gather and publish

Table 12.1

The e-Regulator as Customer-Centric Organization

	Traditional	E-Regulator
Philosophy	Achieve compliance by catching and punishing those who do not comply	Achieve compliance by helping the regulatees to comply
Orientation	Policing	Customer
Effort focused on	Detection after problem Stronger punishment	Making it easier to comply Education—how to comply Sharing best practices
Listen to understand	How do they evade?	Why is it difficult to comply?

data on boating hazards. You create an effective means of gathering the data, publishing and distributing maps, and periodically updating them on a regular basis. As the years pass, the organization recognizes that it has to be more efficient at distributing the maps, and during the 1980s and 1990s goes through various efforts to redesign and reengineer its processes. As the "e-" wave hits in the late 1990s, the organization innovates by placing printers at boating supply outlets so that boaters can print the latest maps, and the outlets do not keep an inventory of outdated maps. This is all progress to be celebrated, but at the same time we should raise a question about the fundamental solution to achieving the mission, based on 1920s–1950s technology, which was distributing maps on paper. If we were tasked with starting a new government department focused on boater safety in the 2000s would we start with the same basic premise of maps? The notion worth considering, one that I have dubbed *government to mission* (G2M) in light of the commonly used government to citizen, business, and government (G2C, G2B, and G2G respectively), is a reevaluation of mission accomplishment in light of the technology and connectivity available in the telecosm era. As shown in Figure 12.9, the efforts at being more efficient and more electronic and streamlining processes that consume many organizations is aimed at the original approaches that were based on long-ago technology. As we show simplistically in the figure, perhaps the data can be transmitted directly to the boating user, taking the need for maps of any kind completely out of the process. This is not intended to be an actual solution, but just an illustration of focusing our attention once again on the mission and considering how we might approach it from a fresh perspective.

For example, if we were designing the educational system for the nation, would our approach to classrooms, textbooks, and departments of education be the same as currently exists? Can the instant connectivity that exists within virtually all members of a community be harnessed to get surplus food more

Figure 12.9   **Attack the Mission Based on Today's Technology**

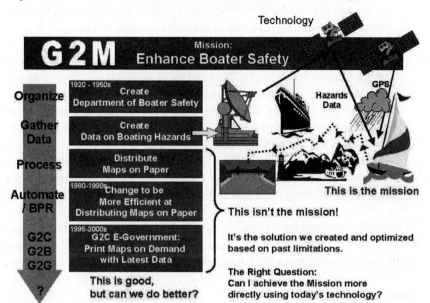

quickly to those in need, as a new approach to hunger? Would our approach to food stamps or medical health be the same? Clearly the answer in many cases is no, which highlights the opportunities for transformation that exist today within government services.

Summary

My mission in writing this chapter has been to stimulate the thinking of government managers in search of better service delivery through electronic means. This chapter has covered a lot of ground, and, to make a point clear, virtually none of it has touched on technology. Our challenge for e-Service has everything to do with our relationship to customers and our focus on the mission, and not our ability to use technology. Certainly technology is both a driver and an enabler, but it is the easier and more obvious issue to deal with in attempting to transform the delivery of electronic government services. To recap a few key themes:

- *Pursue transformation.* The danger is that we will replicate today's stovepipes in cyberspace. We need to focus on what is behind the Web site— the people, processes, culture, and organizations.
- *Shift from agency-centric to customer-centric.* The task is to identify

how customers would group themselves as individuals with similar needs, and then find a way to tune into the dialogue that occurs between customers. When we listen to customers, we need to listen smartly, to understand their underlying needs.

- *Integrate service delivery.* A greater focus on customers will lead to integrated service delivery. We need to identify others who serve the same customer groups and learn to partner with them to meet all the needs of the customer. When reviewing systems and Web sites, do so from the perspective of a customer and recognize that your system or Web site is not the only one that confronts them.
- *Our ultimate goal is the mission.* If customer-centricity alone does not transform our accomplishment of the mission, we may need to think of new ways to attack the mission directly.

As with every challenging goal, recognize that making meaningful progress with e-Service is difficult to do. I hope you will remember to celebrate the small successes while reaching for the big ones.

Notes

The author wishes to thank his many colleagues at Booz Allen Hamilton and in government departments for their contributions of thought to this chapter. He also wishes to thank Laura Bollettino for her editorial contributions and support. The author is grateful to P.K. Kannan of the Robert H. Smith School of Business at the University of Maryland and Dr. Ai-Mei Chang of the National Defense University for their encouragement in publishing this work.

1. See examples throughout David Osborne and Peter Plastrik's (2000) *The Reinventor's Fieldbook: Tools for Transforming Your Government.*

2. Osborne and Plastrik (2000) state explicitly that compliers are not customers. As discussed later in this chapter under "e-Regulators," I believe that a customer-centric approach is valid for those who are regulated. As such, I believe that compliers are a useful subcategory to consider among customers.

3. In this context, "high speed" means at least a typical modem in the 20–50 kilobit-per-second range. While this is not a high data rate compared to other telecommunications technologies, it is a very fast connection mechanism when compared to the amount of data that government customers typically need to transact with their serving agencies. Also, for some customers, such as in government-to-government (G2G) or government-to-business (G2B) applications, much higher data connections are often available through local area or wide area networks.

4. We clearly recognize that there exists a "digital divide" and that some potential e-Service customers do not have ready electronic access to the Internet. While this is an important issue, it is beyond the scope of this chapter in discussing e-Service. However, a point to make here is that if e-Service is implemented in a transformational manner, it will also improve service for customers who continue to access gov-

ernment services through traditional, nonelectronic channels.

5. For example, the congressional appropriation committees are themselves stovepiped.

6. Credit for the term "customer led" goes to author David Siegel (Siegel 1999).

References

Ahlquist, Gary; Jill Albrinck; Gil Irwin; Gary Neilson; Dianna Sasina; Claudia Staub; and E. Alejandro Stengel. 2001. "Click Starting Your Organization: How Traditional Companies Are Mobilizing for E-Business." *www.bah.com.*

Evans, Philip, and Thomas S. Wurster. 2000. *Blown to Bits: How the New Economics of Information Transforms Strategy.* Boston: Harvard Business School Press.

Gilder, George. 2000. *Telecosm: How Infinite Bandwidth Will Revolutionize Our World.* Ashland, OR: Blackstone Audiobooks.

Osborne, David, and Peter Plastrik. 1998. *Banishing Bureaucracy: The Five Strategies for Reinventing Government.* New York: Plume.

————. 2000. *The Reinventor's Fieldbook: Tools for Transforming Your Government.* San Francisco: Jossey-Bass.

Siegel, David. 1999. *Futurize Your Enterprise: Business Strategy in the Age of the E-Customer.* New York: Wiley.

Slywotzky, Adrian J., and David J. Morrison. 1998. *The Profit Zone: How Strategic Business Design Will Lead You to Tomorrow's Profits.* St. Leonards, N.S.W.: Allen & Unwin.

13

Performance Metrics and Successful e-Government Services

Joan Steyaert

Introduction

The federal portfolio is diverse and complex—involving national security, social services, national infrastructure, entitlements, regulation, science, environment, and research and development. Stakeholders include the executive, legislative, and judicial branches of government. Information technology (IT) is a growing segment of the federal budget and a driver in service delivery. Agencies are now challenged with developing an IT enterprise strategy or architecture that links electronic services to the agency's mission and demonstrates value to the public in terms of effectiveness, cost, and efficiency.

In *A Blueprint for New Beginnings* (Executive Office of the President 2001), the Bush administration describes government reform as citizen-centered, results-oriented, and market-based. Reports from Congress, the General Accounting Office, and the Office of Management and Budget (GAO 2000; OMB 2001a, 2001b; U.S. Congress 1992, 1993, 1998) emphasize the need to develop, deploy, and benchmark e-Service projects using performance measures. The administration believes that the World Wide Web offers a new way of governing by delivering customer services seven days a week, twenty-four hours a day. To realize this vision, both federal and state governments are developing "channeled" portals that allow citizens to easily access information and services even if they are not familiar with the inner workings of government. Portals include a directory of services and officials, public key infrastructure (PKI), and e-payment. The challenge for government is to determine and apply performance metrics to strategic management of e-Services and demonstrate the value of these services to the public.

A framework for performance measurement in government electronic services is presented in this chapter, which has three components: methodology, case study results, and discussion and concluding remarks. The methodology section reviews the literature on performance measurement and then defines a proposed set of metrics. The case studies apply the proposed metrics to e-Service programs. The discussion and concluding remarks frame performance measurement in terms of both quantitative and qualitative objectives. The study goes beyond commonly used financial or budgetary measurement techniques and suggests the inclusion of efficiency, productivity, customer value, and satisfaction in making investment decisions relating to Web services.

Methodology

This section focuses on the supporting literature that provides the basis for the case studies and a proposed set of metrics and definitions to be used in measuring the value of agency e-Service projects. It should be noted at the outset that the majority of research continues to concentrate on private-sector electronic business. Recognizing the diversity of goals and objectives of the federal government, this article applies a number of metrics developed for the private sector to the public sector. Given the diversity of federal programs, not all metrics are applicable.

Private-Sector e-Business Literature

To date, most of the e-business literature on measurement has focused on how a company can tie traditional measures of financial performance to strategic goals. Private firms perform investment planning by identifying the projects to be considered in their portfolio and the full consequences of alternative projects. Companies then assign a value to each input and output, and add up the costs and benefits to estimate the total profitability of the project.

One popular approach involves the Balanced Scorecard (BSC) originally designed by Robert Kaplan and David Norton (1992, 1993, 1996; and Kaplan 2000) for private-sector businesses. BSC is a strategic management tool that allows businesses to drive their strategies based on measurement and follow-up. Measures are divided into four perspectives: financial, customer orientation, internal processes, and learning and growth. To succeed, organizations need to supplement traditional financial measures like return on investment (ROI) with three other perspectives: customer satisfaction, internal processes, and the ability to innovate and retain staff. In order to succeed, business leaders need to:

1. clearly delineate their mission (e.g., to become their customers' most preferred supplier);
2. translate the organization's mission into objectives (e.g., to provide their customers with new products) and indicators or metrics;
3. achieve objectives through well-chosen indicators (e.g., percentage of sales generated by new products);

The objective of the BSC is to capture real meaning by including both quantitative and qualitative information on a mix of outcomes (lag indicators) and performance drivers (lead indicators). The BSC offers an alternative approach to the use of incentive payments tied to traditional past performance. It has significant utility to electronic business because the approach adds customer satisfaction and learning as business objectives to traditional financial accounting techniques. Kaplan and Norton's BSC was originally designed for private profit-making companies and thus weighs the financial aspect as the more prominent perspective. Emphasis is given to linking strategies back to financial measures such as return on investment (ROI) and payback. ROI is the ratio of average annual net benefits of the project and the investment. Payback is the period of time that the investor has to wait for the project to repay its initial investment. Other financial metrics include sales, revenue margin, and the number of innovative pricing strategies.

The second BSC perspective focuses on business processes. M. Martinsons et al. (1999) have expanded business processes to include information technology. They suggest that the scorecard can provide a foundation for the strategic management of organizational information technology systems. They recommend efficiency and effectiveness as important metrics for internal information systems development, processes, and information products in the operation of the business (Hansan and Tibbits 2000).

R. Kalakota et al. (1999) also focused on the business process objectives. The authors include IT processes as critical to the successful enterprise both internally and externally. IT not only impacts internal support functions within an organization but also impacts external markets. The e-business IT architecture includes "business processes, enterprise applications and organizational structures necessary to create a high performance business operation."

In the private sector, efficient IT integrates the supply chain and selling chain of the enterprise. Process improvements save time or money by faster service, customized service or clustered service. Both efficiency and productivity improvements result from consolidating and integrating e-business applications.

The following description by R. Kalakota and A. Whinston (1997, p. 3) is useful in this regard.

> From a communications perspective, electronic commerce is the delivery of information, products/services, or payments via telephone lines, computer networks, or any other electric means. From a business process perspective, electronic commerce is the application of technology to the automation of business transactions and workflow. From a service perspective, electronic commerce is a tool that addresses the desire of firms, consumers, and management to cut service costs while improving the quality of goods and increasing the speed of service delivery. From an online perspective, electronic commerce provides the capability of buying and selling products and information on the Internet and other online services. All of the above definitions are valid. It is just a matter of which lens is used to view the electronic landscape.

The third BSC perspective involves the customer. Today, many e-business companies are using customer satisfaction surveys and customer relationship management in addition to ROI and profits to gain customer loyalty and increase market share. In fact, one of the originators of the BSC, David Norton, in a recent seminar series announced that the Balanced Scorecard was being used in nonprofit organizations with the customer perspective given top priority. The Gartner Group (Moaz 2001) and others describe customer satisfaction as "relationship management" and customer loyalty and value as an essential component in retaining and growing markets.

Learning and growth is the fourth BSC perspective. In the IT arena, e-businesses continue to weigh as important staff retention in critical areas such as business applications development and network operations (Strassman 1999).

Public Sector E-Service Literature

The perspectives of many government managers differ significantly from their private-sector counterparts. While the consequences of an e-business project can affect its profitability, the government manager has a much broader range of objectives that would include public health and safety, disaster relief, defense, transportation, and so on. Second, the firm can use market prices to evaluate what it has to pay for inputs and what it receives for outputs. There are many instances where government cannot use market prices in evaluating projects, for example, when the outputs or inputs are not sold on the market or when there is a market failure (Stiglitz 2000). Government managers also face institutional and budgetary constraints.

However, these differences have not deterred OMB and Congress from pushing for greater fiscal accountability. In 1996, both Congress and the executive branch proposed systematic tracking of IT systems. The Clinger-Cohen Act (1992) and the Government Performance and Results Act (1993) require government managers to look at government services in terms of costs and benefits. Specifically, the legislation requires that IT be aligned with business functions through an enterprise architecture, capital plan, and investment process. This means that the investment needs to support work processes that have been simplified or redesigned to reduce costs and improve effectiveness. The legislation also requires agencies to develop performance measures on their investments (Clinger-Cohen Act 1992; Government Performance and Results Act 1993).The Office of Management and Budget in Circulars A-11 and A-130 requires the heads of executive departments to emphasize capital planning and enterprise IT management in preparation of their strategic plans and budget initiatives (OMB Circular A-11 2001a, A-130 2001b).

In achieving financial objectives, a number of agencies are now using GAO's Information Technology Investment Model (ITIM) to improve their capital planning and budgeting process. The GAO's model addresses an agency's financial objectives. It uses an investment framework to assess and improve procedures for deciding what information technology to buy. The model stresses oversight, asset tracking, development of a complete investment portfolio (rather than looking at each project individually), and postinvestment reviews.

The second BSC perspective is also receiving increased attention by public-sector managers, as they begin to focus on efficiency and productivity measures in electronic delivery of services. Process improvements can include performance-based contracting (PBC), cost sharing with industry, seat management, and consolidation of data centers and systems. The process perspective allows managers to look at the entire IT enterprise in order to increase efficiency and productivity. G. Dickson and J. Wetherbe (1985) note that process metrics for e-Services now include more than system availability and downtime. M. Bitterman (2000) develops a performance measurement framework to demonstrate the importance of IT processes in achieving financial objectives in terms of revenues, timeliness of products, and market share. Financial objectives are linked to core, operational, and personnel metrics. Core IT processes include system availability, staff retention, homegrown vs. off-the-shelf applications, and investments in maintenance vs. new initiatives. Operational processes include the staff required to deliver a product, IT performance, and cycle time. Personnel processes include the number of lines of code per function point, desktop moves, and service calls completed or abandoned.

The third BSC perspective has gained importance, as agencies are now required by Congress to increase the accessibility of their Web applications. The customer perspective requires managers to look at the value of their services to consumers. Value cannot be simply measured in financial terms. In fact, financial measures such as ROI and payback have limited utility in determining the value for many functions that are inherently governmental. Value is a much broader concept than benefits (Willcocks 1994), and in the public sector the "qualitative" value of government e-Services is important. J. Stiglitz (2000) identifies measurement challenges in pricing "nonprice" government goods and suggests techniques that will allow government managers to develop "shadow prices" for their services. Examples include customer surveys that focus on the public's "willingness to pay" for a public good or estimating the opportunity costs associated with the loss of a service when there is no other service provider (e.g., environmental protection, disaster recovery, defense). There are a number of studies on customer satisfaction measures: Gartner research on customer relationship management (Moaz 2000), Web research on government sites (CENDI 2001), customer surveys (Fornell et al. 2000; comScore 2001; and National Center for Public Productivity, Rutgers University 1997).

Proposed Case Studies

Approach

This article concentrates on the suitability of a performance measurement framework for federal government electronic services using the four BSC perspectives described by Kaplan and Norton (1992). Case studies provide a vehicle for defining specific metrics used by agencies to achieve financial, process, customer, and learning and growth goals. The cases are chosen for two reasons. First, many of the agencies are participating in measurement programs (required under the Government Performance and Results Act). Second, they are undertaking e-Service projects involving a Web presence with a computer-based customer service system.

The study is based on interviews with management and project leaders and an evaluation of agency Web sites. The data analysis for the research follows the interpretive case study approach of G. Walsham (1995) and the iterative approach of M.B. Miles and A.M. Huberman (1994). It incorporates the four phases of data collection, data reduction, data display, and drawing of conclusions. In the initial stages, evaluation documents, transcripts of interviews, and notes from observations are collected. The resulting collection is then selectively reduced and interpreted in order to identify the issues in the e-Services development that are related to an electronic services scorecard. The proposed performance framework is used to display data before the drawing of conclusions, which are presented at the end of this chapter.

Performance metrics for federal e-government services are defined based on the four perspectives of Kaplan and Norton's Balanced Scorecard (1992). These perspectives include financial, process, customer, learning, and growth objectives. Based on the federal case studies, performance metrics are defined for each score card element. Effectiveness, sales, cost effectiveness, and cost avoidance are proxies for financial success. Efficiency and productivity are proxies for process success. Utility, customer satisfaction, Web traffic, market share, and multichannel delivery are proxies for customer satisfaction. Staff retention is a proxy for learning and growth.

The conclusion and Figures 13.1 and 13.2 provide a "road map" to summarize the case study results. Figure 13.1 relates metrics to BSC perspectives as well as mission objectives. It defines twelve quantifiable success indicators for e-Services. Each indicator is defined in terms of how it can help to improve financial, process, customer, and learning and growth goals of the enterprise. For example, achieving financial objectives in e-Service delivery looks at ways to increase effectiveness, sales and revenues, cost effectiveness, and cost avoidance. Secondly, Figure 13.2 links the metrics defined in Figure 13.1 to federal agencies that are applying measurement techniques. Figure 13.2 illustrates how metrics are applied to e-government services. For example, the U.S. Mint, HUD, and the Veterans Administration showcase portfolio techniques. Process metrics such as productivity and effectiveness are being used by the IRS, the Securities and Exchange Commission, NASA, and the Patent and Trademark Office. Customer metrics are reviewed in the case studies of the Consumer Product Safety Commission, the Federal Consumer Information Center, and the National Institutes of Health. The U.S. Mint provides one example of financial incentives to retain managers, employees, and contractors. These agencies are meant to provide illustrative examples to help managers develop e-Service measurement practices. A questionnaire is presented in the Appendix to encourage agency discussion and e-Service business plans.

As with most qualitative or interpretive approaches, the value of the research comes when explanations of particular phenomena derived from the case studies are valuable to other organizations and contexts in the future.

Figure 13.1   **Proposed Performance Metrics for e-Government Services**

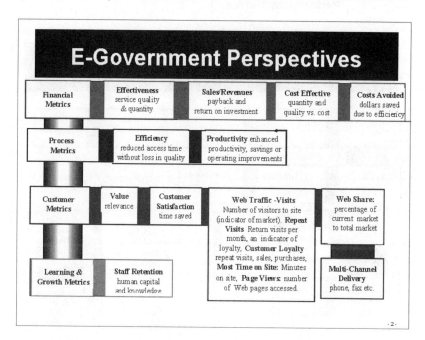

*Proposed e-Government Service Performance Metrics
and Definitions*

The literature on performance measurement supports the development and use of metrics in the context of an agency's e-Service mission and objectives. Twelve metrics are proposed using a framework that highlights financial, process, customer, and growth objectives.

Based on e-business studies, agencies that give priority to financial objectives will rely on four metrics:

1. *Effectiveness* refers to how well government is performing the things it is required to do. It also refers to the degree to which services are responsive to the needs of the community. In e-Services, effectiveness focuses on how well the agency's World Wide Web site responds to its mission and objectives, for example, coverage of agency publications, integration with other government and private-sector Web sites, reach to new constituents or audiences.
2. *Sales and revenues* are traditional business success measures.
3. *Cost effectiveness* refers to dollars saved from electronic services; for

Figure 13.2 **Federal e-Government Programs According to Applied Performance Metrics**

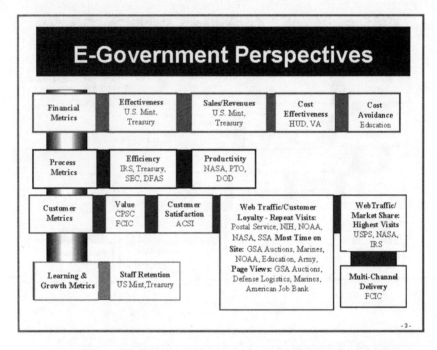

example, the dollars or labor required for a paper-based service versus an electronic service.

4. *Cost avoidance* refers to dollars not spent due to improvements in efficiency or productivity in e-Services.

Agencies that are funded by congressional appropriations and do not generate revenues will focus on process improvements and use two metrics:

1. *Efficiency* requires an agency to increase the value of the service and reduce the cost of labor and technology to provide the service. Efficiency gains can include reducing resource and product costs for services; for example, reducing the cost of creating a Web site, a Web site session, or user services.

2. *Productivity* is defined as enhancing outputs through a combination of efficiency and effectiveness; for example, increasing the availability of IT systems to the public and employees seven days a week, twenty-four hours a day.

Agencies that weigh customer satisfaction as an important driver in e-Service success will use five metrics:

1. *Value* refers to the ability of the service to meet the customer's requirements at the point of need. For electronic service providers, lead indicators can include: usability, clarity and organization of Web site, number of links, time for the e-Service to be provided to the customer, number of customer complaints, existence of a help desk, number of 404 errors, and number of referrals from other Web sites. Lag indicators can include increased consumer productivity or information at the point of need.

2. *Customer satisfaction* refers to the degree that government services meet the customers' expectations in terms of quality, timeliness, and relevance. Agencies frequently use Web statistics as lead indicators in demonstrating customer satisfaction. Statistics can include consumer visits, consumer activity, time on the site, the ratio of unique to repeat sessions, and document downloads. *Visits* refers to the number of visitors and new visitors on an agency's Web site. This number can be used in estimating the size of the current market. *Repeat Visitors* refers to repetitive visits made to the Web site during one month. *Time on the site* refers to the amount of time the consumer spends on the site per visit.

3. *Customer loyalty* involves customer retention over time. This can require surveys, focus groups to segment users, and market intelligence.

4. *Market share* relates to the size or percentage of the agency's electronic market to the total market and to the competitors' market.

5. *Multiple-channel strategy* refers to the ability of the agency to reach customers through the Internet, the World Wide Web, telephone, fax, and in-person service.

Agencies that are developing staff to meet e-Service objectives will concentrate on a single metric: *Staff retention* refers to the time an employee stays with a company and the rate of replacement.

An Overview

Integrating Mission, Objectives, and Metrics

The U.S. Mint

The U.S. Mint provides an illustration of how mission goals can be linked to objectives and metrics. In achieving mission results, the agency effectively balances sales, revenues, productivity, efficiency, and staff retention. The agency's e-business goal is straightforward—to increase the sale of numismatic and commemorative coins. The role of IT involves increasing the agency's effectiveness in sales, processing, planning, and distribution. All elements and activities are integrated through an IT plan. This has meant working with suppliers of coins, as well as the distributors, automating the supply chain, and engaging business partners. To be able to distribute, produce, and logistically meet demand, the Mint has encouraged all offices to work together and fully integrate their applications so that they can identify problems quickly. To anticipate the market, the chief executive officer (CEO) has created a group that focuses on productivity, business intelligence, applications, feedback from customers, and sales and services. In terms of an e-business framework, the Mint is cost-efficient. The agency has:

- multichannel integration of suppliers, distributors, and resellers of information and products through supply chain management;
- stakeholder (chief executive officer, chief information officer [CIO], chief procurement officer [CPO]) involvement through financial, accounting, management, and auditing;
- enterprise resource planning (with stakeholders and customers) in the creation of new markets through sales, distribution, production, and logistics;
- employee-business partnerships to integrate enterprise applications and improve products;
- customer relationship management through communications, sales, and new applications with customers and partners;
- selling chain management to customers and partners.

The U.S. Mint provides an excellent example of implementing an e-business architecture that increases sales and revenues. An enterprise resource plan (ERP) allows managers to integrate financial, personnel, and supply activities across the enterprise in order to reduce costs and improve timeliness. ERP and CRM requires program offices to work together to define data requirements and select best-of-breed software for the enterprise as a whole. Customer relationship management involves the use of trained staff in customer care centers to answer questions and respond to consumer concerns.

Human Resources (HR), Procurement, and Information Technology offices have performance incentives to work together. The CIO and the CPO use business partnerships and performance-based contracting with Internet service providers (ISP). The CIO and HR use financial incentives for career and contract employees based on timely delivery of re-engineered financial processes and products. These activities taken together have progressively moved the Mint from $1 million in sales/month to $1 million in sales/week, and finally to $1 million in sales/day. In 1999, the Mint received $2.5 billion in revenues and $1.1 billion in profits (www.usmint.gov). Customer satisfaction among buyers is an A+ (Fornell et al. 2000).

The U.S. Mint exemplifies an e-business that has created performance incentives to encourage collaboration and retain talent. To be able to distribute, produce, and logistically meet demand, the Mint had to have an enterprise plan that encouraged all offices to work together and fully integrate their applications so that they could identify problems quickly. To anticipate the market, they needed to have a group that was focused on productivity, business intelligence, and applications. This group provides feedback from customers to marketing, sales, and service units. These strategies have ensured the retention of talent and the highest level of performance from contractors and government workers.

E-Service Financial Metrics

The U.S. Mint parallels in many respects an e-business. However, many federal agencies do not have a guaranteed revenue stream. Both the Department of Housing and Urban Development and the Veterans Administration (VA) stress cost effectiveness and cost avoidance using the GAO's Information Technology Investment Model (ITIM).

Cost-Effectiveness Metric

Housing and Urban Development and Veterans
Administration: ITIM

The CIO, chief financial officer (CFO), and CPO of Housing and Urban Development manage a complex series of programs that provide services to low- and moderate-income households. Cost is a driver in balancing conflicting and competing programmatic requirements. To responsibly evaluate these new initiatives, HUD uses portfolio analysis techniques developed by the General Accounting Office. The General Accounting model, called the Information Technology Investment Model (ITIM), (GAO 2000) is designed to improve the capital planning process. The model uses five management "maturity" steps in capital planning. In stage one, the GAO indicates that organizations purchase without an investment strategy. By stage five, organizations make a link between the benefits (results) and the costs of IT projects. To reach stage two, an agency must develop and maintain a project portfolio and a guide that describes the IT inventory. The Department of Housing and Urban Development and the Veterans Administration are using ITIM and a scoring model called Expert Choice. The scoring model supports ITIM by allowing decision-makers to complete portfolio (or alternatives) analysis. Expert Choice is decision-support software for structuring project funding based on an analytical hierarchy of projects, prioritizing business objectives, and pair-wise comparison of projects to identify alternatives and assess risk.

In the case of HUD, managers believe that they have improved capital asset planning by creating investment awareness, building an investment foundation, developing an investment portfolio, and investing in strategic outcomes. HUD stakeholders include the CFO, CPO, CEO, and CIO. The Chief Procurement Office approves a project acquisition strategy. The CFO funds the IT portfolio, working with the CIO to maintain and monitor the working capital fund. The CIO is responsible for setting IT investment policy procedures, establishing thresholds for internal and external project reporting, determining the IT portfolio, monitoring the complete investment portfolio, improving the investment process, and investing for strategic outcomes.

HUD and the VA are now asking questions that focus on:

- whether the investment addresses a material weakness (or an audit finding);
- whether the IT project supports the agency's mission in terms of the agency's business case and budget;
- whether the IT initiative has a project management plan that includes a payback period, an analysis of uncontrolled cost variables (availability of external funding sources, changes in components pricing or maintenance contracts), and a benefit cost analysis;
- . whether the IT program responds to the agency's business case and the relationship of the project to analyses completed by the Office of the Inspector General (OIG), or General Accounting Office.

Projects are ranked from low to high risk based on the impact of the event and the probability of occurrence. For example, HUD's Investment Board requires each project in the portfolio to have at least two performance measures. Performance measures have to be measurable and directly address HUD's mission.

Planning and setting financial benchmarks for IT systems and applications allows managers to track e-Services over time and calculate the total cost of ownership (TCO). This would include looking at the direct effects of projects on the agency's customers, whether investments are reducing costs or improving efficiency, and whether new projects or applications are leveraged on legacy technologies.

Cost-Avoidance Metric

Department of Education: e-Service Cost Sharing

The Department of Education's Student Financial Assistance Program administers several major student aid programs, which provide over $42 billion a year to help millions of students pay for the costs of college. The department uses performance-based contracting to recover payments on defaulted student loans. In 2000, Education introduced a value-engineering project to overhaul business processes that drive operations. The department defines baseline performance levels for contractors, sets measurable results, and provides large incentives for on-time delivery of services. Partnerships with business to re-engineer processes allow the department to avoid costs and increase efficiency and productivity. Expectations for savings at Education are significant. The department predicts that it will save $40–$50 million before the contractor share is paid, and that payment can be anywhere from $14 million to $35 million, depending on the savings achieved. The department has established a system of larger payments in the first year as a way to reduce interest costs, with declining percentages paid over the next two years.

E-Service Technology Process Metrics

To move from paper to electronic services, agencies need to integrate the IT enterprise. Efficiency and productivity are the process metrics in these case studies. Efficiency savings can result from reducing the number of applications that are built vs. bought, reducing investments in IT maintenance in order to increase new initiatives. Efficiency can be measured in terms of time saved in developing applications or dollars saved by streamlining operations. Enterprise integration also can increase productivity. Productivity savings include increasing the speed of data delivery, and the speed and quality of services to the public in terms of time or money. Productivity improvements require accessible applications that integrate the supply chain and selling chain. Productivity improvements include moving toward electronic (rather than paper) procurement processes, using multipurpose smart cards, and 24/7 access to data and services.

Efficiency Metrics

Internal Revenue Service: Public e-Filing

The Internal Revenue Service (IRS) is an agency that faces a complex e-business environment in terms of suppliers, stakeholders, employees, and customers. The agency collects $2 trillion in revenues and has an IT budget of $1.6 billion. Given its complexity, the CIO focuses on standardization and integration of four business processes: filing, reporting, payment, and compliance.

Aligning the business through an enterprise plan is the first step. The second step involves gaining business intelligence and using it to increase the efficiency of electronic transactions. To expand its e-filing market, IRS focuses on accessibility, accuracy, speed, and timeliness via telephone, fax, e-mail, and wireless (a multiple-channel strategy). Electronic filing provides a significant market opportunity. Only 27.8 percent of all taxpayers file online directly or via telefile, but customer satisfaction is high compared to paper filers. IRS states that e-filing on the Web (www.irs.gov): (1) is more accurate than mailing a paper return (less than 1 percent error rate); (2) provides acknowledgment within forty-eight hours signifying that the tax return has been accepted; (3) provides faster and safer refunds with direct deposit in as few as ten days; (4) provides one-stop filing and payment; (5) provides flexible payment using credit cards.

IRS gains e-business intelligence through business and university partnerships. Since 1998, the agency has received survey feedback through the Pacific Consulting Group and the University of Michigan. The University of Michigan uses a customer survey to derive a customer satisfaction index. IRS paper filers are asked how they rank tax filing in terms of clarity, cost of preparation, convenience, timeliness of response, and accuracy. In 1999, the American Customer Satisfaction Index (ACSI) indicated that only 48 percent of IRS customers were satisfied with paper filing. ACSI asked electronic filers how they ranked e-filing in terms of availability and clarity, ease of use (usability), cost of filing, and courtesy of professionals, and it recorded consumer satisfaction at 75 percent. The challenge for IRS is to increase usability and accessibility. In 2002, IRS will add satisfaction indicators to eleven transaction systems (Fornell et al. 2002; American Customer Satisfaction Survey, University of Michigan 2002).

Another source of customer data is comScore's Internet traffic reports of online consumers. ComScore captures surveying and buying activity from large online customer markets. Agencies can gain information on unique filing behavior, audience segments, Web site traffic, and demographic data. ComScore has 1.3 million members who participate in its virtual panels. IRS success can be measured by comScore's online traffic reports (comScore Traffic Report 2001). During the 2001 tax season, there were 7.4 million unique visitors at the IRS Web site. In February, there were 5.8 million visits with 3.5 million visitors at home, 1.9 million at work, and 290,000 at school. On average, the public spent eighteen minutes on the IRS Web site.

The IRS e-business strategy focuses on saving time for taxpayers. This goal has required a strategic plan, business intelligence, financial incentives for customers and employees, and alliances with accounting firms and associations to increase usability. Performance goals focus on increasing IT capacity (to handle scaling), increasing utilization (24/7), increasing efficiency (for customers), improving effectiveness (process performance), reducing cycle time (consumption measures), and increasing quality (personnel performance).

Securities and Exchange Commission: e-filing for Business

The Securities and Exchange Commission (SEC) measures electronic service success in terms of replacing 12 million pages of SEC paper filings annually with electronic filing. The commission meets security goals by using company passwords, digital certificates, encryption, and a secure tunnel for transactions, similar to online banking and other secure Internet and World Wide Web transactions.

Defense Financial Accounting Service: Comparing Public- and Private-Sector Costs of IT Processes

With a working capital fund of $1.7 billion, the Defense Financial Accounting Service (DFAS) is responsible for accounting and payroll systems for more than 3 million people. Facing the need to cut costs, DFAS aligns its business strategy and business operations to reduce the cost of developing and integrating financial systems. It has consolidated the number of processing centers from 300 to 26 and reduced the number of data centers. Two centers now process all payroll requirements. Twenty-six civilian pay systems have been reduced to one.

DFAS has partnered with the Gartner Group for over seven years in benchmarking and cost analysis. DFAS uses the benchmarking approach of Gartner's Performance Measurement Team (Bitterman 2000) and Gartner cost data (Bergstrom 2000). DFAS benchmarks its applications, maintenance, and development costs against private-sector organizations and government installations of similar size and complexity. Performance goals relate to increasing infrastructure availability, reducing cost per transaction and cost per function, as well as the time to implement new applications (or functions).

Productivity Metrics

National Aeronautics and Space Administration: Seat Management

NASA is using performance-based contracting to improve the IT environment for scientists. IT performance metrics include 24/7 availability (99.8 percent uptime), maintainability, interoperability, and value. NASA's enterprise strategy focuses on mainframe consolidation, wide area network (WAN) support, and outsourcing the desktop. Total costs for providing IT services in personnel and finance are calculated. WAN metrics include cost/bandwidth and customer satisfaction. Given that NASA engineers analyze satellite images, and network traffic can be as much as 80 percent video graphics at some facilities, bandwidth is critical. Internal customer metrics for desktop outsourcing or seat management includes customer satisfaction, availability, and average cost per seat. IT performance targets are to improve information technology infrastructure and service delivery, capability, and efficiency, while maintaining high customer ratings and IT security.

Department of Defense: Smart Cards

The Department of Defense (DOD) plans to improve productivity by using smart cards that can provide instantaneous information to authorized users on troop readiness, building access, purchasing, and network security. One example of smart card innovation is the Common Access Card (CAC), of which the Navy is executive agent. Adding more information to the card has required DOD to address cultural issues.

Patent and Trademark Office: Integrating Enterprise Processes

The Patent and Trademark Office (PTO) is a leader in using IT to increase business and employee productivity. Since 1994, PTO has integrated its e-business through an enterprise architecture that defines information technology standards, services, interfaces, supporting data formats, protocols, and products (i.e., information is created once and used often). This enterprise architecture ensures that the office meets business requirements for high availability, maintainability, interoperability, and value. Productivity is defined in terms of accessibility, production, operations, and customers. Access measures include the number of documents delivered per month; the number of Patent and Trademark Depository Libraries serving the most populated Metropolitan Statistical Areas; and the usability of information. Process metrics focus on reducing the time for patent application approval, data capture, and retrieval. System performance metrics include availability of network servers, the network backbone, external gateways, e-mail services, and the number of Web transactions with a three-second response time. Customer metrics focus on time to answer and handle calls, average and total voice calls, voice mail calls, and e-mail calls handled per month, the number of automated system queries per month, and the number of Web pages delivered per month.

The public can check the status of U.S., Japanese, or European patent applications over the Internet and the World Wide Web without compromising confidentiality or security because of public key infrastructure (PKI). Patent applicants can get automated assistance in preparing transmittal information as well as real-time acknowledgment of patent submissions. These enhancements have resulted in an 11 percent increase in customer satisfaction (Fornell et al. 2000) and an 8 percent increase in productivity (as determined by the number of transactions processed).

E-Service Customer Value Metrics

Value Metric

Consumer Product and Safety Commission: Value

The Consumer Product and Safety Commission was recently cited by Brown University's Taubman Institute (West 2001) as one of the best federal Web sites in terms of customer value. It registers more than 1.5 million hits and 400,000 visits a month. The site is bilingual and searchable back to the commission's creation in 1973. The site reaches a target audience of young families that might not have access to recall information on consumer appliances and products through the press.

Customer Satisfaction Metrics

University of Michigan: American Customer Satisfaction Survey

The American Customer Satisfaction Index provides comparative customer satisfaction data on government service provision. The University of Michigan Business School started working with private companies in 1994 to gain insights into customer satisfaction. Over the last six years, the ACSI survey has been expanded to more than thirty federal agencies in twelve departments and seven nondepartment agencies. There are thirty-one customer segments (type of service provided). Segments are grouped by local and state, earned benefits, public information, recreational land users, international travelers, applicants and users, household consumers, tax filers, and regulatory users. Agencies participating in the survey select a customer segment relevant to their central mission.

The 1999 ACSI is one of the first cross-agency studies of customer satisfaction using a methodology that provides comparisons across customer segments. The survey includes 90 percent of the government's public customers.

Satisfaction varies across customer segments depending on whether customers receive services, collect earned benefits, seek information, visit recreational facilities, return from international travel, apply for a program, file a tax form, or are subject to regulation. Agencies that have increased their customer satisfaction rankings include the Department of Education's Student Financial Loan Program (electronic applicants), NASA (educators), and the U.S. Mint (e-buyers).

Agencies are also using the ACSI results to improve business processes. For example, the National Science Foundation (NSF) modified its grant review process when it learned that applicants were not getting timely feedback. With a customer satisfaction rating of 57 percent (among electronic grant applicants), the NSF moved to streamline the grant review process through benchmarking the proposal process. This provided performance goals for reviewers and shortened the time for grant review and award. With more than 30,000 grant applications per annum (amounting to more than $1 billion), a move toward 100 percent electronic submission forced realignment of IT operations and project selection.

Customer Loyalty and Web Traffic Metrics

National Library of Medicine and National Institutes of Health: Integrated Content and Trusted Source of Information

The National Library of Medicine and the National Institutes of Health use sophisticated Web metrics to evaluate their electronic services. In the past, market researchers estimating customer satisfaction had to contend with reliability and validity problems because forms were paper-based and took months to analyze. With the Internet and the Web, it is possible to obtain instantaneous feedback from consumers as they use Web services. It is also possible to set up focus groups to accelerate customer feedback. Web surveys are a cost-effective way of capturing reliable customer feedback.

A combination of Web statistics and satisfaction measures can be used to better understand e-Services markets. Web data provide an indication of a site's popularity but not the whole story. For example, unique visits can be an indicator of new customers. The number of visits per visitor can be an indicator of customer loyalty, and pages per visitor and minutes per site can be an indicator of value when used in combination with repeat visits.

The concept of Web evaluation is clearly maturing as well as the use of Web metrics (CENDI 2001). With regard to Web performance and Internet connectivity, the National Library of Medicine (NLM) is a leader in monitoring Web site performance. The NLM uses traditional Web metrics, unique hits, unique visitors, page views, sessions, page demands, hosts, file requests by type, files downloaded, errors in completing user requests, megabytes of information transferred, kilobytes transferred to network per Web performance, html pages per hour and html pages each day, and accessibility.

However, the library is also relying on new techniques to provide the most complete source of health information on the Web. This includes analysis of comparative/competitive Web sites through virtual panels of users (using essential attributes) and usability as an important requirement in Web design. To increase transactions, the agency is partnering with comScore to gain information through virtual panels of about 120,000 participants. On average customers are predominantly female (67 percent), forty years or older (44 percent), and college educated (66 percent). NIH analysts compare the at-home market for government medical information (medline.gov and nih.gov) to private-sector providers (allhealth.com, Webmed.com) as well as other popular government sites such as irs.gov, ed.gov, and ustreas.gov. To determine customer loyalty, the NLM uses a series of indicators that include repeat monthly visitors to the site. They also ask randomly sampled visitors to their site (3,000 users) if they access the site one or more times per month. Thirty-six percent of the visitors indicate they visit the site one or more times per month, 61 percent indicated they repeatedly access the site from home, and 63 percent indicated they are highly interested in special health questions.

Timeliness of service delivery is also a factor requiring IT managers to look at peak congestion, capacity (bandwidth), and end-to-end Internet connectivity. Capacity metrics includes the speed of the search, the pathway between hosts, transfer capacity, and connectivity quality. Channel metrics include download times, throughput, and latency.

In the long term, the NLM plans to focus on value metrics for information. Fred Wood, a Web advisor to NLM, says that the "real economic gains of integrating the enterprise is improving health decisions and outcomes. In information dissemination this involves reductions in demographic disparities in the use of health information and increasing alternative/complementary medical information" (CENDI 2001).

Market Share Metrics

ComScore: Standard Traffic Measurement Reports

ComScore provides a database infrastructure for comparative analysis of Web sites nationally and internationally. The company provides a view of Internet and Web behavior by 1.5 million opt-in users and captures detailed information of their online and offline buying. Marketing companies (such as comScore) can provide comparative data for determining the market potential of Web services. ComScore's traffic volumes for California, Texas, and Florida provide an indication of the potential market for federal services. In June 2001, 3.3 million consumers accessed California's Web site. The site showed high customer loyalty with three to seven repeat visits per month. On average, ten pages were accessed by consumers, and they spent about thirteen minutes on the site. For the same period, Texas registered 2.9 million visitors to its site. The site also showed high customer loyalty with 2.7 repeat visits per month and twenty pages viewed. Governmentguide.com (a commercial site for federal information) registered 2.8 million visits per month, and 2.9 million visitors worldwide, with 1.5 repeat visits and 7.4 pages viewed over 7 minutes per visitor.

Only ten federal departments and agencies in June 2001 had traffic comparable to these states (i.e., 1.5–4 million unique visitors). These agencies included the U.S. Postal Service, which had 3.9 million unique visits per month, 2.5 visits per visitor, 12.6 pages viewed and about 10 minutes per visit; and the National Institutes of Health with 2.5 million U.S. visitors and about 1.8 million international visitors per month, 2 repeat visits per month, and 11–20 pages accessed. NIH registered about 14 to 30 minutes per visitor. Other high-volume sites include the National Oceanographic and Atmospheric Administration, the Department of Education, the Internal Revenue Service, the National Aeronautics and Space Administration, the Treasury Department, the Army, the Department of Justice, the Social Security Administration, and, the Navy.

Multichannel Delivery Metric

Federal Consumer Information Center: Multiple-Channel Marketing and Delivery

One of the significant trends in e-Services is multichannel marketing of products and services. The Federal Consumer Information Center (FCIC) is using the Internet and the Web, catalogs, and voice to seamlessly market and integrate its offerings. The FCIC relies on telephone calls and customer surveys to measure consumer satisfaction. The telephone center handles about 2.7 million telephone calls per year, approximately 10,000 telephone calls per day. The center also answers requests for information through the blue pages, Google, and FirstGov search engines on the Internet and the Web.

The FCIC actively surveys customers sending surveys with its reports and publications. Customers are asked to rank quality, timeliness, and the information channel. The response rate is high, from 20 to 30 percent. From 1997 to 2000, the FCIC has moved to a multichannel service strategy that includes the Web, toll-free phone service, and specialized marketing to new customer groups: women and Hispanics.

Discussion and Concluding Remarks

Services make up the vast majority of our economy. This is reflected by both the growth of this sector and the growth of services' importance within the goods sector. Services are also a critical component of the public sector. To move forward in e-government programs, agency leaders will need to become experts in managing IT investments. Building an effective enterprise brings together government managers, stakeholders, financial planners, program officers, employees, and customers. The e-business plan should include objectives, strategies, and quantifiable metrics that are developed through a consensus process across the agency. The case studies support the importance of metrics in project planning, implementation, and evaluation. The financial metrics that proved to be relevant to agencies implementing e-Service programs included effectiveness, sales, revenues, cost savings, and cost avoidance. The process metrics that proved to be relevant to decision-makers included efficiency and productivity. Customer metrics centered on value, customer satisfaction, customer loyalty, market share, and multichannel delivery. Learning and growth metrics focused on staff retention.

To explain and defend financial and process objectives to the executive branch and to congressional committees, managers should consider the development of metrics that can be easily understood and tracked over time. Such indicators would include *effectiveness, sales and revenues, cost savings, cost avoidance, efficiency,* and *productivity.* Effectiveness is measured in terms of how well the e-Services are accomplishing the agency's mission. Cost avoidance is measured in terms of how well the agency increases savings by consolidating data centers, standardizing hardware and software platforms, replacing legacy applications, outsourcing, and performance-based contracting. Efficiency can include the replacement of paper-based processes and online filing. Productivity can include streamlining enterprise applications and increasing the availability and access to information through integrated systems.

Agencies also need to demonstrate value to the public. To do this, they should consider measures that focus on *customer satisfaction, customer loyalty, market share,* and *multichannel delivery.* Customer relationship management is an important factor in increasing value. The Internet and the World Wide Web can provide instantaneous and inexpensive feedback. Many agencies are now using Web surveys and focus groups to improve the quality and content of their services. A multichannel delivery strategy requires a dedicated help desk that is equipped to provide timely customer service. The case study on the U.S. Mint identifies *staff retention* as a critical metric where learning and growth are important to consistent delivery and increased market share.

Figures 13.1 and 13.2 summarize the findings from the case study results in the last section. Section 7 proposes metrics and simple definitions for e-government services (Figure 13.1) and identifies federal e-government programs according to applied performance metrics (Figure 13.2). A sample performance measurement questionnaire (Appendix) uses the metrics developed in Figures 13.1 and 13.2. The questionnaire is intended to increase agency discussions on e-business and e-Services goals and objectives.

In the case studies where metrics are being used to evaluate e-Service investments, government executives report (1) reductions in the total cost of IT; (2) reductions in the number of nonstandard platforms, redundant data centers, duplicative applications; (3) reductions in maintenance and service costs through outsourcing and performance-based contracting; and (4) consistently high customer satisfaction scores.

Government managers also note limitations in developing quantitative metrics in an uncertain political and budgetary environment. Constraints include:

1. establishing clear lead and lag indicators for electronic services in terms of the efficiency and effectiveness;
2. setting performance benchmarks to measure quality of service and usability;
3. gaining executive support and public trust in service delivery;
4. tracking and measuring savings due to productivity and efficiency gains in IT operations over time;
5. providing consistent and comparable statistical information across diverse programs;
6. gaining market intelligence to understand consumer demand for electronic services;
7. tracking trends in "e-Service" best practices to quickly adapt to change.

The American Customer Satisfaction Survey completed by the University of Michigan and studies by Gartner and comScore are steps in the right direction. Performance studies that rank government services will allow citizens to compare programs both horizontally and vertically in terms of quality and value. Government agencies should consider creating focus groups to simplify data formats for reporting, filing, licensing, and applications across government. Clustering e-Services to increase efficiency is already happening at the state and international level, and this has dramatically increased traffic on state government sites. One of the important advantages of Web technology is that the public can seamlessly access multiple sources of information rapidly and inexpensively. This capability will increase citizen demand for service delivery systems that directly respond to their needs and requirements.

At the state level, the CIO of New Jersey believes that the Internet and the World Wide Web offer a new way of governing by delivering customer services twenty-four hours a day, seven days a week (i.e., 24/7). To realize this vision, New Jersey has developed a "channeled" portal. The portal allows citizens to easily access information and services even if they are not familiar with the inner workings of the New Jersey government. The portal includes a directory of state officials, public key infrastructure, services, and e-payment.

Ontario, Canada, has an e-justice program that uses an enterprise-wide infrastructure, policies, and standards to consolidate twenty departments into six cluster organizations—police; criminal, civil, and family courts; the judiciary; Crown attorneys; the private bar; and corrections staff. The integrated justice project implements a province-wide information network to link all agencies. Once information is captured, it is (electronically) stored for reuse by authorized officials. The integrated justice project aims to provide up-to-date information, instant access to facts across the system, less paperwork, faster prosecution of crime, and better support to victims. The implementation includes public key infrastructure with planned implementation of 34,000 certifications. A secure network is relied upon for transmission and sharing of sensitive information.

The promise of the Internet and the World Wide Web is to encourage public participation in our democratic institutions. It offers the potential of a more responsive and accountable government. By establishing a clear vision and road map for electronic services, we can increase the ability of citizens to make decisions that are more informed and improve the quality of our government institutions.

Appendix: Performance Measurement Questionnaire

Background

Why all the emphasis on performance metrics by Congress and the GAO? Republican Senator Fred Thompson of Tennessee, in reviewing federal agency compliance with the Clinger-Cohen Act (CCA) in 2000, concluded that seventeen of the twenty-four agencies covered by the CCA were not fully implementing information technology capital planning and investment controls. Thompson also noted the lack of quality data for the assessments of major IT investments. Many agencies do not link IT performance to agency program performance. Senator Thompson concluded that links to performance reports are often too broad to provide sufficiently robust measures of the impact that information technology has made on an agency's overall objectives (GPRA P.L.103–62). These agency reports are required by the Government Performance and Results Act, Clinger-Cohen (P.L. 104–106), and the Government Paperwork Elimination Act (P.L. 105–217). Additionally Thompson found that sixteen agencies neither developed nor submitted IT management reports that included whether the project met original goals or described agencies' accomplishments, progress, or areas requiring attention. Finally, one-fourth of the agencies reported significant deviations of projects from cost or schedule goals. Is his report, Thompson stated that agencies were not using sound business procedures, and because of this, they were unable to improve program performance and meet their mission goals.

It is hard to measure the success of government programs. This is because many of today's output measures do not tell you how to improve; do not identify or clarify issues driving current performance; are retrospective measures that expose symptoms not causes; do not link to business objectives or increasing customer value; do not relate metrics to IT management and individual performance.

The following questions are meant to help focus managers on performance metrics for e-Services.

1. Financial metrics
   - Effectiveness
     (a) Does your agency have a strategic plan that links electronic services to corporate goals, vision, and mission?
     (b) Is your e-Service initiative consistent with your agency's legislative mandate and responsibilities?
     (c) Is there a capital asset plan and does it include electronic service projects? Have you completed an alternatives analysis on different e-Service options? How much funding is required and for how long? Is your funding and revenue stream secure?
   - Sales and revenues, cost effectiveness, and cost avoidance
     (a) Can you calculate a return on investment (ROI)? What are the potential savings? Are there congressional or budgetary restrictions in terms of procurement?
     (b) Have you calculated other funding options if there are changes in installation schedules?
     (c) How will changes in funding impact the project? What additional funding is required before and after the e-business installation?

(d) Can the private sector or nonprofits be your partners? How would this impact funding? What risks do they face?

(e) Are you willing to track operating and maintenance costs as financial performance targets for new and existing (legacy) systems? Identify applications that can be brought online first and short-term and longer-term cost savings. Identify upgrades needed, time, cost. Estimate the cost of concurrent systems (hardware/software) that will be required during the transition to electronic services.

2. Process metrics
   - Efficiency
     (a) Can you make a business plan with metrics or benchmarks for process improvements in terms of efficiency, effectiveness, productivity, or service?
     (b) What is your current technology platform? Do you have an enterprise architecture? What is required for improvements in efficiency? Identify hardware/software applications that need to be integrated to provide an integrated supply chain and customer service chain for electronic services.
   - Productivity
     (a) Can you standardize applications or consolidate data centers to improve productivity?
     (b) How does paper flow through the organization? What processes can be immediately put online to increase productivity?
     (c) How accessible are the services for employees and the public? Can you benchmark public access time for paper vs. electronic services and cost?

3. Customer satisfaction
   - Value
     (a) Have you set customer satisfaction targets in terms of customer access to services?
     (b) What techniques are being used to estimate relevance and timeliness of e-Service products?
     (c) Have privacy and security issues associated with electronic provision of data been addressed?
     (d) Can you calculate improvements in customer satisfaction in terms of faster service, more complete and accurate information, and so on? Are you incorporating Web statistics as a lead indicator of satisfaction?
     (e) What is your customer relationship strategy? Have you surveyed your customer base in terms of customer expectations?

- Web traffic and customer loyalty
  - (a) What Web metrics do you plan to use to evaluate customer satisfaction, for example, quality, usability, and effectiveness?
  - (b) How will you incorporate user feedback into business processes?
- Web traffic and market share
  - (a) Are there value-added companies or agencies that have similar product offerings? What is the position of value-added companies in the marketplace? Are your products and services tailored around a niche market or national market?
  - (b) How many customers do you currently have? Is the customer base national or regional, citizens, businesses, or employees?
- Multichannel delivery
  - (a) What are your sources of business intelligence about your customers?
  - (b) What are the channels that you will need to access or provide service delivery, for example, government to business, government to government, government to the public?
4. Learning and growth
- Staff retention
  - (a) Is there support for your initiative at the CEO level?
  - (b) Does the culture of your agency support new ways of doing business? Can your agency quickly adapt to change?
  - (c) Do you provide financial incentives for performance? What benefits are provided to employees and contractors that meet performance targets in terms of savings, productivity, efficiency, and reduced costs?
  - (d) Do you have a CRM training strategy within your agency, and are you planning to "train the trainer" or use contractors?
  - (e) Are you developing incentives for collaboration in delivery of e-Services with executives?
  - (f) How are you creating a knowledge management environment to increase business intelligence and anticipate customer demand?
  - (g) What are your current incentives for employee retention? Have you developed learning and growth strategies for your employees?

References

Bergstrom, L. 2000. *IT Spending: Its History and Future*. Stamford, CT: Gartner Group, Performance Measurement Group.

Bitterman, M. 2000. "Building an Integrated Performance Management Systems." *Gartner Measurement Newsletter*. Stamford CT: Gartner Group.

CENDI (Departments of Commerce, Energy and Environment; National Aeronautics and Space Agency; National Libraries of Agriculture, Education, Medicine; Department of Defense). 2001. "Evaluating Our Web Presence: Challenges, Metrics, and Results." National Library of Medicine, National Institutes of Health, Washington DC: www.dtic.mil/cendi (April 17).

ComScore. 2001. "Federal Government Internet Scorecard–The Top 10." *govScore Standard Traffic Report* (June), p. 3.

Dickson, G., and Wetherbe, J. 1985. *The Management of Information Systems*. New York: McGraw-Hill.

Executive Office of the President. 2001. *A Blueprint for New Beginnings*. Washington, DC: Government Printing Office.

Fornell, C.; B. Bryant; and E. Anderson. 2000. *Special Report: Government Satisfaction Scores*. National Quality Research Center, University of Michigan Business School.

———. 2001. *Special Report: Government Satisfaction Scores*. National Quality Research Center, University of Michigan Business School.

———. 2002. *Special Report: Government Satisfaction Scores*. National Quality Research Center, University of Michigan Business School.

General Accounting Office. 2000. Accounting and Information Management Division. *Information Technology Investment Management: An Overview of GAO's Assessment Framework Exposure Draft*, Version 1: www.gao.gov/specialpubs/ai00155pdf (May).

Hansan, H, and H. Tibbits. 2000. "The Evolution of an Information System for Managerial Use: A Longitudinal Study." *Australian Journal of Information Systems* 2, no. 2: 88–93.

Kalakota, R., and A. Whinston. 1997. *Electronic Commerce: A Manager's Guide*. Reading, MA: Addison-Wesley.

Kalakota, R.; M. Robinson; and D. Tapscott. 1999. *E-Business: Roadmap for Success Guide* (Information Technology Series). Reading, MA: Addison-Wesley.

Kaplan, R. 2000. *The Balanced Scorecard for Public-Sector Organizations*. Boston: Harvard Business School.

Kaplan, R., and D. Norton. 1992. "The Balanced Scorecard–Measures that Drive Performance." *Harvard Business Review* 70 (January–February): 71–79.

———. 1993. "Putting the Balanced Scorecard to Work." *Harvard Business Review* 71(5) (October): 134–142.

———. 1996. "Using the Balanced Scorecard as a Strategic Management System," *Harvard Business Review*. 74(1):75–85.

Martinsons, M.; R. Davison; and D. Tse. 1999. "The Balanced Scorecard: A Foundation for the Strategic Management of Information Systems." *Decision Support Systems* 25: 71–88.

McClure, C., and T. Sprehe. 2001. "Comprehensive Assessment of Public Information Dissemination, June 2000–March 2001." *Final Report*, vol. 1. Washington, DC: Government Printing Office.

Miles, M.B., and A.M. Huberman. 1994. *Qualitative Data Analysis*. Thousand Oaks, CA: Sage.

Moaz, M. 2001. "Relationship Value as Measured by Mutual Advantage" (Notes COM-13-1953). Stamford, CT: Gartner Group.

National Center for Public Productivity. 1997. *A Brief Guide for Performance Measurement in Local Government*. Newark, NJ: Rutgers University.

Office of Management and Budget. 2001a. *OMB A-11*, Transmittal Memorandum # 74 for Heads of Executive Departments and Agencies: www.whitehouse.gov/omb/circulars/a11.

————. 2001b. *Exhibits A-130* , Transmittal Memorandum #4 for Heads of Executive Departments and Agencies, Management of Federal information Resources: www.whitehouse.gov/omb/circular/A130.

Stiglitz, J. 2000. *Economics of the Public Sector*, 3d ed. New York: Norton.

Strassman, P. 1999. "Measuring and Managing Knowledge Capital, Report on Knowledge, Technology, and Performance." www.strassman.com/pubs/measuring-knowledge.

U.S. Congress. 1992. *Clinger-Cohen Act*, Section 5123, P.L.104–106.

————. 1993. *Government Performance and Results Act*, P.L. 103–62.

————.1998. *Government Paperwork Elimination Act* (GPEA, Title XVII), P.L. 105–217.

Walsham, G. 1995. "Interpretive Case Studies in IS Research: Nature and Method." *European Journal of Information Systems* 4(2): 74–81.

West, D. 2001. *State and Federal E-government in the United States 2001*. Taubman Institute, Brown University. Available at www.brown-edu/departments/Taubman-Center/polreports.

Willcocks, L. 1994. *Information Management: The Evaluation of Information Systems Investments*. London: Chapman and Hall.

About the Editors and Contributors

Mary Jo Bitner (Ph.D., University of Washington) is the AT&T Professor of Services Marketing and Management at Arizona State University and research director for the Center for Services Leadership at ASU. She is faculty coordinator for the ASU M.B.A. services marketing and management concentration. Bitner is coauthor of the text *Services Marketing: Integrating Customer Focus Across the Firm,* 2d ed. (2000). She has consulted with numerous businesses on service quality and customer satisfaction and is a frequent presenter on these topics at conferences and executive education programs. Bitner's research focuses on how customers evaluate service encounters and the role of self-service technologies and front-line employee behaviors in determining customer satisfaction with services. Her research has been published in the *Journal of Marketing, Journal of the Academy of Marketing Science, Journal of Retailing, Journal of Business Research, International Journal of Service Industries Management,* and other publications.

Jeffrey O. Bollettino leads the Digital Transformation practice within Booz Allen Hamilton's information technology team. Having worked for Booz Allen for fifteen years, he is a vice president and partner with the firm, based in McLean, VA. Bollettino's personal focus is on digital strategy—working with government clients to achieve transformation in serving their customers, using the Internet as an enabling technology. Bollettino is a thought leader in electronic government, and has been a guest lecturer on this topic for the Council for Excellence in Government, the National Defense University and the Kennedy School of Government. Bollettino's major areas of work have included wireless and enterprise networking technologies. He has a bachelor of science degree in electrical and computer engineering from Clarkson University. He lives in Oakton, VA, with his wife Laura and daughters Alessandra and Francesca.

Irina Ceaparu is a Ph.D. student in the Department of Computer Science at the University of Maryland, College Park. She is currently working in the Human-Computer Interaction Laboratory, under the guidance of Dr. Ben Shneiderman.

Charles L. Colby is president of Rockbridge Associates, a Washington, DC–area market research firm that deals with technology marketing issues for services firms. For more than twenty years, he has consulted for companies such as Discovery Channel, Verizon, VeriSign, Marriott, MCI, Capital One, BP, and the U.S. Postal Service. He is an expert in strategic planning, advanced research design, and data analysis. He has contributed extensively to the body of knowledge on technology adoption, having written numerous articles and presented at conferences. He recently coauthored a book with A. Parasuraman titled *Techno-Ready Marketing: How and Why Your Customers Adopt Technology* (2001). He is a senior fellow at the Center for E-Services at the University of Maryland.

Dina Demner is a graduate student in the Computer Science Department and a graduate research assistant in the Computational Linguistics and Information Processing Laboratory at the University of Maryland Institute for Advanced Computer Studies.

Robert F. Easley is an assistant professor of management information systems in the Management Department of Mendoza College of Business, University of Notre Dame. He holds a Ph.D. in decision and information systems from Indiana University, Bloomington, an M.B.A. from Pennsylvania State University, and a B.A. from the University of Illinois. His research interests include decision support systems, market structure analysis, and technology acceptance. His current research focuses on economic modeling of Internet auctions and B2B market structures, recommendation systems, and collaborative technologies. His research has appeared in *Journal of Marketing Research*, *Journal of Accounting and Economics*, *European Journal of Operational Research*, *Mathematical and Computer Modeling*, and other journals.

Rashi Glazer is professor at the Walter A. Haas School of Business, University of California, Berkeley, codirector of the Berkeley Center for Marketing and Technology, and director of the Berkeley Portfolio of Marketing Management Executive Education Programs. His teaching and research interests are in the areas of competitive marketing strategy, technology and information strategy, interactive and database marketing, e-commerce, and consumer and managerial decision-making. He is the founding coeditor of the new *Journal of Interactive Marketing* (formerly *Journal of Direct Marketing*) and an associate editor of *Management Science*. His articles have appeared in *Marketing Science*, *Journal of Consumer Research*, *Journal of Marketing*, and other publications, and he is the coauthor of three books, *The Marketing Information Revolution* 1994), *Readings on Market-Driving Strategies* (1997), and *Cable TV Advertising* (1989). He is the developer of the Infovalue program for measuring the value of a firm's information, and SUITS, an interactive computer simulation for teaching the strategic use of information and the integration of information technology strategy with business strategy.

Weiyin Hong is an assistant professor in the Department of Management Information Systems, University of Nevada, Las Vegas. She received her B.Sc. in management information systems from FuDan University, China, and her Ph.D. in information and system management from Hong Kong University of Science and Technology. Her research interest is user acceptance of emerging technologies, such as electronic commerce and digital libraries, and human-computer interaction. She was an ICIS doctoral consortium fellow in 2000 and has published in *Journal of Management Information Systems*.

Edward Hung is a Ph.D. student at the Department of Computer Science, University of Maryland, College Park (UMCP). He is supported by scholarships from the Croucher Foundation for his Ph.D. research. He received his B.Eng. in computer engineering and M.Phil. in computer science from the University of Hong Kong in 1998 and 2000 respectively. He received his M.S. in computer science from UMCP in May 2002. He was awarded a number of scholarships, including the Epson Foundation Scholarship, the Hong Kong and China Gas Co. Ltd. Postgraduate Scholarship, Stephen Kam-Chuen Cheong Memorial Scholarships, and the Hong Kong Institution of Engineers Student Prize. He has written three journal and conference papers related to data warehousing and parallel data mining. His current research area is semistructured databases. More information about his research and publications can be accessed from www.cs.umd.edu/~ehung.

P. K. Kannan is Safeway Fellow and associate professor of marketing at the Robert H. Smith School of Business at the University of Maryland, where he is associate director for the Center for e-Service. His current research focuses on pricing information products and product lines, e-coupons, online loyalty, and marketing and product development on the Internet. Dr. Kannan has served as a panelist in the National Science Foundation Workshop on

Research Priorities in e-Commerce and a Fellow of the AMA Consortium on e-Commerce. He serves on the editorial boards of *Journal of Service Research* and *International Journal of Electronic Commerce*. He is also guest editor of a special issue on marketing on the E-Channel for *International Journal of Electronic Commerce*, and is the past chair of the AMA Special Interest Group on Marketing Research. He has corporate experience with Tata Engineering and Ingersoll-Rand and has consulted for companies such as Frito-Lay, PepsiCo, Giant Food, SAIC, Fannie Mae, Proxicom, and IBM.

Katherine N. Lemon, Ph.D., is an expert in the areas of customer equity, customer relationship management (CRM), and wireless CRM. She is currently a member of the marketing faculty at Boston College's Wallace E. Carroll School of Management. Previously, Lemon was a visiting professor at the Harvard Business School and was on the marketing faculty of Duke University's Fuqua School of Business. She received her Ph.D. from University of California at Berkeley. Lemon's academic research appears in a number of marketing journals, and she has coauthored two books: *Wireless Rules: New Marketing Strategies for Customer Relationship Management Anytime, Anywhere* (2001) and *Driving Customer Equity: How Customer Lifetime Value Is Reshaping Corporate Strategy* (2000). Lemon has conducted research in numerous industries, including emerging e- and m-commerce companies, and has consulted with and taught executives of many global businesses.

Loren J. Lemon, J.D., is an attorney with over eighteen years of legal experience in business and corporate transactions, including extensive negotiation and documentation of e-commerce arrangements. He has represented enterprises ranging in size from Fortune 100 multinational companies to entrepreneurial start-ups. He is in private practice in Lexington, MA, and has been admitted to practice in the states of Massachusetts, California, North Carolina, and Kansas. Lemon served as the chief researcher and technical advisor for *Wireless Rules: New Marketing Strategies for Customer Relationship Management Anytime, Anywhere.*

Matthew L. Meuter received his Ph.D. in marketing from Arizona State University in 1999. He is currently associate professor of marketing at California State University, Chico. Meuter's research focuses on the impact of technology on the marketing function. He is specifically interested in the changing nature of technology-based service encounters, customer satisfaction with self-service technologies, customer adoption of technologically based service delivery innovations, and organizational e-commerce issues. His research has been published in *Journal of Marketing, Journal of Applied*

Psychology, Journal of the Academy of Marketing Science, and other publications. He also has an article forthcoming in *Journal of Business Research.*

Frederick B. Newell is CEO of the international consulting firm Seklemian/ Newell. Newell is an industry expert in customer relationship management and the planning, development, and implementation of customer-focused marketing programs. A member of the Retail Advertising Hall of Fame, he has worked with large multinationals as well as small businesses around the world. He speaks to and consults with executives on CRM, customer loyalty, and wireless CRM. Newell is the coauthor of *Wireless Rules: New Marketing Strategies for Customer Relationship Management Anytime, Anywhere* (2001) and the author of *loyalty.com* (2000) and *The New Rules of Marketing* (1997).

Richard W. Oliver is the CEO of the American Graduate School of Management. He is an adjunct professor of management at the Owen Graduate School of Management at Vanderbilt University, where he teaches competitive strategy and strategies for biotech. He is also a Senior Fellow, Health Policy, at the Vanderbilt University Institute for Public Policy Studies. Oliver is the author of *The Coming Biotech Age: The Business of Bio-Materials* (1999), and *The Shape of Things to Come: 7 Imperatives for Winning in the New World of Business,* (1998) and is coauthor (with William Jenkins) of *The Eagle & the Monk: 7 Principles of Successful Change* (1998). He has published widely in academic and popular journals. Prior to joining the Owen School in 1992, he was vice president, corporate marketing, Nortel. He serves on the board of four companies (two of which are listed on NASDAQ) and serves as chairman of the board of directors of Symmetricom Inc., a California-based high-tech firm. He is active in Nashville-area education and cultural organizations.

Amy L. Ostrom is assistant professor of marketing at Arizona State University. Her research focuses on issues related to services marketing, including customers' evaluation of services, customers' role in creating service outcomes, and customers' adoption and evaluation of self-service technologies. Her work has appeared in a number of journals including *Journal of Marketing, Journal of Consumer Psychology,* and the *Advances in Services Marketing and Management* series.

Roland T. Rust holds the David Bruce Smith Chair in Marketing at the Robert H. Smith School of Business at the University of Maryland, where he is director of the Center for e-Service and chair of the Department of Marketing. His honors include the American Marketing Association's Gilbert A. Churchill Award for Lifetime Achievement in Marketing Research, as well as lifetime achievement awards in advertising and statistics. He has won awards for articles in five journals, and his seven books include *Driving Customer Equity: How Customer Lifetime Value Is Reshaping Corporate Strategy* (2000), which he coauthored with Katherine Lemon. He is the founder and chair of the AMA Frontiers in Services Conference, and serves as founding editor of the *Journal of Service Research*. He has consulted with many leading companies worldwide, including American Airlines, AT&T, Chase Manhattan Bank, Dow Chemical, DuPont, FedEx, Nortel, Procter & Gamble, Sears, Unilever, and USAA, and he serves on several corporate boards.

Michael J. Shaw is Leonard C. and Mary Lou Hoeft Endowed Chair Professor in Information Technology Management and director of the Center for Information System and Technology Management at the University of Illinois at Urbana-Champaign. He is also affiliated with the Beckman Institute for Advanced Science and Technology. His major research interests are electronic commerce, information technology for supply chain management, decision support systems, and computer-integrated manufacturing. He has published more than sixty refereed scholarly papers in journals such as *Management Science, Information Systems Research, INFORMS Journal on Computing, Communications of the ACM, IEEE Internet Computing, IIE Transactions*, and *Decision Support Systems*. He is the chief editor of the recently published *Handbook on Electronic Commerce* (2001) and is also the editor of *Information-Based Manufacturing* (2000).

Ben Shneiderman is a professor in the Department of Computer Science, founding director (1983–2000) of the Human-Computer Interaction Laboratory, and member of the Institutes for Advanced Computer Studies and for Systems Research, all at the University of Maryland at College Park. He is the author of *Software Psychology: Human Factors in Computer and Information Systems* (1980) and *Designing the User Interface: Strategies for Effective Human-Computer Interaction*, 3d ed. (1998). Shneiderman's 1999 book, coauthored with S. Card and J. Mackinlay, is *Readings in Information Visualization: Using Vision to Think*. His treemap visualization is used by www.smartmoney.com/marketmap, for whom he is an advisor.

David Simms is CEO cofounder of IntiMetrix, and previously was president of The Idea Factory Consulting. Mr. Simms has ten years' experience in consulting and senior-level marketing, sales, and management with Fortune 30 companies PepsiCo and IBM. He holds a B.A. degree in economics from the University of California, Irvine, and an M.B.A. from the Owen Graduate School of Management at Vanderbilt University. He currently lives with his wife, Victoria, and daughters Taylor and Devon in Collierville, TN, where he teaches Sunday school and enjoys coaching youth soccer.

Joan Steyaert joined General Services Administration as its deputy associate administrator of governmentwide information technology policy in 1997. The Technology Policy was created in 1996 to spur the implementation of technology policy across government. With five divisions within GSA working in electronic commerce, accessibility, and enterprise management, the Governmentwide Policy Office provides assistance to departments, bureaus, and small agencies by promoting partnerships and collaboration across government. Dr. Steyaert is currently working with the National Defense University and GSA on customer satisfaction measures for electronic government services. She has a Ph.D. degree from the University of Pennsylvania. Before her appointment, she was chief information officer of the United States Trade Representative (USTR), the international trade office for the president. The most senior IT official within USTR, she was responsible for planning and managing an international network that provided telecommunications to government officials worldwide. She was also recognized for planning and installing secure connectivity with the Department of State that eliminated millions of dollars of paper.

Kar Yan Tam is currently professor of information and systems management and director of the Center for Electronic Commerce at Hong Kong University of Science and Technology. His research interests include electronic commerce applications, digital copyright protection technology, and electronic payment. His papers have appeared in major information system journals, including *Management Science, MISQ, Information Systems Research, Decision Support Systems,* and *Journal of Management Information Systems.* He is currently on the editorial board of a number of IS journals.

Sajeev Varki is an assistant professor at the University of Rhode Island. He holds an undergraduate degree in engineering from the Indian Institute of Technology, Kharagpur, an M.B.A. from the Institute of Management, Ahmedabad, and a Ph.D. in management from the Owen School of Management, Vanderbilt University, Nashville, TN. Varki's research interests include substantive and methodological areas. Among his substantive areas of interest are strategy and service marketing. His papers in strategy have been published in *Marketing Letters, Journal of Business Research*, and *Marketing Management.* His papers in service marketing have been published in *Jour-*

nal of Retailing, Journal of Service Research, European Journal of Marketing, and *International Journal of Service Industry Management*. His methodological interests are in the area of mixture models and choice models. His papers in methodology have been published in *Journal of Marketing Research* and *Marketing Research*.

Chih-Ping Wei is an associate professor in the Department of Information Management at National Sun Yat-Sen University in Taiwan, R.O.C. He holds a Ph.D. and an M.S. in management information systems from the University of Arizona, and a B.S. degree from the National Chiao-Tung University in Taiwan, R.O.C. He was a visiting scholar at the University of Illinois at Urbana-Champaign from 2001 to 2002. His papers have appeared in *IEEE Transactions on Engineering Management, IEEE Intelligent Systems, IEEE Transactions on Information Technology in Biomedicine, Decision Support Systems, Journal of Organizational Computing,* and *Electronic Commerce.* His current research interests include knowledge discovery and data mining, information retrieval and text mining, multidatabase management and integration, data warehouse design, and knowledge management.

Chi Kin (Bennett) Yim is associate professor of marketing at the University of Hong Kong and Thunderbird: The American Graduate School of International Management. His primary areas of research include services marketing, Internet marketing, customer satisfaction and loyalty, China marketing, and brand-choice modeling. Yim has published articles in *Journal of Marketing Research, Marketing Science,* and *Journal of Business Research,* and he has presented many papers in conferences in the United States and Europe. One of his *JMR* articles was a finalist for the 1995 William F. O'Dell Award for making the most significant long-run contribution to the marketing discipline. Yim received his Ph.D. in management (marketing) from the Krannert Graduate School of Management, Purdue University.

Haixia Zhao is a Ph.D. student in the Department of Computer Science, University of Maryland, College Park. She received her B.S. in computer science from Zhejiang University, Hangzhou, China, and her M.S. in computer science from Academia Sinica. She was a group leader on the Chinese Labor Market Statistic and Analysis System project, a nationwide distributed data warehousing system. Her current research interests include information visualization and databases.

INDEX